IN THE
Wake
OF THE
Exxon Valdez

IN THE
Wake
OF THE
Exxon Valdez

THE DEVASTATING IMPACT OF THE ALASKA OIL SPILL

Art Davidson

**SIERRA CLUB BOOKS
SAN FRANCISCO**

The Sierra Club, founded in 1892 by John Muir, has devoted itself
to the study and protection of the earth's scenic and ecological
resources—mountains, wetlands, woodlands, wild shores and rivers,
deserts and plains. The publishing program of the Sierra Club offers
books to the public as a nonprofit educational service in the hope
that they may enlarge the public's understanding of the Club's basic
concerns. The point of view expressed in each book, however, does
not necessarily represent that of the Club. The Sierra Club has some
sixty chapters coast to coast, in Canada, Hawaii, and Alaska. For
information about how you may participate in its programs to preserve wilderness and the quality of life, please address inquiries to
Sierra Club, 730 Polk Street, San Francisco, CA 94109.

Library of Congress Cataloging in Publication Data:
Davidson, Art, 1943–
    In the wake of the Exxon Valdez: the devastating impact of the
Alaska oil spill/by Art Davidson.
        p. cm.
    Includes bibliographical references.
    ISBN 0-87156-614-1
    1. Oil spills—Environmental aspects—Alaska—Prince William
Sound Region. 2. Tankers—Accidents—Environmental
aspects—Alaska—Prince William Sound Region. 3. Wildlife res-
cue—Alaska—Prince William Sound Region. 4. Exxon Valdez
(Ship) I. Title.
TD427.P4D39 1990
628.1'6833'097983—dc20   89-29294
                                                              CIP

Production: Susan Ristow
Editor: Linda Gunnarson
Jacket design: Bonnie Smetts
Book design: Abigail Johnston
Maps: Hilda Chen
Printed in the United States of America on acid-free paper
containing a minimum of 50% recovered waste paper, of
which 10% of the fiber content is post-consumer waste
10 9 8 7 6 5 4 3

This book is for the people and wild creatures affected by the oil spill, and for all those who did whatever they could to help

Contents

PART III: THE WAKE

Acknowledgments

Many people have helped with this book. My heartfelt thanks go to Karen Serieka, my assistant, who worked tirelessly to make this book as full and complete as possible. I have been very fortunate to have two extremely capable and supportive editors, Linda Gunnarson at Sierra Club Books and Suzanne Lipsett, a creative and insightful writer herself. For their special contributions, I want to thank Chris Swartz, Tom Sexton, Dr. James Butler, Barbara Faeo, Tammie Smith, Aardvark, Mei Mei Evans, Karen Brewster, Betty Berensen, Patti Saunders, Dr. John Farrington, and Susi Alexander. I appreciate the support of the Alaska Conservation Foundation. A number of other writers have been encouraging and helpful; in particular, I'd like to thank Pamela Abramson, Harry Hurt III, Lynda Wright, Paul Jenkins, Mark Dowie, Patti Epler, Stan Jones, Charles Wohlforth, Ron Dalby, Shannon Lowry, Rosanne Smith, David Hammock, and Steve Lindbeck. Finally, many people shared their experience and insights; to each one I extend my gratitude for adding immeasurably to the telling of this story.

Introduction

After the wreck of the *Exxon Valdez*, I asked an oil company executive what he thought went wrong, what this was all about. "It's simple," he said. "A ship hit a rock."

This is, indeed, a book about how an oil tanker hit a submerged reef. It is also about how the politics of oil collided with our responsibility to the earth. And I found this to be a story of addictions: not just a tanker captain's addiction to alcohol but widespread addictions to power, money, and energy consumption.

The fateful journey of the *Exxon Valdez* begins, in a sense, with the discovery of oil-saturated sands 8,708 feet beneath the tundra of Alaska's North Slope in January 1968. I was in Alaska at the time, but I was busy climbing mountains and, for a while, didn't give much thought to what the discovery meant. However, I became increasingly apprehensive about how the oil industry's intensifying activities would affect life in Alaska. Further test wells confirmed a pool of at least 10 billion barrels of oil and 26 trillion cubic feet of gas—one of the world's largest accumulations of these resources. Within three years, oil companies had paid a record $900 million to the state of Alaska for leases on the North Slope. The federal government, eager to get the oil revenues flowing, scraped a winter haul road from Fairbanks to the new oil field. When spring came, permafrost beneath the roadway began eroding, prompting one University of Alaska scientist to label this hastily built road "the biggest screwup in the history of mankind in the Arctic." But a more prevalent attitude was voiced by the executive assistant to Alaska's governor: "Hell, this country's so goddamn big that even if industry ran wild we could never wreck it. We can have our cake and eat it too."[1]

The oil companies wanted to build an 800-mile pipeline through the heart of Alaska—from Prudhoe Bay at the edge of the Arctic Ocean to Valdez in Prince William Sound. And they wanted their pipeline right away. New country would be opened up; there would be airstrips, haul roads, construction camps, and pump stations where there had been only the sounds of wolves and the wind. Of even greater concern, supertankers would pick up the oil at the pipeline's terminus in Valdez and carry it through the remote and incredibly abundant waters of Prince William Sound. With storms, drifting ice, narrow passages, and submerged reefs, these were treacherous waters for oil-laden tankers the length of three football fields. An accident could devastate colonies of sea birds and kill eagles, sea otters, seals, salmon, whales, and many other creatures.

By this time, I was working for Friends of the Earth, and we filed suit against the proposed pipeline. This would be the first test of the Environmental Policy Act of 1969, which requires an assessment of the social, economic, and environmental implications of activities on federal lands. This law does not require that the safest or wisest decision be made, but in our view it did require a thorough examination of both potential problems and alternatives to proposed development. We felt there were safer alternatives to the oil industry's proposal. For example, an all-overland pipeline through Canada would eliminate the need for tankers, thus avoiding the risk of oil pollution at sea. Better yet, the oil could simply stay in the ground for a while longer, on reserve until we knew how to transport it more carefully and use it less wastefully.

Because the U.S. Department of Interior and the oil industry had made only a cursory assessment of the pipeline's potential environmental problems, a federal judge granted a preliminary injunction against the pipeline's right-of-way permit. Fishermen, fearful of oil tankers in Prince William Sound, also filed suit against the proposed pipeline. Having already invested nearly $3 billion in North Slope leases and development, seven oil companies formed a consortium called Alyeska and pleaded their case before a sharply divided Congress. It took intensive lobbying from the state of Alaska and a tie-breaking vote by Vice President Spiro Agnew to clear the way for the Trans-Alaska Pipeline and the tanker route.

Congressional approval of the pipeline rested on a key condition: that the oil industry pledge to spare no effort to protect the environment. To make certain the industry kept this pledge, the state of Alaska created its Department of Environmental Conservation.

In December 1973, construction crews were mobilized, and by the time the pipeline was completed it was the largest and, at $8 billion, the most expensive private construction project in history. When oil started flowing through the pipeline in 1977, my own fears about the project had been somewhat allayed. It is true that the safer, all-overland pipeline route through Canada had been rejected, but the industry, the state of Alaska, and the federal government were all promising the American public the safest pipeline and tanker system in the world. I remember one very high-ranking British Petroleum official confiding to me that "You environmentalists drove us crazy, throwing up all those ecological concerns. We fought you. But if you hadn't slowed us down, we'd have made a real mess of things. Now we have a truly superior oil transport system."

From my experience in the pipeline battle, I knew that it was going to take persistent monitoring and an occasional lawsuit to make certain the industry maintained the required safeguards. The oil companies could be powerful adversaries—tough-minded and determined to get their way. If a corner could be cut, they would find and cut it. I expected the oil industry to develop its oil as efficiently as it could, taking only those environmental precautions it was required to take by law. Despite their gestures toward wildlife and wild places, the oil companies hadn't come to Alaska to nurture caribou. They came to make money.

The stances and actions of the state and federal governments were harder to predict. The federal government has environmental protection responsibilities, but it is also in the business of leasing oil. The U.S. Department of Interior and the U.S. Coast Guard were supposed to help safeguard Alaska from oil spills, but would their resolve be firm? The state has a constitutional obligation to protect the lands and waters of Alaska, but the prevailing attitude in Alaska was to jump-start the economy with oil development—as much, and as soon, as possible. When oil started coursing through the pipeline, the state assumed the primary watchdog role over industry. After being ardently pro oil development, could the state transform itself into a conscientious guardian of the environment?

In any event, after the pipeline was built I went on with my life, building a log cabin for my family and a career for myself in resource planning. Like other Alaskans, I soon became accustomed to the benefits of having the oil industry in the state. With the advent of North Slope oil money, state income taxes were abolished, and each resident began receiving an annual windfall check of at least $800 from the state's oil revenues. Oil development was soon producing 85 percent of state revenues, creating jobs, and paying for new highways, schools, libraries, and performing arts centers. For nearly twelve years, we enjoyed the prosperity of our state's oil wealth without having to face its trade-offs—until the wreck of the *Exxon Valdez*.

Like many Alaskans, my first reaction was a mixture of anger and loss. For years, I have gone out to Prince William Sound to fish and explore its remote coves and fjords. In one of my favorite places to visit by sea kayak, I am surrounded by the thunder of waterfalls and glaciers breaking over dark cliffs, sending house-size blocks of ice crashing into the sea. There are streams where one can catch a salmon with bare hands, coves to set pots for shrimp and crab. I've drawn my kayak closer to a surfacing whale than I really cared to be. More than anything, Prince William Sound is a place for an intimate experience of the forces of nature: ocean currents churning over reefs, tides flowing like rivers, and great migrations of whales and birds.

Just after the spill, I tried to convince myself that the oil was going to be contained. State-of-the-art oil spill equipment would be on call twenty-four hours a day. Industry and government alike had assured Alaska's citizens that, if there ever was a large spill, the oil would be quickly cleaned up.

It wasn't. And as the world watched in horror, the *Exxon Valdez* oil spill became an ongoing event, a complex disaster. For weeks and months, the oil flowed along thousands of miles of Alaska's coastline. As fishermen, Natives, and other Alaskans struggled to save the wildlife, the fisheries, and their own way of life, it often seemed as if dozens of separate oil spills were occurring at once. The oil was forever moving, and wherever it touched its impact was different.

In writing about this event, I've tried to draw the myriad strands together to show the fabric of the spill. On one level, this is a story of people reacting to a crisis. At 4 A.M., an oil company president in Texas is awakened by a phone call from Valdez, Alaska, and tries to mount a response to an oil spill he realizes may already be beyond control. State officials, who feel "ambushed" by their worst fears, scramble to fight a crisis they haven't prepared for. Oil spill experts find that all their specialized knowledge, all their advanced equipment, can't begin to control a spill of this magnitude. Alaskans and people from around the world try to rescue stricken birds and sea otters, often to no avail. To some, the spill becomes another gold rush: the spillionaires, as they come to be called, find they can make big money from Exxon's cleanup efforts. As the oil runs out of control, so does greed, carelessness, jealousy, carpetbagging, and lying. And in the midst of so many things going wrong, some unlikely heroes emerge.

Yet another story unfolds with more difficulty: understanding the wreck of the *Exxon Valdez* means coming to grips with the moral and legal responsibility not only for the accident but for the cleanup as well. How on earth could this nightmare have happened? Is this only the fault of the tanker crew? Of a careless oil company? Of the oil industry as a whole? What should the state and federal governments have done? And to what degree are those of us who use oil and vote responsible? The wreck is not just an environmental disaster, but a moral crisis as well.

Finally, this is a story of public complacency in the face of potential disaster. Here you will meet a lot of people eager to believe industry's promises, to enjoy the benefits of oil without carefully considering the risks. Here are the perennial choices—profits versus safety, cheap fuel versus a clean environment, prevention versus reaction—and the troubling questions that arise when choices are made. Why was no one prepared? Did the oil industry deceive the public? Did government agencies meet their responsibilities? Is there any defense against a large oil spill? How far are we willing to risk our planet's health to enjoy the benefits of its resources?

To bring a sense of perspective to the complex, interwoven, and far-ranging elements of the oil spill, I have arranged this book in three parts. "The Spill" follows the events of the crucial first four days, hour by hour, sometimes minute by minute. "The Response" examines the ways in which Exxon, the state, and the federal government tried to fulfill their promise to contain the oil, save wildlife and fisheries, protect communities, and restore the environment. "The Wake" follows the oil as it hits national parks, wildlife refuges, and one coastal community after another.

In the course of preparing this book, I have drawn on literally thousands of hours of investigative hearings, court proceedings, town meetings, and my own discussions with people coping with the spill. I am grateful to every person who took the time to share with me his or her experience of this crisis. I have also respected the request of some to remain anonymous for fear of reprisal. People appearing in this book have vastly different views of what happened or should have happened. Some will be fighting each other in court for a decade or two. I've striven to afford each a clear presentation of his or her view.

Here, often in their own words, are the oil and government officials, the scientists, Native villagers, fishermen, beach cleaners, wildlife rescuers, and many others who fought the continent's most devastating oil spill. As the author, I've tried not to intrude but to let these people speak for themselves and allow the events—each crisis within the crisis—to unfold as they did in the spring and summer of 1989.

This chaotic and devastating oil spill occurred in Alaska, but a similar disaster could happen wherever the world's tanker fleets transport oil. In Canada and the United States, 75 percent of the people live within an hour's drive of the coast: this could happen to them.

Part I

The
Spill

Chapter 1

Passages Through the Sound

Prince William Sound is a region shaped by water in many forms—rivers, rain, snow, ice, ocean currents. Glaciers sculpt sharp granite ridges along the coastal range. Turbulent rivers, swollen with spring melt, rush to the sea. Waterfalls tumble through time-worn grooves cut into cliffs. Surf rolls and thunders; waves rise and recede. And wind-driven breakers roll and explode against rocky islets and headlands.

Here in the northernmost reach of the Pacific Ocean, spring stirs in the sea before it is felt on land. In late March of 1989, snow lay deep among the spruce stands and along the beaches, but migrations were underway out in the sound. Salmon drawn landward from the open sea had begun their restless search for spawning streams. Gray whales from Mexican waters would soon breach in the swells of the sound. Seabirds were coming in from across the Pacific. Swans, geese, cranes, and flocks of shorebirds were flying the coastal winds. Tiny rufous hummingbirds were on their way from Central America; terns were coming from Antarctica.

Humans share Prince William Sound as well. Fishing families

and Native villagers make their homes among its quiet bays and thickly wooded islands. "Where else can I find this kind of solitude?" muses Brooke Adkinson, who lives alone on Hinchinbrook Island, at the southern entrance to the sound. "Sometimes I get up early in the morning, especially in spring, to watch rays of sunlight work in through the mist, hit the rocks, and light up those silvery-gray shadows. For about half an hour everything turns rosy. The kittiwakes start flying, light and quick in the air. Sometimes the killer whales come up. I just love to watch 'em. They're huge, but so graceful. It's like watching ballet dancers— what's that movement they do? I used to know. . . . Oh, pirouette, that's it. The whales are out there doing their pirouettes."[1]

Waters of the Gulf of Alaska slip past Hinchinbrook Island into Prince William Sound. The prevailing current, flowing like a separate river within the sea, forms a migratory passage for fish, dolphins, and whales. This entrance to the sound has also been a favored route of mariners since Captain Cook sailed here in search of the elusive Northwest Passage. Cook found no route to the Orient, but he named the sound for England's young Prince William. He named one island for his trusted mate, Hinchinbrook, and another for his friend, the great navigator Captain Bligh. Now, sailing ships and coal-fired steamers have faded into the past, and oil tankers ply this passage to the Trans-Alaska Pipeline terminal at Valdez.

Valdez was once a small, closely knit village, ringed with mountains and therefore known as "the little Switzerland of Alaska." A gateway to interior Alaska, Valdez became wedded to oil when Alyeska, the consortium of six oil companies that owns the Trans-Alaska Pipeline, chose it as the base port for shipping North Slope oil. In 1973, Alyeska erected in Valdez eighteen enormous storage tanks, five floating tanker berths, a ballast-receiving facility, a group of giant incinerators, and a maze of feeder lines and valves. Nowadays, seventy to seventy-five tankers come to Valdez each month, and local bumper stickers and baseball caps sport the phrase "Valdez, home of the supertankers." From the beginning, the people of Valdez understood the benefit of the oil industry moving into their hometown: money, lots of it.

On Thursday, March 23, 1989, at the port of Valdez under gray evening skies, the crew of the *Exxon Valdez* readied the ship for the five-day run to Long Beach, California. The three-year-old, 987-foot tanker was the newest, best-equipped ship in Exxon's fleet. Its captain, forty-two-year-old Joseph Hazelwood, had sailed for Exxon Shipping for nineteen years and had made the Valdez–Long Beach run many times. By 6:00 P.M. that Thursday, the *Exxon Valdez* was loaded with 1,264,164 barrels of North Slope crude, and Captain Hazelwood was anticipating a routine passage through Prince William Sound and down along the West Coast.

Meanwhile, Alyeska oil executives and technicians were celebrating a "safety dinner" at the Valdez Civic Center. Two months earlier, the British Petroleum tanker *Thompson Pass* had lost 1,700 barrels of oil while berthed at the Alyeska terminal. Over the years there had been many spills, but none as large as that from the *Thompson Pass*. Alyeska employees had corralled most of the oil. The Coast Guard's port commander, Steve McCall, had termed the response adequate, and the Alyeska celebrants were now congratulating themselves on a job well done.

However, not everyone was happy with the way Alyeska had handled the *Thompson Pass* spill. Four hours before the *Thompson Pass* had arrived at the Valdez terminal, Chuck Hamel, a former tanker broker, had been alerted by friends in the industry that a spill was likely to occur. The tanker had been leaking before coming to Alaska, but British Petroleum had sent her north anyway, hoping to get in another run to Valdez before repairing her. When the *Thompson Pass* berthed at the terminal, "they placed a boom around the ship, but they didn't watch her," Hamel said. "Suddenly, there was a lot of oil in the water. When oil started dribbling over their containment boom, they tried dragging out a long line of absorbent boom with work boats. The first boat that tried hit some rocks. The next guy made a turn in shallow water, so a second boat was knocked out of commission. The third boat backed in safely, but tore up the boom pulling it over rocks. This circus went on for *two weeks*. The oil was sitting right there, right in front of them, but it took them fifteen days to lift 1,700 barrels from the water to the dock. And Alyeska called it a 'textbook' response."

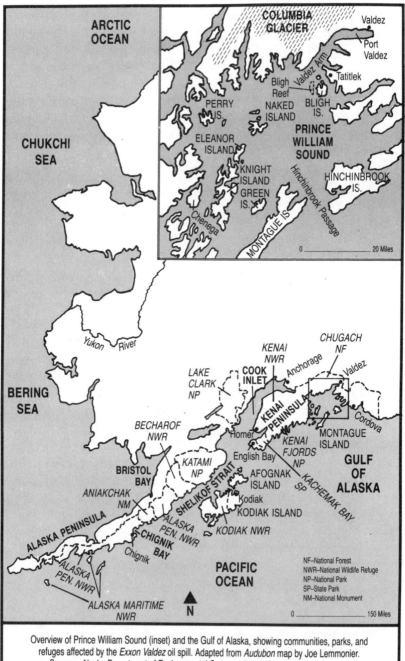

Overview of Prince William Sound (inset) and the Gulf of Alaska, showing communities, parks, and refuges affected by the *Exxon Valdez* oil spill. Adapted from *Audubon* map by Joe Lemmonier. Sources: Alaska Department of Environmental Conservation and National Park Service.

When Valdez mayor John Devens heard what had happened, he assembled a citizens committee to investigate safety problems at Alyeska. "Now, I've always been prodevelopment," said Devens, an articulate man who serves as both mayor of Valdez and president of the area's community college. "I've given lots of speeches about 'our good industrial neighbors.' But these tankers are getting out of hand. We've got to make sure they don't hurt our fisheries and tourism."

Devens's citizens committee discovered that ships making the Valdez run constituted 13 percent of the nation's total tanker traffic but accounted for 52 percent of its accidents. This discovery, along with the *Thompson Pass* spill, confirmed longstanding fears. Devens said, "In 1982, Alyeska dismantled its team dedicated 100 percent to oil spill response, and workers started coming to us saying, 'Don't use our names, but we don't like what's happening. People who know how to handle oil spills are getting laid off. Equipment's breaking down and not being replaced. Alyeska's cutting corners to save money.' We decided we'd better be able to take care of ourselves—just in case.

"We planned to build up our own oil spill protection over a five-year period," Devens continued. "We instituted a new property tax to raise money to buy our own boom and skimmers. Pretty soon, Alyeska told us, 'You all don't really need that stuff.' Then the state tried to talk us out of getting it. We went ahead anyway and collected about $20 million from the new tax, but the state sued us to cease and give it the collected funds. So while the lawyers argue over it, that money sits in a bank instead of buying oil spill equipment."

On the same Thursday evening, March 23, while the *Exxon Valdez* crew readied their tanker and Alyeska employees celebrated, Devens convened a town meeting to discuss the risks oil development might pose to Valdez. When Alyeska declined an invitation to send a speaker to the meeting, Devens invited Riki Ott from Cordova to voice her concerns about tankers passing through the sound. Ott is a fisherwoman and environmentalist who each summer dons rubber boots and raingear to fish the Copper River Delta, in treacherous channels known as "the flats." Riki Ott the fisherwoman is also Dr. Fredricka Ott, with a master's degree in oil pollution and a doctorate in sediment pollution. She has a quick, almost impatient wit, and if you can discuss hydroxylated derivatives and dibenzothiophene, you are talking her language.

Fog prevented Ott from flying the 70 miles from Cordova to Valdez, so she spoke by teleconference line to the thirty people gathered in the Valdez council chambers. Riki exhorted her listeners to recall the 1973 suit initiated by her fellow Cordova fishermen to block the Trans-Alaska Pipeline from exiting in Prince William Sound. At that time, Ott noted, the fishermen had considered themselves neither antioil nor environmental extremists. They had simply wanted to protect the sound and the fisheries that supported their way of life.

The town of Cordova had once been a port for shipping copper to market, but when the ore played out fishing became the mainstay of the community. Kids grew up, became fishermen, had kids of their own, and grew old. For more than eighty years now, life in Cordova has revolved around the herring that spawn in spring and the summer runs of pink, red, chum, coho, and king salmon. The harbor, ringed with snow-capped mountains, is the center of town. Houses look out over multicolored fishing boats and an occasional pleasure craft. Streets wind down to the water's edge. Boats leaving the harbor enter a maze of channels, bays, fjords, islands, islets, and reefs. When oil tankers began transiting Prince William Sound, the people of Cordova felt vulnerable. It seemed inevitable that some day a tanker would run aground in this wild reach of sea and mountains that is their home.

"Congress overrode the fishermen's lawsuit in 1973," Riki Ott pointed out, "but not the fishermen's concern about water quality. Congress acknowledged these concerns and stipulated in Trans-Alaska Pipeline System (TAPS) legislation that there would be an oil spill contingency plan and a wastewater treatment system. We were assured that the best available technology would be utilized."

Ott then cited deficiencies in Alyeska's wastewater treatment and questioned its ability to handle a large spill. "We have already had a close call," Ott cautioned. She was reminding her listeners of a 1980 incident involving a fully loaded tanker, the

Prince William Sound. The vessel had lost power in 70-knot winds, and tugs had been unable to attach towing lines to her. The helpless tanker had been out of control for seventeen hours. "That thing was drifting around out there like a billiard ball going across a table," Coast Guard Admiral Edward Nelson, who observed the incident, had remarked. "It didn't hit Naked Island and it didn't go aground on a glacier, but it sure came close. We were all holding our breath." Minutes before the tanker *Prince William Sound* would have wrecked on a reef, its captain had managed to restart the engines.

In the wake of this event, the state of Alaska insisted that towing bridles be attached to the tankers. Despite this improvement, Riki Ott warned, "We're playing Russian roulette here. It's not a matter of 'if.' It's just a matter of *when* we get the big one."

While Ott was voicing her concerns and the Alyeska staff was celebrating its safety record, Captain Joseph Hazelwood was taking shore leave as the *Exxon Valdez* loaded oil. He had pulled into port at 11:00 P.M. the previous evening; later Thursday night he would command the tanker's return to Exxon's Long Beach, California, refinery. For six months of the year, on rotations of sixty days on and sixty off, Hazelwood's home was aboard ship. A few hours' relaxation in Valdez helped to relieve the monotony.

At 5:00 P.M., Hazelwood and his chief engineer, Jerzy Glowacki, stopped in at the Pipeline Club, a popular bar and dining room. With a seaman's cap set over his prominent forehead and his dark beard laced with silver, Hazelwood's appearance reflected his experience. After graduating from maritime college in 1968, he had advanced quickly through the Exxon ranks. He had earned his master's license at age thirty-two, ten years earlier than most Exxon captains.

In one corner of the dim, smoky Pipeline Club a dart board was posted. Sheets of cribbage scores were tacked to the wall. Small trophies gathered dust on a shelf, and a poster advertised an ugly-bartender contest. Behind the bar hung a chunk of steel from the pipeline cut into the shape of Alaska; the Yukon River was etched into the metal, mountains were welded to the shiny surface, and a thin replica of the pipeline itself stretched across the state.

Hazelwood, nursing vodka straight up, told Glowacki that there had been a report of a heavy flow of Columbia Glacier ice into the sound. They discussed the possibility of waiting for daylight before setting out. They had already lost time making turbocharger adjustments on the northbound leg of the trip, but Exxon had allowed them three extra days before their arrival at Long Beach, so a delay was feasible. Still, Hazelwood wanted to set out. He had been making the Valdez run for ten years and had encountered ice in the dark before.

On the way back to the tanker, Hazelwood and Glowacki stopped at the Club Valdez for pizza to go. The captain ordered another drink. At 8:10 P.M., they called a cab to run them back to the terminal. A guard cleared them through the security entrance.

By 9:00 P.M., the *Exxon Valdez* was ready to depart. Earlier, Third Mate Gregory Cousins had tested the vessel's navigation equipment: radar, gyro compass, automatic pilot, course indicator, rudder control, and other sophisticated instrumentation. At 9:12 P.M., the tanker's last mooring line was detached from the pier and two tugs nudged the *Exxon Valdez* from its berth. On the bridge were harbor pilot Ed Murphy and Captain Hazelwood. Coast Guard regulations require that harbor pilots—who are trained to know about navigational hazards in local waters—be contracted to guide tankers from port to open water. Earlier, when they were boarding, Murphy had smelled alcohol on Hazelwood's breath but had said nothing about it.

At 9:21 P.M., Murphy, directing the vessel's speed and course settings, began to steer the *Exxon Valdez* out of the harbor toward Valdez Narrows, 7 miles from port. The Narrows, a channel that forms the entrance to Valdez Bay, is 1,700 yards wide. Middle Rock, a rock in the channel sometimes called "the can opener," reduces the minimum usable width to 900 yards. In computer simulations before the route was sanctioned, pilots repeatedly wrecked their imaginary tankers on Middle Rock. However, with the help of escort tugs and harbor pilots, tankers three football fields long had successfully negotiated the Narrows for eleven years. "We all know what the stakes are," said one longtime Valdez harbor pilot. "You've always got to be on your toes. I see these ships as eggs that are a quarter of a mile long. You can't make mistakes with them. A mistake ends your career."[2]

The *Exxon Valdez* steamed through the Narrows in relatively calm weather: a 10-mph breeze from the north, with 4-mile visibility through low clouds and some snow and fog. With Murphy at the helm of the vessel, Hazelwood left the bridge, which was highly unusual and against company policy. But the two men had known each other for years and had eaten together that afternoon. Murphy mentioned nothing; he knew Hazelwood well and respected his seamanship. On a previous passage through the Narrows, when Murphy was piloting the ship, Hazelwood had helped avert disaster. "It was a winter night with very limited visibility. I was making a course change on Potato Point, and we were accelerating," Murphy recalled later. "The quartermaster applied the helm the wrong way. . . . The loaded vessel was rapidly swinging toward the beach. Captain Hazelwood picked up that mistake even before I did."[3]

On this March 23 evening, the *Exxon Valdez* passed through the Narrows without mishap. Fourteen miles out of port, the tanker reached Rocky Point, where harbor pilots normally transfer command of a ship back to the captain. Murphy had to order Hazelwood called back to the bridge. When Hazelwood returned to the control room, Murphy again noticed the smell of alcohol on the captain's breath. However, a Valdez harbor pilot had never challenged a captain's command of his vessel. A pilot's continued employment by a given vessel can depend on the captain's good will. Murphy decided that Hazelwood looked fit and focused enough to assume command. At 11:20 P.M., Captain Joseph Hazelwood took control of the *Exxon Valdez*.

In the dimly lit radar room atop the three-story Coast Guard station in Valdez, civilian radar man Gordon Taylor watched a bright orange ring on the radar scope. The ring represented the *Exxon Valdez* as it moved from the terminal out through the Narrows. At Rocky Point, radar coverage became fainter and Taylor found it difficult to read. "You can pick up vessels off Bligh Island if there are no squalls, no heavy seas, no wind, and the radar is tuned up and working well," Taylor explained later. He added that it's easy to lose track of a tanker. "The vessel is there one sweep; the next, no vessel."

In 1981, James Woodle, then the Valdez Coast Guard commander, had recommended that the Coast Guard radar system be improved. He had wanted to ensure sharp vessel coverage between Bligh Island and the leading edge of the Columbia Glacier. The U.S. Geological Survey had predicted even more extensive glacial ice floes over the next ten to thirty years, and Woodle had argued that "placement of a radar site on either Glacier Island or Bligh Island could prove to be an invaluable tool. . . . Expanded radar coverage in this area is strongly recommended."

The Coast Guard had not acted on Woodle's recommendation, because it deemed the additional radar sites, at $100,000 a year, "cost prohibitive." In fact, budget cuts and the transfer of personnel to President Reagan's war on drugs had continually drained money from the Valdez Coast Guard budget and had whittled its staff from thirty-seven to twenty-four since the pipeline's completion in 1977.

Far from pushing for the recommended additions, Commander Steve McCall, who took over as the Coast Guard's ranking officer in Valdez in 1986, favored a downgraded system. "It's been twelve years since the tankers began operating, and nothing major has gone wrong," McCall had commented regarding the recommended radar upgrade. "So a lot of things have changed from what people thought was necessary in 1977. . . . We started downgrading in 1984. . . . We changed the radars in '82, and made manpower cuts. . . . How much do you really need to watch a ship that is going in and out, all by itself, with nobody around it?"

As the *Exxon Valdez* approached the edge of radar coverage, Hazelwood radioed the Coast Guard that he was "heading outbound and increasing speed."

At 11:24 P.M., harbor pilot Ed Murphy, who had already turned over command to Hazelwood, left the tanker and boarded a pilot boat that would speed him back to the port of Valdez. Hazelwood radioed Traffic Valdez, the Coast Guard's radio monitoring station:[4]

HAZELWOOD: We've departed a pilot. At this time hooking up to sea speed. And ETA [estimated time of arrival] to make it out [past Naked Island] on 0 100 [1:00 A.M.]. Over.

TRAFFIC VALDEZ: Roger. Request an updated ice report when you go down through there. Over.

HAZELWOOD: Okay. Was just about to tell you that judging by our radar I will probably divert from TSS [Traffic Separation Scheme] and end up in an inbound lane. Over.

TRAFFIC VALDEZ: No reported traffic. I got the *Chevron California* one hour out and the *ARCO Alaska* is right behind him. But they are an hour out from Hinchinbrook.

HAZELWOOD: That'd be fine, yeah. We may end up over in the inbound lane, outbound track. We'll notify you when we . . . cross over the separation zone. Over.

Shortly after Hazelwood notified the Coast Guard that he was going to divert from the Traffic Separation Scheme (designated one-way inbound and outbound tanker lanes), he radioed that he was going to angle left and reduce speed in order to work through some floating ice: "At the present time I am going to alter my course to 200 [degrees] and reduce speed about 12 knots to wind my way through the ice. And Naked Island ETA may be a little out of whack. But once we're clear of the ice, out of Columbia Bay, we'll give you another shout. Over." However, despite Hazelwood's assurance to the Coast Guard, the ship's speed was not reduced.

At 11:40 P.M., the night shift took over at the Coast Guard station back in Valdez. Radar man Taylor had seen the *Exxon Valdez* "blinking on and off the screen" but had lost the vessel by this time. Before heading home, Taylor told his replacement, Bruce Blanford, that the *Exxon Valdez* was crossing into the separation zone—possibly into the northbound lane to avoid the ice.

However, Hazelwood did not notify the Coast Guard when he left the traffic separation zone. And instead of ending up in the inbound lane, he went on through the inbound lane, taking the tanker farther off course. In one transmission, he mistakenly identified his vessel as the *Exxon Baton Rouge*, and his speech was slurred.

At the Coast Guard station, it was now Blanford's responsibility to track tankers and warn of impending danger. Instead of trying to locate the *Exxon Valdez* on radar or trying to monitor its movements by radio, Blanford began to rearrange the tanker traffic data sheets. To track the progress of the tankers traveling in and out of Valdez, he moved stacks of paper, each representing a different vessel, around the room.

"As soon as [Taylor] left and I got everything sorted out in my mind, I checked all of the vessel data sheets," Blanford would report. "We each have our little way of keeping things straight in our heads and keeping our watches flowing smoothly. I'm left-handed. The rest of them are right-handed, so they all set their sheets up [one] way and I set mine up this way. And so I go through and get them where I can understand them. And I generally lay [the sheets for each tanker] from left to right. . . . When their sheets end up all the way on the right-hand side, a tanker would be in Valdez."

By the time Blanford had arranged his stacks of paper to represent vessels going to and from the port, the *Exxon Valdez* was nearing the ice. "After I got things squared away, so to speak, I went down and got a cup of coffee," Blanford said. "I may have been gone a couple of minutes. I really couldn't say how long."

Meanwhile, on the *Exxon Valdez*, Third Mate Gregory Cousins had joined Hazelwood on the bridge to make a navigational fix on the vessel's position in the sound. The night was too dark for the seaman on watch to see any bergs, but ice was silhouetted on the radar screen. It was an extensive floe—thousands of chunks of ice had broken from the Columbia Glacier and were being massed together by the current. Cousins and Hazelwood discussed skirting the ice. Some of the ice, broken into pieces the size of a car and smaller, were of little consequence to a tanker. But the massive bergs—those the size of a house and larger, the ones they called growlers—caused concern. However, Cousins couldn't tell from the radar screen whether there were any growlers out there in the night.

The northern edge of the floe appeared to be two miles dead ahead. At their current course setting, they would run into it. The ice was backed up to Columbia Glacier, so they couldn't pass it to the right. To the left of the ice was a gap of nine-tenths of a mile between the edge of the ice and Bligh Reef. They could wait until the ice moved, or reduce speed and work their way through the ice. Captain Hazelwood chose another option: turn and en-

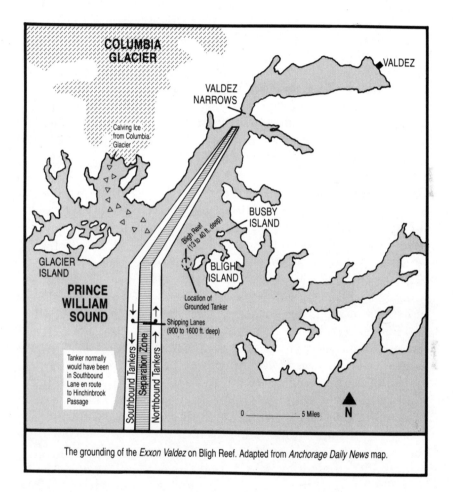

The grounding of the *Exxon Valdez* on Bligh Reef. Adapted from *Anchorage Daily News* map.

ter the gap between the ice and the reef. The ship was still accelerating.

Hazelwood ordered the helmsman to alter their course "180 degrees to port"—to turn left across the 2,000-yard-wide zone separating inbound and outbound traffic and continue across the 1,500-yard-wide inbound lane. A well-timed right turn would be necessary to avoid Bligh Reef, which lay six miles ahead in the darkness. There would be little room for error. The vessel needed at least six-tenths of a mile to make the turn, and the gap between the ice and Bligh Reef was only nine-tenths of a mile wide. The tanker itself was nearly two-tenths of a mile long. The tanker would have to start its turn well before the gap between the ice and the reef if it was to make it through.

At 11:46 P.M., Maureen Jones left her cabin to go on duty. Captain Hazelwood relayed an order to her to stand on the bridge wing instead of standing her watch from the bow. Although 800 feet farther from the front of the boat, she would have the advantage of watching for hazards and buoy lights from a high position. She went to the bridge as requested.

As Jones came on duty, Helmsman Harry Claar's shift was coming to an end. Claar's job as helmsman was to physically move the steering wheel at the direction of the captain or qualified mates. Hazelwood gave him two last orders: to accelerate to sea speed and to put the ship on automatic pilot. Both commands were highly unusual. Speed was normally reduced when ice was encountered, both to minimize impact with bergs and to allow the crew more time to plot vessel position, make course adjustments, and react to an emergency. The automatic pilot—almost never used in the sound—would have to be released if any course changes had to be made.

Though puzzled by Hazelwood's orders, Claar increased speed and locked the controls on automatic pilot. He was then replaced at the helm by Robert Kagan.

On the bridge, Hazelwood told Cousins he was going below and asked if he felt comfortable navigating alone. Cousins had made only a few voyages with Hazelwood, and he had never maneuvered the *Exxon Valdez* in tight quarters. Nevertheless, he replied, "Yes, I feel I can manage the situation."

Standard Coast Guard procedure dictates that in the presence of danger, two officers must be on the bridge. The junior of the two is responsible for fixing the location of the vessel. The senior officer is responsible for directing the vessel's course based on this navigational information. Before leaving Cousins alone on the bridge, Hazelwood told him to make a right turn when the ship was across from the Busby Island light and to skirt the edge of the ice—but he neither gave Cousins an exact course to follow nor plotted a line on the chart. If he had, Hazelwood might have noticed that it was virtually impossible to turn abeam the Busby light and also miss the ice.

Hazelwood left the bridge at 11:53 P.M. "to send a few messages from [my] cabin." Cousins was now the only officer on the bridge. The chief mate and second mate were off duty, resting. Moments after the captain left, Cousins, who had not heard Hazelwood's orders to Claar, discovered that the vessel was on automatic pilot, and he shifted it back into manual mode. The ship was still headed on a 180-degree course toward Bligh Reef, and Cousins faced a critical maneuver: he had to avoid the ice but couldn't wait too long before turning. The vessel was increasing speed.

At 11:55 P.M., Cousins called Hazelwood to say, "I think there's a chance that we may get into the edge of this ice."

Hazelwood said, "Okay," and asked if the second mate had made it to the bridge yet. Cousins replied that the second mate hadn't arrived. They talked for less than a minute and neither mentioned slowing the vessel down.

Once more, Cousins assured the captain that he could handle things and then told the helmsman to make a 10-degree right turn. Cousins turned again to the radar, trying to locate the leading edge of ice. As he concentrated on the ice, Cousins may have lost track of time for a few minutes. He was peering at the radar screen when the tanker slipped past the Busby Island light without beginning to turn.

It was nearly midnight, the beginning of Good Friday, March 24, when Maureen Jones, now on watch, noticed that the red light on the Bligh Reef buoy was to the ship's right. Red navigational lights are placed to the right of ships returning to port, and almost every seaman knows the adage "red, right, returning." Since the *Exxon Valdez* was leaving port, the light should have been on the left side, to port. Jones alerted Cousins that "a red light was flashing every four seconds to starboard."

At virtually the same moment, though the ship was turning slowly, Cousins concluded that the tanker had not responded to his 10-degree right-turn command. He immediately ordered a 20-degree right turn, and this time he noticed the vessel responding.

Jones called Cousins a second time. She had a more accurate count on the red light; it was flashing every five seconds. It was still on the wrong side of the ship.

Cousins ordered a hard right and called Hazelwood, saying, "I think we are in serious trouble."

At 12:04 A.M., the *Exxon Valdez* shuddered. Hazelwood raced to the bridge. After first impact, the tanker advanced 600 feet before it ground to a halt on Bligh Reef.

Hazelwood didn't try to back off the reef. With the engines running full speed forward, he ordered a hard right, then a hard left. In the engine room, the chief engineer did not know they had grounded; he couldn't figure out why the system was overloading.

Chief Mate James Kunkel had been sleeping in his quarters, but awoke at first impact. "The vessel began to shudder and I heard a clang, clang, clang. I feared for my life. I thought I would never see my wife again. I knew my world would never be the same," Kunkel recalled.

Realizing they might capsize, Kunkel went to the bridge and quickly calculated their stability on the ship's computer. The vessel was leaning 4 to 5 degrees to starboard. "We weren't stable enough to move."

However, Hazelwood continued his attempts to force the tanker ahead. For fifteen minutes, he held the throttle forward on sea speed, spinning the wheel right to left. The ship swung slightly and groaned as rock ground metal, but Hazelwood could not dislodge the tanker from the reef. It was too dark to see oil on the surface of the sea, but the stench of crude oil filled the air.

Control room gauges confirmed that they were rapidly losing oil. Hazelwood turned to Chief Mate Kunkel and said, "I guess this is one way to end your career."

At 12:27 A.M., twenty-three minutes after grounding, Hazelwood finally radioed the Coast Guard traffic control in Valdez.

HAZELWOOD: Yeah. It's *Valdez* back. We should be on your radar there. We've fetched up, run aground north of Goose Island, around Bligh Reef. And evidently we're leaking some oil. And we're going to be here awhile. And if you want to say you're notified. Over.

TRAFFIC VALDEZ: *Exxon Valdez*, Valdez Traffic, roger. Are you just about a mile north of Bligh Reef?

HAZELWOOD: Yeah, that's correct. Over.

TRAFFIC VALDEZ: Roger that.

HAZELWOOD: Okay. We'll give you the status report as to the changing situation. Over.

TRAFFIC VALDEZ: Standing by.

At 12:30 A.M., the Coast Guard officer on duty woke Commander Steve McCall, asleep at home. "This is the big one. We have the *Exxon Valdez* aground at Bligh Reef."

"What? You must be kidding. Okay, I'm on my way," McCall said.

The Coast Guard officer then radioed the *Stalworth*, a tug in the Valdez harbor, "for possible assist" and closed the port of Valdez to all commercial traffic. Tankers loading oil at Alyeska's terminal were put on hold "until further notice," and incoming tankers were ordered to drop anchor and wait. The Coast Guard called for the *Silver Bullet*, a speedy pilot boat, to run out to Bligh Reef.

Commander Steve McCall sped through the empty streets of Valdez. He had been looking forward to retirement in just three months, and he had hoped to wrap up his Valdez duty without a crisis. As soon as he arrived at the Coast Guard traffic control center, McCall radioed Hazelwood, with whom he had gone to maritime school many years before.

McCALL: *Exxon Valdez*, this is the captain of the port, Commander McCall. Do you have any more of an estimate as to your situation at this time? Over.

HAZELWOOD: Oh, not at the present, Steve . . . but we are working our way off the reef . . . the vessel has been holed. Right now we're trying to steer off the reef. And we'll get back to you as soon as we can.

McCall: Roger on that. You know, we've got all our planned mechanisms in place to give you what assistance we can. . . . Take it, take it slow and easy and, you know, I'm telling you the obvious, but . . . take it slow and easy and we are getting help out as fast as we can.

Hazelwood: Okay. We're in pretty good shape right now stabilitywise. We're just trying to extract her off the shoal here and you can probably see me on your radar. And once I get underway I'll let you know.

McCall: Roger. Yeah. Another thing, now again, before you make any drastic attempt to get underway you make sure you don't . . . start doing any ripping. You got a rising tide. You got another about an hour and a half worth of tide in your favor. Once you hit the max I wouldn't recommend doing much wiggling. Over.

Hazelwood: Okay. Yeah, I think . . . the major damage has kind of been done. We've kind of . . . rolled over it and we're just kind of hung up in the stern here. We'll just drift over it and I'll get back to you. We'll be standing by. *Exxon Valdez*, clear.

Chapter 2

Day One: The First Twenty-Four Hours

Moments after Captain Joseph Hazelwood radioed Valdez from Bligh Reef, ringing phones began to break the early morning quiet.

At 12:30 A.M., March 24, the Coast Guard called Alyeska and alerted night-shift superintendent Dave Barnum that the *Exxon Valdez* had run aground and was leaking oil. Barnum notified a crew that was loading a tanker.

During the first years of pipeline operation, Alyeska's oil spill response personnel had operated much like firemen at a firehouse. Before Alyeska began tightening its budget in 1981, the response team ran drills, maintained equipment, and stayed on duty twenty-four hours a day. Commenting in retrospect on the dismantling of the team, Alyeska's managing engineer, William Howitt, said, "Alyeska did not have to obtain permission to make this change."[1] The idea was that personnel assigned to other jobs would be available to fight an oil spill. The change was noted in

Alyeska's oil spill contingency plan, which described the consortium's strategy for emergency response. On the morning of the spill, therefore, Alyeska had no trained spill response team in place and ready to act.

At 12:35 A.M., Alyeska terminal superintendent Chuck O'Donnell was awakened by the phone. Told that a tanker had "possibly gone aground," O'Donnell called Alyeska marine supervisor Larry Shier and sent him over to the Coast Guard office to see what was going on. Then O'Donnell went back to bed.

At 1:23 A.M., Darryl Warner, president of the Exxon Pipeline Company in Houston, was notified of the spill. He immediately called Frank Iarossi, president of Exxon Shipping (also in Houston), who, at his bedside phone, initiated Exxon's response. Meanwhile, in Valdez, Alyeska's Larry Shier assured the Coast Guard and Dan Lawn, of Alaska's Department of Environmental Conservation (DEC), that Alyeska was implementing its contingency plan. However, after alerting Alyeska night crews of the spill, Shier grabbed a sleeping bag to catch some sleep in O'Donnell's office.

At 1:59 A.M., Coast Guard Commander McCall radioed the *Exxon Valdez* for a status report. He was told that no one knew how many of the tanker's sixteen oil-storage compartments had ruptured or how much oil had been lost.

By 3:00 A.M., Coast Guard Lieutenant Thomas Falkenstein and Dan Lawn (DEC's man in Valdez) had reached the *Exxon Valdez* aboard the *Silver Bullet*. Falkenstein asked Captain Hazelwood the nature of the problem. Hazelwood said, "I think you are looking at it."

Lawn ascended the pilot's ladder and saw a turbulent pool of oil rising two feet higher than the surrounding water. He would later describe what he saw as "a boiling cauldron. The oil was rolling up, boiling up, like it was cooking."

At 3:19 A.M., Falkenstein radioed Valdez. He informed McCall that at least 138,000 barrels of oil had already been lost and that 20,000 barrels were escaping every hour. As the oil rushed out, the tanker balanced precariously over Bligh Reef. Falkenstein warned McCall that the vessel was in danger of either breaking apart on the rocks or capsizing, and that an additional one million barrels of oil might escape. McCall, in turn, warned

Alyeska of this crisis and advised that lightering (transferring the *Exxon Valdez*'s oil to another tanker) be commenced as soon as possible.

At 4:00 A.M., DEC's Dan Lawn called Alyeska from the tanker's satellite phone and then stared into the darkness, awaiting the light of Alyeska's response boat.

Alyeska's contingency plan stated that a vessel with containment boom and skimmers would arrive at the scene of a spill in no more than five and a half hours, and that period was now nearly over. Lawn got back on the radio phone. "What's going on? This ship is still leaking. You need to send out every piece of equipment you've got right away."

At Alyeska, Larry Shier replied that the equipment was on its way and would arrive at first light.

By 5:00 A.M., thirty-nine workers had arrived at the Alyeska terminal expecting to be handed equipment and assignments. However, the boom required to contain the oil and skimmer attachments needed to suck it up were not on the response barge—and the barge itself was in dry dock. Battered by a storm early in February, the barge was awaiting repair to a crack in its bow. Now an Alyeska official decided that the barge was seaworthy without the repairs.

The large skimmers and deep-sea boom missing from the barge lay in a warehouse, buried under tons of lightweight harbor boom. A forklift and a crane were deployed to begin sorting skimmers and sections of boom and loading them onto the barge. However, for several hours there was only one operator for both pieces of equipment.

An observer likened the scene to something out of a slapstick movie: "The operator would snag containers of boom with the forklift, drive to the barge, climb into the crane to swing each container onto the deck, jump from the crane to the forklift, and speed back to the warehouse for another pickup."

"Describing this as some sort of Keystone Kops routine is ridiculous. Utter nonsense," countered Alyeska spokesman Tom Brennan. "You don't keep the barge loaded, because each spill is different. You load up as you need to."

However, as soon as the boom and skimmers were loaded onto the barge, it was discovered that the barge and its tug were needed for a task considered even more urgent—getting lightering equipment to the stricken tanker. The tug stood ready to run the large inflatable fenders and other lightering gear out to Bligh Reef, but first the equipment had to be found. After an hour's search, someone noticed the fenders buried under a snowdrift. The boom that had been loaded onto the barge was unloaded to make room for the lightering equipment. As Exxon spokesman Don Cornett described the process later, "It took us additional time to put the [boom and skimming] equipment on the barge and then take that off when the priority changed to a lightering operation. And it took additional time to dispatch lightering equipment and load it back on the barge."[2]

At 6:00 A.M., Mayor John Devens was awakened by a call from the local radio station. "You'd better put on your mayoral hat. We've got an oil spill."

"Oh, come on, now. It's six o'clock, for God's sake," Devens mumbled, half asleep. "We've had others. They'll take care of it."

"No, no, John. This is a different kind of oil spill. This is big."

Before rushing to his office, Devens tried to call Alyeska and Exxon but couldn't reach anyone. He left messages on their office answering machines, saying that the city of Valdez would help in any way possible, with both money and personnel. He requested calls back. He never got any.

Shortly after 6:00 A.M., as dawn crept over Prince William Sound, Alyeska officials flew over the spill for the first time. They saw a slick three miles long and two miles wide drifting south from the tanker. They couldn't see the depth of the black pool from several hundred feet in the air, but rising fumes stung their eyes. The slick hadn't yet hit a beach, and they saw no dead birds or animals. The oil was just drifting.

At 6:30 A.M., Dan Lawn on the *Exxon Valdez* called Larry Shier again at Alyeska. "You need to get that equipment to Bligh Reef. The oil is moving away from the ship and has to be contained immediately."

Shier assured Lawn that boom and skimmers were en route. In fact, however, this equipment would sit on the dock in Valdez for another four hours.

The gap between Alyeska's oil spill contingency plan and its actual performance was widening. The plan acknowledged that "speed in deploying booms is essential in order to contain the maximum amount of spilled oil" and promised that "the necessary equipment is available and operable to meet oil spill response needs . . . [R]apid and effective operations are necessary to limit the spread of oil."

"I told them where to go with their goddamn boom and with their cleanup equipment, and to get their butts out here!" Lawn would rage. "They told me they were coming, that they had all the stuff coming, that they'd be right out there. And we waited, and we waited, and we waited, and we waited."

At 7:00 A.M., March 24, warm morning light was flooding into the Cordova home of Jack and Paula Lamb when their phone rang. Paula Lamb watched her husband pick up the receiver and listen in silence. The Lambs run a tender that collects salmon from fishermen in the sound, and for the past weeks they had been readying their boat for the salmon runs. When Lamb hung up the phone, his wife recalled, "He looked like someone had died." After quickly telling her what had happened, he went straight to the union hall, home of Cordova District Fishermen United (CDFU). Paula Lamb would see her husband just three times in the next four weeks.

When Jack Lamb arrived at the union hall at 7:10 A.M., CDFU director Marilyn Leland was already there. The two tried to call Riki Ott, but her phone was off the hook. Jack left to get her.

At 7:30 A.M., Riki Ott flew down the stairs in her nightgown to answer the banging on her door. Lamb was out of breath. "How long will it take you to get dressed?" he panted. Ott ran upstairs to throw on her work clothes, yelling back down to Lamb to build a fire in her wood stove so her cabin would be warm when she returned that night. It would be more than five weeks before she got back home.

At the CDFU office, Lamb, Ott, and Leland began making preliminary phone calls. The Coast Guard office in Valdez confirmed that something had happened, but "they were noncommittal and provided little information," Leland said. "They referred me to someone in Juneau."

Leland called the Alyeska emergency number in Valdez, but no one answered. "We've got to get on top of this," she said. She and Lamb began to alert the fishermen. Ott ran out to the airport to hitch a plane ride to Valdez.

It took Ott's plane eight minutes to circle the periphery of the slick. "It was perfectly calm. But I was stunned," she said. "There was no boom, no containment. Just a tanker on the rocks with two fishing boats coming up to it. Where *was* everybody?"

They flew through a blue haze that was lifting from the slick, the air thick with the stench of evaporating hydrocarbons. By the time Ott reached Valdez, she had a headache. Government officials and reporters were already pouring into town and offices were jammed. Ott asked the Avis rental car agency at the airport if she could use their phone. Their counter became her first Valdez command post.

Back in Cordova, thirty fishing boats were ready to leave the harbor. "The fishermen weren't asking about being reimbursed. They just wanted to help, get some boom out there, run the skimmers, do whatever they could," Leland said.

Shortly after 9:00 A.M., someone answered the phone at Alyeska and told Leland, "We are putting together a list of boats that can get out on the spill immediately. We'll get back to you." When Leland hadn't heard from Alyeska by noon, she called back to tell them that seventy-five fishing boats were now ready to help. Alyeska told her, "We have a person on this and he'll call you back." He never did.

At 9:30 A.M., Joseph Hazelwood was given a sobriety test aboard the *Exxon Valdez*. Hazelwood told a state trooper who witnessed the test that he had drunk only one beer in town before reboarding the ship but had drunk a low-percentage alcoholic beverage after the accident.

By 10:00 A.M., the *Exxon Baton Rouge*, en route to load oil in Valdez, was diverted to Bligh Reef to take on oil from the *Exxon Valdez*. The stability of the *Exxon Valdez* was uncertain, and unless it was lightered rapidly it would split apart and spill its remaining oil. Before tying the two ships together, the pilots wanted to survey and resurvey the seabed around Bligh Reef to make certain that a submerged rock wouldn't cause another shipwreck. The captain of the *Baton Rouge* radioed the stricken tanker:

BATON ROUGE: I am going to be going past you and making a round turn, coming in on your stern. And I guess I'll have good water all up alongside you.

VALDEZ: Yeah. . . . There's that 35-, 36-foot lump [submerged rock] a couple of hundred yards out. But everything else is in order. It's pretty clear. To the south side we haven't sounded yet. I wouldn't suggest going down there. There's a lot of rocks and junk. What kind of drift you coming in with?

BATON ROUGE: Okay, I'm coming up now. I'll probably be 29 feet aft, something like that. . . . I'll come off your quarter and then with the tugs I'll be able to kind of come in for a nice, nice soft landing. I hope.

VALDEZ: Okay. Thanks a lot. We'll talk to you when you get here. We'll have the pilot boat run around and get some more soundings for you up the starboard quarter area.

BATON ROUGE: Okay, yeah. It'll be just like a runway approach. . . . What tugs are there?

VALDEZ: The *Stalworth*'s here. The other two I guess will be coming from town, the *Sea Flyer* and the *Pathfinder*. . . .

BATON ROUGE: What's the ETA for the tug coming out from the terminal with the fenders?

VALDEZ: As far as we know they're still not under way yet. Stand by and I'll check. Have you ordered another tug, or has the pilot ordered another tug for maneuvering?

BATON ROUGE: We kind of made the assumption that the tug would be alongside by then based on the fact that she is supposed to be bringing out the transfer hose. If she hasn't gotten underway yet, I'd appreciate it if she'd get underway as soon as possible. . . .

VALDEZ: I never thought I'd see the day I'd be doing something like this.

BATON ROUGE: We never thought we'd see it either.[3]

Meanwhile, back in Valdez, Mayor Devens waited at the airport for Governor Steve Cowper to arrive. Alyeska president George Nelson motioned Devens to a corner. "I thought Nelson was going to tell me how badly he felt about the oil spill," Devens said later. "But he squints at me with those little eyes of his and rebukes me for holding the citizens oil-safety meeting. He said, 'What did you do last night, asking for more DEC involvement? . . . You trying to cause trouble? That's not playing fair. We expected more of you, Devens.'"

By 4:00 P.M., Governor Cowper had arrived in Valdez from Fairbanks and Dennis Kelso, the commissioner of Alaska's Department of Environmental Conservation, had flown in from Juneau. Together they boarded a float plane, flew out through the Narrows, and landed near the *Exxon Valdez*. A small Coast Guard boat ferried them to the tanker, and they boarded the crippled vessel. Commissioner Kelso told the governor that "Alyeska's contingency plan is very specific about what kind of equipment they would have here within five and a half hours. It's quite clear that what was promised has not been delivered."

The Alyeska barge, loaded with 50,000 pounds of boom and skimmers, hadn't set out from Valdez until 11:00 A.M., ten hours after the grounding. It arrived at Bligh Reef at 2:30 P.M.—more than fourteen hours after the accident. Kelso noted that one DEC official had left his home 250 miles away that morning, had driven over two mountain ranges, and had still arrived at the *Exxon Valdez* before Alyeska's initial response equipment.

Kelso and the governor did see two open skiffs with skimming apparatus mounted on their bows that were crossing and recrossing the oil. However, in minutes these skimmers were filled to capacity, and Alyeska had sent no storage barge. The skimmers, with nowhere to unload their collected oil, wandered around the slick like two waterbugs on a pond, trying to look busy. Kelso saw that "the skimmers had short lengths of boom deployed. It looked as if they were set out to direct oil into the skimmer. We didn't see any boom on the leading edge of the spill or around the tanker the way it should have been."

Cowper said that they were going to have to consider using dispersants in areas where the environmental risk would be minimal and acceptable. Kelso responded that the state had already "preapproved" the use of dispersants in offshore areas in order to reduce the likelihood of uncontained oil moving into more ecologically sensitive areas. On the premise that the chemicals might be as damaging to the environment as the oil itself, state approval was still required for near-shore areas.

By now the oil had spread out to the southwest farther than Cowper and Kelso could see from the deck of the tanker. Acrid fumes burned their eyes and filled the sky with blue haze. As he was leaving the *Exxon Valdez*, Governor Cowper said, "I've never seen such a goddamned mess in my life."

By 5:30 P.M., an estimated 240,000 barrels of oil had escaped the *Exxon Valdez* into Prince William Sound. Since first light, the slick had spread from 6 to more than 18 square miles. "I couldn't believe when we flew over there this morning that nothing was being done," Riki Ott said. "And now they are talking about dispersants. I can't believe any of this."

By that evening, Commissioner Kelso had assumed overall command of the spill for the state. At forty-one, the commissioner looked fit enough to run a marathon and emanated a relaxed charm that masked a sharp command of detail. Kelso had an undergraduate background in sciences and a law degree from Harvard and had become commissioner of the Department of Environmental Conservation in 1987. His responsibility was to direct the state's three-part role in the crisis: to oversee the industry's spill response, assess the damage, and monitor the cleanup. Within twenty-four hours of the grounding, DEC had twenty-five of its staff members headquartered in the Valdez courthouse. That night, Kelso had no idea that another response to the spill had been generated—by Exxon—thousands of miles away.

Reflecting on the moment when he had received word of the grounding early Friday morning in Houston, Frank Iarossi, president of Exxon Shipping, said, "My first thought was that I couldn't believe this was happening to us just two weeks after the other one."

"The other one" was the *Exxon Houston*. Exxon Shipping had sailed through more than twenty years without a major oil spill—until March 1989. The *Exxon Houston* had been moored 1,000 yards off the reef line at Oahu in Hawaii. Midway through the discharge of the tanker's oil, heavy winds had picked up and the terminal's mooring chain had broken. The vessel was blown onto the reef, where it spilled 200 barrels of fuel. Disconnected terminal lines spilled 600 barrels of oil.

"We initiated our response plan and it worked effectively," recalled Iarossi. "The Coast Guard called it a model response, and we were absolved of any blame." Iarossi had visited the site and returned from Hawaii feeling that his people had performed well. Two weeks later, he awoke to the *Exxon Valdez.*

"It is kind of ironic," Iarossi said, "that it should happen to us with the newest ship, probably the strongest drug and alcohol policy of any company, and probably the strongest enforcement."

Iarossi had faced challenges before. After graduating from the Coast Guard academy in 1959, he had remained on active duty for ten years, earning master's degrees in mechanical engineering and naval architecture while still in the service. After leaving the Coast Guard, Iarossi had gone on to earn an M.B.A., with plans to open a consulting firm with a friend. When he noticed that Exxon was seeking a job candidate with a master's in engineering, he decided to go for an interview, "not because I wanted the job, but because I had never gone through an interview in my life. So I bought a new pair of shoes . . . and I was totally relaxed because, quite frankly, I did not want the job. But when Exxon offered me a position, I ended up taking it, not because I wanted to go to work for Exxon, but because I thought it would be a pretty good place to start to find out what the business world was all about. I figured in two years I'd be done and get back with my friend to start our own firm. That was twenty-one years ago."

While his friend went off to sail charter yachts in the Bahamas, Iarossi rose through the ranks at Exxon. He supervised company tanker construction in Japan and helped Exxon develop its oil spill response plan. In 1982, Iarossi was made president of Exxon Shipping, responsible for eighteen tug and barge units and nineteen ocean-going tankers. Iarossi's Houston headquarters housed Exxon's oil spill response plan, not a site-specific plan like Alyeska's, but rather twenty-eight volumes of response-mobilization guidelines. In a glass case near the entrance to his office was a six-foot replica of the *Exxon Valdez*.

At 1:30 Alaska time on Friday morning, Frank Iarossi was in his bedroom on the phone with Ulysses LeGrange, senior vice president of Exxon U.S.A. "I told him we had a problem and I didn't know the magnitude of it yet." LeGrange gave Iarossi full authority to do whatever had to be done, "no limits, no bounds, total open authority."

During the next two hours, Iarossi made phone calls from his bedside, waking executives and oil spill specialists. One of Exxon's managers contacted Captain Hazelwood on the *Exxon Valdez*. "We couldn't tell if we had a couple barrels out in the water or a lot more than that," Iarossi recalled. "The real shock came at 3:30 A.M. Alaska time, when George Nelson [Alyeska president] called to say the vessel had lost an estimated 138,000 barrels. I didn't feel panic, just a tremendous sense of urgency. We had an unbelievable problem on our hands. I told him that we were going on full mobilization. He was obviously relieved to know that we'd be in Alaska that evening."

Before driving to his office, Iarossi recalled a few moments of quiet. "I'm not sure what I was doing at the time, maybe praying or trying to gather my strength," Iarossi said. He realized that an uncontrollable amount of oil had escaped. No one had ever faced a spill like this before. It was the largest spill ever to occur in North American waters and, to complicate matters, it had not occurred on the high seas, where the oil might have more easily dispersed and broken down. This oil was loose in Prince William Sound, where, unless it was quickly contained, the tides, currents, and wind would carry it into some of the most ruggedly beautiful coves and fjords in the country.

At 7:00 A.M. Texas time (4:00 A.M. in Alaska), Iarossi arrived at his office to meet with his top managers. Calls were made to mobilize skimmers and boom in San Francisco and Southhampton, England. Half an hour into the meeting, Harvey Borgen, Exxon Shipping's West Coast fleet manager, called Commander McCall to ask if dispersants could be used. Borgen understood McCall to say that Exxon Shipping could use dispersants on the spill. Iarossi recalled that "this was critical to us. There was no way we could have misunderstood it."

Based on McCall's apparent approval of dispersant use, Iarossi contracted two 707 jets to transport dispersants to Alaska. A C-130 equipped to spray was sent from California to Phoenix, Arizona, where it would take on dispersant equipment and then head to Valdez.

At 11:36 A.M. Texas time, Iarossi and Exxon oil spill response coordinator Craig Rassinier left Houston for Valdez in an Exxon jet. They were accompanied by Gordon Lindblom, a scientist who had helped pioneer the use of chemical dispersants on oil spills, as well as a lawyer, a claims adjuster, and one of Exxon's senior mariners. As they flew north, the executives discussed strategy and made periodic air-to-ground calls. They learned that drums of dispersants were being delivered to the Houston airport; communications equipment was being diverted from Long Beach, California, to Valdez; lightering fenders were being located; and helicopters and fixed-wing planes were being contracted in Alaska.

Exxon's corporate jet refueled in Seattle at 1:48 P.M. Alaska time. On that stop, Rassinier called Alyeska to discuss the possibility of in situ burning—the ignition of a floating pool of oil cordoned off with fireproof boom. Other calls, to the Houston command center, confirmed that planes were en route: a DC-8 from Oakland and a C-130 from Houston as well as the C-130 picking up dispersant equipment in Phoenix. Once again airborne, Gordon Lindblom called Valdez and was disturbed to learn that Alyeska was making a dispersant test with a large bucket slung from a helicopter. Iarossi later recalled that "Lindblom came back muttering, saying that they were going to use a helicopter and that that was a mistake; it would never work; it would only screw us up."

Meanwhile, data from the grounded tanker was being relayed to Houston so that an Exxon marine expert could evaluate the stability of the *Exxon Valdez*. He foresaw problems. The tanker was unbalanced. Divers would have to assess the structural damage to determine how firmly the tanker was lodged on the reef. Lightering was delayed, because moving oil at this point would further unbalance the ship.

At 5:37 P.M., Exxon's corporate jet landed in Valdez, and Frank Iarossi immediately opened the company's command post at the Westmark Hotel. On his way to a press conference, Iarossi ran into Coast Guard Commander McCall. "He said we needed to test dispersant. That was the first time we heard that we were required to do tests," Iarossi said.

That afternoon, Alyeska had made the first dispersant trial from a helicopter, and as Gordon Lindblom had predicted, the test failed. It also aroused opposition to using dispersants. As one DEC official later remarked, the helicopter test "clearly demonstrated that because of the calm conditions and thickness of the oil, dispersants were not effective."

"A helicopter using a drop bucket never works, and it greatly complicated our life," Iarossi said. "A C-130 will spray about 5,500 gallons, compared to 300 for a helicopter, so it's really not enough to make a noticeable difference on a large spill. Plus, the control of the droplet size is very difficult. The governor and Kelso were watching, and the results were not immediately apparent, so I think everyone decided dispersant was a hoax. Between that failed test and all the pressure he was starting to get from the fishermen and from the governor, McCall began to have second thoughts about dispersant. At the time I felt that once we got that first load of dispersant down we'd be able to proceed. I did not comprehend what a delay it would turn out to be. If I'd realized the agony we'd go through over the next two days, I think I'd have started screaming and shouting."

At the press conference, Iarossi announced that Exxon accepted responsibility for the spill. He then drove to the Valdez tanker terminal and assumed responsibility from Alyeska for the lightering operation, dispersants, and public relations. Exxon let Alyeska remain in charge of mechanically picking up the oil with skimmers.

Commissioner Kelso was puzzled by Exxon's assumption of responsibility for the spill response. He assumed that Alyeska was still in charge legally, because its obligation was clearly spelled out in the contingency plan: "Alyeska will maintain full responsibility and control in the event of an oil spill unless a government agency specifically notifies Alyeska they have assumed responsibility and control." This was the first of many confusions regarding actual, legal, and moral responsibility—not to mention authority. Together, these confusions would add up to the most profound unanswered question surrounding the cleanup: Who, in fact, was in charge?

State approval of Alyeska's response plan had been predicated on the company's guarantee that it would have workers and equipment on a spill within five and a half hours. Alyeska's contingency plan included charts, graphs, and lists of equipment, but it made no mention of Exxon or any other parent company taking charge of a spill. When notified that Exxon was taking over from Alyeska, Commissioner Kelso said, "There is no authority for such a transfer. We expected Alyeska to take care of the spill. In my view, the handoff is inappropriate. We are seeing a pattern of promised activity and broken promises. Alyeska has dropped out of the picture completely, washed their hands of this mess. Exxon says they are assuming responsibility, but there is a lack of organization."

The emerging questions of authority and responsibility were critical. The state expected Alyeska to act, as specified in its state-approved contingency plan. However, Alyeska's parent companies, anxious to disassociate themselves from the disaster, looked to Exxon to take over. Exxon said it was responsible for the spill and, according to a prior agreement with Alyeska, was mobilizing. However, when Exxon started to assume command, the state was surprised. Iarossi expressed surprise in turn. "I am very puzzled by Kelso's comments about never being informed of our taking over a large spill," he said. "I don't think Dennis Kelso was ever aware of all the correspondence between his department and Exxon. I mean, we clearly stated all the way back in 1982 that in the event of a major spill we would mobilize the spill response."

In 1982, Exxon had written in a letter to the Alaska DEC that "for most tanker spills the response outlined in the Alyeska plan will suffice. However, in the event of a major spill by an Exxon owned and operated vessel it is anticipated that Exxon Company, U.S.A.'s oil response team would be activated." Iarossi said that again "in 1987 we spelled out our mobilization plan and where the equipment would be coming from. The state came back to us and said, 'Should Exxon vessels be limited to trade with the Trans-Alaska Pipeline Service Company and limited to Prince William Sound traffic, no contingency plan would be necessary.' The Alaska Department of Environmental Conservation never once raised any objection. So we said fine."

Although informed years before that Exxon would be in charge of a large spill of its own making, the state had never bothered to ask Exxon how it would respond. Now, in response to a crisis, Exxon had to mobilize from thousands of miles away. "We started from ground zero," Iarossi said. "There was no logistics system in place." First, Exxon shipped its equipment to the Anchorage airport. Then the company set up a feeder airline and trucking system to transport equipment from Anchorage to Valdez. Finally, the equipment had to be deployed by boat, float plane, and helicopter to the oil slick 25 miles out in Prince William Sound. By Iarossi's estimate, Exxon had spent well into the millions by the close of Friday, March 24. "Some of the flights were costing $300,000 to $400,000."

While Frank Iarossi and the other Exxon people scrambled in an attempt to mobilize equipment, state and local observers were beginning to sense what one called "a nightmare within the nightmare." Not only was a tremendous amount of oil loose on the waters of Prince William Sound, but Alyeska, which they had counted on to recover the oil, was disappearing. Kelso had expected fast and effective action from Alyeska, whose contingency plan even listed the names and phone numbers of employees who would fight a spill. However, Valdez mayor John Devens noted that "many Alyeska employees got dressed and waited by the phone to be called out on the spill. For some reason these people, who were trained and ready to go to work, were never called."

Not only were Alyeska employees absent from the scene, but the company's top managers—such as William Howitt, Chuck O'Donnell, Larry Shier, and George Nelson—were pulling back from active participation in the response. Alyeska was disappearing.

At 10:00 P.M. Friday, Captain William Deppe, Exxon's marine expert, boarded the *Exxon Valdez* to take charge of the precarious process of salvaging the tanker without losing any more oil. Joseph Hazelwood was being relieved of command and, after questioning by authorities in Valdez, would be free to return to his home and family in Huntington, New York. As Deppe took over command of the *Exxon Valdez*, he cautioned a shaken Hazelwood, "This is something much bigger than you can imagine while sitting out here. Prepare yourself for a lot of attention when you get to shore."

Captain Deppe quickly met the various state and Coast Guard officials aboard ship and immediately began formulating a plan to save the vessel. Deppe had come up through the Exxon ranks, signing on as a mate in 1972 and becoming a master in 1981. He had commanded the *Exxon Long Beach*, the near-identical sister ship to the *Exxon Valdez*, and had been chosen by Exxon to supervise four vessels in its West Coast fleet. Maneuvering the *Exxon Valdez* off Bligh Reef without spilling the remaining oil would be his most harrowing experience in nearly twenty years at sea.

"We were sitting there with our survival suits, life jackets, and very little information about what the bottom of the ship looked like. We didn't know whether she'd make it through the night," Deppe said. "We certainly wanted to try to get as much oil off as possible, but our first consideration was all the people on board, making sure that we had an emergency response plan in case the ship did break in half or did start to capsize if she slid off the reef. No one knew whether the ship might break in half at any time."[4]

As the first day of the oil spill came to a close, deeply troubling questions were beginning to appear. Was Alyeska shirking its responsibility and letting Exxon shoulder both the burden of and accountability for spill response? Or had the state been unaware of an established chain of responsibility in the event of a large spill? Should the state have been reviewing oil spill plans of the shipping companies, such as Exxon, as well as that of the consortium? Why had the Coast Guard failed to observe that there wasn't an adequate oil spill response system in place? While these questions might be answered in court years hence, the most pressing concern now was whether Exxon's people, flying into Alaska from thousands of miles away and marshaling equipment from around the world, could actually contain the disaster unfolding at Bligh Reef.

Chapter 3

Day Two: "A House on Fire"

B y Saturday morning, March 25, estimates of the amount of oil spilled had risen to 240,000 barrels. This spill was 140 times larger than the *Thompson Pass* spill, which Alyeska had taken fifteen days to clean up right in Valdez Harbor; 300 times larger than the *Exxon Houston* spill in Hawaii; and 1,000 times larger than most of the terminal-related spills the industry was used to dealing with.

Dr. James Butler, a Harvard University professor who had chaired a National Research Council oil spill study group said, "A spill of this magnitude is virtually impossible to respond to adequately."

Exxon took command of what barges, boom, and skimming equipment Alyeska had, and Frank Iarossi pressed for permission to do controlled burning and to use chemical dispersants. However, Iarossi knew he faced an even more pressing problem than the 240,000 barrels of oil in the water. Perhaps only he and his closest advisors realized how close the *Exxon Valdez* was to capsizing and dumping the remaining 1,000,000 barrels— 42,000,000 gallons— of oil into Prince William Sound.

Throughout the early hours of Saturday morning, divers descended into the dark waters beneath the *Exxon Valdez* to assess the damage and help determine the vessel's stability. After diving through a foot of oil just to reach the sea, the divers were forced to wipe the sludgy crude from their faceplates and headlamps. "It was real scary," diver Mark Dione said. "It was totally black down there, no light at all."

The divers descended 50 feet down the vertical wall of the tanker, and then another 70 feet to its ripped underbelly. "Mindboggling," Dione said. "We felt our way in the darkness while this enormous ship was creaking and groaning. The hull is seven-eighths-inch steel, but it was like a tin can with holes punched in it. Big chunks of metal were hanging down. There were dozens of holes, some large enough to drive a truck through. Structural ribs were bent and crippled. There was a boulder in there the size of a Volkswagen."

The divers' survey revealed "very substantial underwater damage over about 50 percent of the vessel's bottom." Eight of the tanker's thirteen cargo compartments were ruptured, and more than 600 feet of hull lay cracked or broken. The tanker's midsection had sustained the most damage, possibly from Hazelwood's attempts to force the ship off the rock.

The divers also found that the ship's stability was more precarious than had first been thought: "The vessel is balanced on a rocky pinnacle at about its midsection." Had Hazelwood dislodged the *Exxon Valdez* from the reef, the tanker almost certainly would have rolled and sunk. As it was, it sagged where it hung over the reef. Reports from the divers and data from the ship's gauges were being fed to Exxon's marine engineers in Houston. Their analysis was relayed back to Iarossi in Valdez: at low tide the vessel would flex further, possibly cracking apart and disgorging the remaining 1,000,000 barrels of oil.

"I got confirmation from our people in Houston that the vessel was in danger of capsizing," Iarossi said. "We had to proceed very, very carefully. The first real decision I had to make was, with between thirty and forty people on the ship, do we risk lightering at all? It's one of those decisions that was made instinctively. We just had to go all out to get the oil off the ship.

"The way we tried to cover the risk was to carefully plan an evacuation, in case anything started to go wrong—if the vessel started to slide off the reef, if we had any signs of structural failure. We made sure everybody had exposure suits. Both life boats were rigged. We had four tugs and two Coast Guard vessels alongside and they were ready to pick up anybody who was forced to jump into the water."

By early Saturday morning, the waiting *Exxon Baton Rouge* had tied up next to the *Exxon Valdez*. William Deppe began the removal of the remaining oil with extreme caution, lest the *Exxon Valdez* capsize while being offloaded. To counterbalance the precarious position of the *Exxon Valdez*, seawater had to be used to displace oil removed by lightering. Any appreciable weight shift might have dislodged the damaged vessel.

"We attempted to start the cargo pump using that system to pump cargo out," Deppe said. "When we did that, we noticed that cargo was coming out the starboard side. So we shut down the system and, rather than risk any additional oil being spilled, we decided to pump all the oil using portable pumps."[1]

When that decision was made, 10,000 barrels of oil had been transferred to the *Baton Rouge*. Lightering was now at a standstill, leaving 990,000 barrels in the unstable tanker until portable pumps could be located. That afternoon the Coast Guard offered three pumps, and Exxon ordered nine others from Anchorage, Seattle, and Detroit.

Meanwhile, Exxon was trying to mount a three-pronged attack to retrieve the oil from Prince William Sound: burning, skimming, and using dispersants. Burning required specialized fireproof boom to contain a manageable pool of oil. At the time of the grounding, there was only 500 feet of fire boom in Alaska, hardly enough to make an appreciable difference. However, by noon Saturday, Exxon had transported another 2,500 feet of fire boom to Valdez, and a test burn was scheduled for that evening.

Twenty-four hours into the spill, Alyeska's skimming boats had reclaimed fewer than 1,000 barrels of oil, far less than their contingency plan projected. Exxon's skimming attachments were arriving from San Francisco and England, but no one had yet developed an effective method of transferring oil from the skimming boats to a collection barge—even though such a transfer had been a foundation of Alyeska's contingency plan for twelve years. Dispersants appeared to Exxon to be the only real remaining hope of controlling the spill.

However, dispersants are controversial. They do not remove oil from the water; rather, they act like dishwashing detergent, breaking the oil into tiny droplets that descend from the surface down deeper into the water column—the subsurface water directly below the spill. Some view dispersants as a quick fix for making oil vanish. However, critics argue, the oil doesn't disappear; dispersants just transfer the problems of oil from the surface into the water column itself, where it could harm marine organisms.

"There have been a lot of rumors regarding the use of dispersants," said Dr. Alan Maki, Exxon's chief environmental scientist in Alaska.[2] Iarossi had Maki explain dispersants to a skeptical crowd in Valdez. "Let's look at what's happening out in the sound now," Maki said. "What we see is the slick spreading on top of the water. That's [because] oil and water don't mix. Oil is not soluble in water. When you add oil to water, eventually you will see a natural breaking up of the slick due to the motion of waves, but the process takes quite a bit of time. Naturally, the slick can travel in the process.

"Usually we see the formation of what we refer to as mousse, which is an oil/water emulsion, and the formation of tar balls, large balls of oil in water," Maki said. "Dispersants act as an aid to the natural weathering process of oil in water. . . . [Their] effect is to pull the slick apart into tiny micron-sized oil droplets. . . . [Oil] is much more likely in this state to undergo the natural processes of evaporation, photolysis [breakdown from light], and biodegradation." But, Maki cautioned, "the circumstances that dictate the use of dispersants are seldom clear-cut, and the choice is necessarily a compromise between . . . conflicting priorities for protecting different resources."

For several years, the U.S. Environmental Protection Agency had been working on developing federal guidelines regarding dispersant use. Recognizing the potential conflicts, the agency's team of scientists determined that dispersant decisions would have to be "made on a case-by-case basis. . . . It is not, for example, inconsistent that one state or region placing a high priority on its shellfish industry would have very different policies and even procedures than a state or region assigning highest priority to waterfowl protection."

Recognizing that trade-offs are often involved with dispersant use, the EPA devised a national contingency plan that allowed each state to decide if and when dispersants would be used. Still, in the stipulated protocol, for dispersant use to proceed, a Coast Guard on-scene coordinator (OSC) must obtain agreement from both the affected state and the U.S. Environmental Protection Agency representative on the regional response team (RRT). The latter is an interagency team established under federal law to respond to spills of oil and other hazardous substances.

A survey of nineteen coastal states reveals widely divergent attitudes toward the use of dispersants. On the conservative end of the spectrum, Oregon prohibits all use of dispersants. Maryland, Rhode Island, New Hampshire, and Washington authorize dispersant use only under compelling circumstances, such as life-threatening situations to people or endangered species. Mississippi considers dispersant use on a case-by-case basis in the open waters of the Gulf of Mexico but not in waters inside its barrier islands. New York and New Jersey preauthorize use of dispersants in designated areas, while Massachusetts relies on the U.S. Coast Guard for dispersant decisions. Maine would not consider giving preapproval to a federal on-scene coordinator and retains autonomous control.

The state of Alaska had spent several years developing dispersant guidelines that would balance speedy emergency approval with the protection of sensitive ecosystems. Alyeska's spill response guidelines, which the state approved, are among the most liberal in dispersant policy. They state that "dispersants will be considered as a possible response option only when mechanical containment and recovery response actions are not workable." Alaska DEC Commissioner Dennis Kelso explained: "It's important to keep in mind that dispersants don't take oil out of the water. They are to be used on a case-by-case basis. They are a tool to be kept in the kit—and used in the right circumstances."

So that this tool could be used quickly in an emergency, the state established three dispersant-use zones. Zoning considerations included currents, water depths, habitats, fish and wildlife concentrations, near-shore human activities, and required response time. Regions far from sensitive shorelines were designated zone 1; for these the EPA and the state of Alaska gave the Coast Guard's on-scene coordinator preapproval to use dispersants. The large, open areas in Prince William Sound, including the tanker route from the Narrows to the open sea, are identified as zone 1.

In the more ecologically sensitive zone 2 areas, dispersant use depends upon case-by-case EPA and state approval. In zone 3 areas, which are in and around resources requiring protection, such as intertidal areas, small coves, and fjords, the use of dispersants is not recommended at all. As in zone 2, the use of dispersants in zone 3 requires case-by-case EPA and state approval.

Bligh Reef, onto which the *Exxon Valdez* crashed, was designated zone 3. However, the oil was spreading through a zone 2 area and soon extending into the more open waters of zone 1. Within hours of the grounding, Exxon had phoned Commander McCall, the Coast Guard's on-scene coordinator, to ask if dispersants could be used. Iarossi had understood McCall's answer to be yes, and since only McCall's approval was necessary for zone 1, the matter seemed to be settled with regard to the open waters into which most of the oil was moving. Based on this understanding Iarossi had called for dispersant in drums and planes to spray it on the slick.

However, the word *preapproval* in Alaska's dispersant guidelines may have been used erroneously. Alaska's dispersant guidelines also state that "in all cases, the use of dispersants will be based on the determination that their impact will be less harmful than that of non-dispersed oil." McCall, as on-scene coordinator, had yet to determine that dispersant use would cause less damage than the crude itself. There were no guidelines for making this pivotal determination, and McCall was neither a chemist nor a marine biologist. He would be advised by his regional response team, but he would also be hearing from Cordova's Riki Ott and Exxon's Gordon Lindblom plus fishermen, environmentalists, and industry experts. Assailed from all sides, Commander Steve McCall was in a very difficult position of personal responsibility. In making a critical decision that might minimize the spill's impact, he was caught between the urgency to use dispersants quickly and concern that they might do more harm than good. "Above all, rapid response is important," Dr. James Butler's National Academy of Sciences committee emphasized. "As the oil spreads out, it becomes more viscous and hard to disperse." Precious hours were disappearing.

"An oil spill is like a house burning down. You've got to be ready," Dr. Butler said. "You just can't stand around trying to figure it out—'Well, let's go out and buy some hose now, and let's hook up the water mains.' 'No, we can't do it today, let's wait until tomorrow.' If you wait, you might as well not bother at all. You have to think of it as a house on fire. If you go into a house three days after the fire starts to begin putting the fire out, you're going to be disappointed."

The clock was ticking away hours of optimal cleanup conditions in Prince William Sound. Twenty-four hours had elapsed by the time Exxon's first spray plane arrived. Iarossi, bolstered by the opinion of advisors such as Dr. Gordon Lindblom and Dr. Alan Maki, was anxious to begin using dispersants. However, from the early hours of the spill, the decision of whether to use dispersants was stalemated by conflicting needs. Further, it was mired in confusion.

Earlier, on Friday, March 24, at 6:30 A.M., McCall had requested that Alyeska fax him a written request for dispersant use. By 8:00 A.M., Alyeska had handwritten a ten-page emergency request for dispersant use and had faxed it to the Coast Guard station in Valdez. However, the Coast Guard's fax machine had been malfunctioning, so, as an alternate route to approval, Alyeska had faxed the same handwritten request to the regional response team in Anchorage. More than seven hours after Alyeska's initial attempt to fax their emergency request, McCall had given his approval for a dispersant trial.

At the press conference Friday evening in Valdez, Frank Iarossi emphasized "the need to move quickly to disperse oil." However, Governor Steve Cowper expressed caution at that same press conference: "Everybody realizes the risk that [dispersants] pose to marine life. We are already seeing some effect on marine life just because of the oil. I want to assure everybody that dispersant is not going to be used in anything other than a carefully targeted way. We want to try to make sure that we check back with the fishing community, that we check with the Department of Fish and Game, and do as little damage as possible. You can't use dispersants without doing damage to marine life. That's clear. But we want, if possible, to keep oil off the beaches."[3]

Caught among conflicting opinions of the state, Exxon Shipping, and the public, McCall decided he needed further trials.

At 6:12 A.M. Saturday, Exxon's C-130 plane, equipped with dispersant spray, arrived in Anchorage from Phoenix. At this point, there were 365 50-gallon drums of dispersant in Alaska— not enough to disperse even half of the oil, but still enough to get started.

It was noon before McCall approved a test run. At 4:00 P.M. the plane took off from Valdez loaded with 3,700 gallons of dispersants. It laid down a 150-foot-wide swath just south of the *Exxon Valdez*. "The test in my view clearly was successful," said Iarossi. "Two important things happened. Light reflection was different where sprayed. And the surface action was different, a clear rippling effect where dispersant had been sprayed."

McCall, however, saw it differently. "We couldn't really tell how well it was working, mainly because of the lack of wind and lack of surface action in the water. It looked like it was working, but you couldn't really tell because it wasn't being churned up."[4] Exxon's planes were reloaded for spraying dispersant the following day, but McCall told Iarossi he needed "unequivocal" proof that dispersants were working.

"Not using dispersants because the water is too calm is a fallacy. I don't know where they learned that spraying the dispersant on the oil slick would cause [the slick] to disappear immediately," Dr. James Butler said. "When the wind came up, the dispersant that had stayed with the slick would mix with the oil and the slick would begin to disperse. Even if the slick didn't disappear, oil washed ashore with some dispersant wouldn't stick to shoreline surfaces so much. But they were still saying, 'Well, if it doesn't disappear instantly, then it isn't working.'"

As night fell, the unseasonably calm weather held. A fisherman anchored a few hundred yards from the slick watched the setting sun ripple red-orange over the water and than saw a wall of flame shoot suddenly into the sky near his boat. "Goddamn," he yelled to his crew, "the ocean's on fire! Let's get the hell out of here!"

The fishermen expected to see the *Exxon Valdez* shoot skyward at any moment in a fiery explosion. They escaped unscathed, but some of the residents of the nearby village of Tatitlek reported sore throats and stinging eyes from the smoke of Exxon's first test burn.

Some, fearful of dispersants and disillusioned with skimmers, had suggested torching the tanker and all the oil in one big blaze. "To my knowledge, this was never seriously considered," Iarossi said. "The problem is, you've got a tremendous amount of fuel, a million barrels of oil, still in the tanker. When flames reached the tanker, you wouldn't know what's going to happen. That kind of fire is totally uncontrollable. I mean, we could have blown away Tatitlek village and half of Prince William Sound."

As it was, smoke from the relatively small test burn prompted the state to require Exxon to obtain a permit from DEC before doing any further controlled burning. The company had hoped this test burn would clear the way for continued burning. The test had successfully burned off approximately 15,000 gallons of oil in less than an hour, and now only a small pool of tarlike residue remained where the fire had burned itself out. By now, Exxon had 3,000 feet of fire boom in Valdez, enough to run four simultaneous burns. If its permit came through in time, Exxon could work through the night, burning off approximately 50,000 gallons (nearly 1,200 barrels) per hour. Said Frank Iarossi, "Getting that permit right away was absolutely critical, because burning is just as sensitive to the time factor as dispersant. Once you let the oil emulsify and it begins to take on water content, you can't burn it."

By midnight Saturday, forty-eight hours after the *Exxon Valdez* had run aground, mechanical cleanup had made little headway, and Exxon had yet to receive permission to proceed with burning and dispersants. Response to the spill was becoming paralyzed by indecision, a struggle over authority, and vastly different and conflicting expectations as to which measures would work.

Commissioner Kelso, frustrated by the stalled cleanup, blasted the "inertia and incompetence of both Alyeska and Exxon, which are not entirely separate entities."[5] Kelso was still relying heavily on assurances within the Alyeska contingency plan that skimmers could recover a significant amount of oil, but by the end of the second day of the spill, they had made no appreciable progress with the enormous pool of oil.

On the other hand, Frank Iarossi said, "It was pretty clear that this spill was way beyond the capability of any mechanical pickup, even if you mobilized all the equipment in the world. Meanwhile, the oil is spreading through Prince William Sound and we're wasting all this quiet weather debating whether or not we could use dispersant. Dr. Butler says it's like arguing whether to use water to put out a fire while a house is burning. That's exactly what we were doing."

Chapter 4

Day Three: Time Runs Out

E aster Sunday crept coral pink over Prince William Sound as sharp, white mountains emerged from the darkness. In Valdez, Easter celebrations of resurrection and renewal were overshadowed by the ominous presence of oil drifting southwest from Bligh Reef. Most of the oil was concentrated in a 15-square-mile pool, but thick tendrils swirled out over more than 100 square miles. Two dead sea otters were sighted, as were seventy-five oiled seabirds—white-winged scoters and golden eyes.

At the Valdez civic center, a church was holding its Easter services. On the other side of a thin partition, Exxon was holding its morning press conference, jammed with frustrated people wanting to know why so little oil had been retrieved, why Exxon wasn't moving faster, and why the company wanted to throw chemical dispersants on the sea. Angry shouts about skimmers and dispersants mixed with the sound of hymns coming through the wall.

According to Alyeska's prespill projections, more than 100,000 barrels of oil should have been recovered by now, but total recovery stood at fewer than 3,000 barrels. Skimming boats were still scooting over the slick with no effective means of transferring skimmed oil. Exxon was still awaiting a burning permit, but the main question at hand was dispersant authorization. The decision-making process, much like the town of Valdez and the state of Alaska, was being consumed by strained emotions and conflicting information.

"The one word that describes it best is confusion," Coast Guard Admiral Edward Nelson said of the chaotic situation he found when he arrived in Valdez that weekend. "On Sunday, Frank Iarossi had sixty-eight of his people up there. They knew how to get oil out of the ground and move it from point A to point B, but these guys were not crisis managers. When I walked in and saw Exxon's place, it looked like a political caucus room—packed with people, long tables, phone lines, people running in and out with doughnuts. This was supposed to be the operations setup where they were trying to make decisions. The state didn't have anybody in there: they were sitting down at a court building and weren't a whole heck of a lot better off. There were guys down there who wanted to get hired, and you had to crawl over them to get to a meeting. At Coast Guard headquarters, Steve McCall was supposed to be doing business as usual, but he was getting hounded from all sides. He had the regional response team holding their meetings, some of the cleanup folks, fishermen, and the telephone guys who were stringing lines so we could talk between the three headquarters. . . . It was a zoo."

By Sunday, Exxon's employees in Valdez were outnumbered by radio and television crews and journalists who became part of the general turmoil. As the media relayed images of the spill to people around the world, they both reported and fueled the atmosphere of growing anger, frustration, and mistrust.

"We've got hysteria, a real stampede," said Alyeska's Tom Brennan. "The crowds are getting angrier and nastier. Valdez has become a black hole, sucking in every nut and screwball in the universe. Some of these clowns tried running our people off the road. I told our employees, 'Don't drive Alyeska's red Suburbans, drive your own cars.'" Brennan even "discreetly asked about getting a bulletproof vest. My hotel room was across from Iarossi's, and I know he got a death threat."

"There were a couple death threats," Exxon's Frank Iarossi

acknowledged. "The company sent up security people, who maintained a close watch over me. But I didn't think anybody wanted to hurt me, because I was trying to do everything I could to help."

Tumultuous, general-admission-style press conferences were now being held every morning and evening, and these became a forum for public debate. Some Exxon managers considered these press conferences distractions from the work of fighting the spill, but many people saw them as a means of pressuring Exxon into taking more decisive action.

Ironically, Exxon's attempts to accommodate the press at these twice-daily events helped shift the public's attention away from a negligent Alyeska. "It's interesting, but somehow Alyeska slid right out from under everything," observed Coast Guard Admiral Edward Nelson. "Alyeska didn't get yelled at, yet they are the ones who failed to do the job they were supposed to do.

"Those so-called press conferences were Roman circuses," Nelson continued. "They went on interminably, so you didn't have time to do anything else. We'd get through at 11:00 P.M., and in the morning it was time to have another press conference. There was no control—so many issues being thrown up, so much time spent arguing, that it took away everyone's ability to work on the spill."

Admiral Nelson was now the ranking Coast Guard officer in Valdez. While Commander Steve McCall served as on-scene co-ordinator, Nelson became a behind-the-scenes coordinator. "I was there to represent more horsepower," Nelson said. "Steve McCall was doing a fine job, and I was supposed to back him up. But it was clear to both of us that I was a camel with his nose in the tent. And it wasn't long before I was in the tent."

It was at the press conferences that the public had its say regarding the critical issue of dispersant use, and Nelson considered the outcry to have a significant impact. "Those press conferences created a certain amount of pressure on those who had to make the dispersant decisions," Admiral Nelson remarked later. "The attitude was, 'You're going to throw these dangerous chemicals in the water and they are going to destroy our fish and our water column. No one is concerned about the environment. If you allow dispersants, you're letting big oil off easy.' "

Riki Ott took full advantage of the opportunity to counter the case Iarossi made for using dispersants. "The contingency plan makes mechanical pickup the number one priority," she said. "So let's get the stuff out of the water first, before relying on dispersants. Exxon is jumping on dispersants as the cure, but dispersants are like soap. They just break up oil. . . . [The water] looks better, but the oil is still there."

"We'll still be here a year from now if we have to use only skimmers," Iarossi countered.[1]

"Mechanical pickup removes the oil. Dispersants shove it down into the water," Ott responded. As an aside she muttered, "Oh, Iarossi. *That* guy. He'd never make it as a fisherman."

In reflecting on those raucous press conference/town meeting forums, Iarossi said, "It seems like Riki Ott took up half of every town meeting, with me responding to her concerns, which of course didn't help any. It absorbed a lot of our energy and attention. We should have been out fighting the oil spill, but here we were in a public forum, trying to get permission to go fight the oil spill. All those press conferences are on videotape, and I'm sure anyone who studies them will find a perfect case of how not to address a crisis.

"This is the heart of the dilemma we have," Iarossi said. "Here is the commander [McCall] in the middle of battle, and he's supposed to figure out a scientific question. My personal view is that McCall was put in a box in which there was no way he could get out. Even though McCall had preapproval, he still had to determine if the environmental impacts associated with chemical dispersant would be less than those occurring without chemical dispersion."

It was not only the press conference turmoil that was stalling the decision-making; it was also the fact that definitive answers to the questions being debated did not really exist. "The reason for the debate surrounding dispersants is that the effects of their use depend on a lot of different factors—spraying technique, sea surface state, ocean currents, water depth, and the biological communities being impacted. Nobody knows all of the possible effects," Harvard University's Dr. James Butler said. "In order to know for sure what might happen, you'd have to know the toxicology of every organism in the marine community and all of the currents. The mathematical model would be enormous. It would probably take five years, and then it would be five years too late."

However, enough was known about dispersants to warrant their use in open water areas. As Dr. Butler said, "Throughout the dispersant arguments, few people seemed to comprehend that even if the oil were dispersed in the upper layer of water over a large area, it would be rendered much less harmful than the untreated slick. The water of Prince William Sound was hundreds of feet deep, and tidal currents would carry oil dispersed in the water column to the open ocean, where it would be still further diluted."

Commander McCall, ever cautious, called for further dispersant tests. Sunday's trials began with a 9:00 A.M. dispersant spray flight, which the Coast Guard judged inconclusive. At 2:00 P.M., a C-130 dropped 5,100 gallons of dispersants on the slick, and in Iarossi's opinion the results were "spectacular." A breeze that had begun stirring the water's surface may have helped to catalyze the dispersant. McCall had not witnessed this test, but after reviewing the videotapes he acknowledged that "the Sunday afternoon test seemed to work pretty well."

Meanwhile, at 3:00 P.M. Sunday, Iarossi received word that the state had finally granted a permit for controlled burning. But permission to use dispersants was still being withheld. "I pleaded with Admiral Nelson to give us the authority to use dispersants," Iarossi said. "He told me that he agreed with me and that we had to move. He was getting very frustrated."

At 5:00 P.M., Iarossi was still trying to convince Commander McCall to approve dispersants when DEC's Dennis Kelso, his staff, and additional Coast Guard and Exxon officials arrived to join the discussion. Kelso said that the state was not ready to permit an open-ended use of dispersants. He was concerned about the trade-offs between dispersing oil into the water column versus allowing it to wash ashore. Admiral Nelson recalled that "Kelso was still very, very cautious about using dispersants, extremely cautious."

Iarossi feared that the decision makers were "slowly being consumed with political issues versus spill issues. We were fighting amongst ourselves rather than fighting the oil spill."

Although Kelso and Iarossi disagreed on response methods,

their personal relationship remained cordial. At one point in the midst of the dispersant debate, Kelso, noticing that Iarossi was wearing a Colorado "Outward Bound" cap, mentioned that he had once been an instructor in that program. "We got into a fine discussion about climbing mountains," Iarossi recalled later. "I told him that I only went on one mountain climb in my whole life, and that was in 1985 when, at the age of forty-nine, I climbed Mt. Elbert in Colorado. There were no hard feelings between Kelso and myself, but everybody was very anxious. We were attempting to state our case. Kelso was listening, but he always came back to his preferred way to fight an oil spill: exhaust opportunities for mechanical pickup before using dispersants. I told him that was correct for a 1,000-barrel spill but we were way beyond that. He never did say that the state agreed to the use of dispersants."

By 6:45 P.M., Commander McCall had deliberated long enough. "We finally have agreement to use dispersant in zone 1," he told Iarossi. McCall's use of the word *agreement* indicated his desire to mediate among the opposing parties. Though the dispersant controversy was far from resolved, the question of whether to use dispersants on this spill was finally answered, sixty-six hours after the grounding.

"My objective was to get all the dispersant we could down onto that slick just as fast as we could," said Iarossi, who was keenly aware that the *Exxon Valdez* might break apart at any time. At Bligh Reef, lightering had commenced and continued without further delay, although the stricken tanker still contained 940,000 barrels of oil.

By Sunday evening, fewer than 3,000 barrels of oil had been collected from the waters of Prince William Sound. "That's 3,000 barrels under ideal conditions," Mayor Devens said. "And we know the weather's going to change."

"We are trying to keep from being overwhelmed," Iarossi said during that night's press conference. "We're concentrating on three major priorities: the million barrels on the ship, the ship itself, and the oil on the water. We have been so frustrated today, just as frustrated as everyone else, at the pace of recovery. And the reason for that frustration is that we have been limited to mechanical pickup. It's not gonna do the job. . . . It is the slowest and least effective tool. That's why it was so important to get the state's permission to burn, and so important to get the permission of all the authorities to begin to use dispersants."[2]

However, with dispersant-use authorization in hand, the application of the chemicals was by no means an accomplished fact. Exxon still lacked the amount of dispersants required to treat a spill the size of the *Exxon Valdez*. As Exxon flew in dispersants from around the world, it became apparent that there was not enough *anywhere* to treat a spill of this magnitude. In fact, on Friday, the first day of the spill, Exxon had ordered plants in Houston and England to manufacture more. While this action ostensibly displayed determination to respond to the oil spill, it also illustrated the extent to which DEC, Exxon, British Petroleum, and the other Alyeska owner companies had all grossly underestimated the means necessary to disperse a large spill.

Commissioner Kelso calculated that the total amount of dispersants available in Alaska on Sunday was enough to treat only 9 percent of the spill. Iarossi responded that "critics will say we didn't have 100,000 or 400,000 gallons of dispersant on hand. That's absolutely true, but that's never the way the system was intended to operate. The dispersant was there in 365 drums, which is exactly what's called for in the Alaska Department of Environmental Conservation–approved Alyeska contingency plan. This is an issue that Dennis Kelso sidesteps. But the plan approved by Kelso's department spells out exactly how much dispersant is required to be on hand and where it is to be stored: 160 drums in Anchorage, 160 drums in Kenai, and 45 drums in Valdez. That's exactly what was there in Alaska on the day of the spill, exactly according to the plan. The concept is that 365 drums is enough for your first day's run using one airplane. From there you set up a shuttle system moving dispersants from other stockpiles around the country."

Regardless of the amount of dispersants Exxon mobilized, there was still not enough; nor was there a guarantee that dispersants would work. Dispersant effectiveness varies with timing, oil composition, water temperature, and wave agitation on the surface of the sea. "It's important to note that all the talk about the use and effects of dispersants on big spills is hypothetical," emphasized Dr. James Butler. "It's based on lab data and a few small field tests. No one has successfully treated a spill of this size."

Before returning to his hotel room Sunday night, Frank Iarossi said, "Starting tomorrow we are going to have all three tools—skimmers, burning, and dispersants—at our disposal. By tomorrow morning we're going to be going all out."[3]

However, that night the weather turned. For three days the wind had stayed below 15 knots, keeping the oil pooled close to Bligh Reef. The waves had been less that 3 feet high, ideal for oil recovery. The sun shone brightly Sunday morning, but in the afternoon a high overcast seeped into the sky and the wind started picking up. By nightfall, small craft advisory warnings were posted for Valdez Arm. Gusts up to 25 knots buffeted the port, and in the fading light whitecaps raced across Prince William Sound.

Chapter 5

Day Four: The Storm

By dawn Monday morning, a spring blizzard was howling down out of the Chugach Mountains, driving snow and sleet through the streets of Valdez. A gust tore the roof off a hangar at the airport. Boats were pinned in the harbor. Planes were grounded. Twenty-foot waves raced across Prince William Sound. Gale-force winds whipped the heavy crude into a frothy mixture of sea water and oil. The massive oil slick was spreading out, breaking into separate slicks and running southwest with the wind.

"The slick is moving like it's on a superhighway," said Exxon's Frank Iarossi. "Our worst fears happened. The wind just shot us down. Those winds stampeded the slick out of the center of the sound over to the islands."[1]

The main pool of oil moved 40 miles overnight. Stygian waves, heavy with oil, hammered the headlands of Knight Island. Purplish-black tendrils twisted along the tidal rips. Currents carried oil into coves. Great swaths of iridescent sheen overran rafts of kelp. The beaches of Smith and Naked islands were awash with the black crude; in places waves tossed oil 40 feet above the tidal rocks. The time of grace, those three calm days when the oil might have been contained, had been squandered. Within twenty-four hours the spill had grown from 100 square miles to approximately 500 square miles.

It had been a long night on the *Exxon Valdez* for Captain Deppe, his crew, and the envoy of Coast Guard and DEC officials that had gathered onboard. Dressed in survival suits, they had stood watch through the hours of darkness, prepared to abandon ship, listening to the steel hull groan as it shuddered and twisted upon the reef. The *Exxon Valdez* had been tied to the *Exxon Baton Rouge* and four giant tug boats. By morning, the storm had turned *all six vessels* 12 degrees, as if, lashed together, they had become a giant weather vane pivoting on the rock and swinging with the wind. On the tanker's deck, sea spray had frozen into sheets of ice.

The urgency of transferring oil from the stricken tanker was so great that the lightering pumps continued to run throughout the storm. Frank Iarossi said that he and his people were "gaining confidence by the hour. They are getting a handle on this, beginning to make some progress."[2]

But Valdez mayor John Devens was frustrated. "We've got a tanker out there that is severely damaged. The wind is blowing, we are well past the 72-hour mark, and we still haven't got any cleanup done. I don't know what you would call Frank Iarossi. Any man who can say that 'we're growing more confident' after a tanker with a million barrels of oil still on board just rotated 12 degrees because of the wind . . . has got to be a very optimistic soul."[3]

Iarossi later responded. "Hell, anybody faced with 240,000 barrels of oil on the water and another million on a ship ready to capsize has got to be very optimistic to keep going. To keep going you had to bolster yourself and the people working with you. It would have been very easy to give up."

At the time, Iarossi elaborated Exxon's position. "I know the operation's not spectacular, the ship just sits there, but I can't overemphasize the concern we've had from the beginning that we had a 240,000-barrel problem, and the last thing in the world we could stand is having a 1,240,000-barrel problem. So we have just been going all out to keep this situation from getting any worse than it is.

"We've got approximately 30,000 feet of 18-inch boom deployed. We've got another 20,000 feet of absorbent boom available. We've got ten helicopters and four fixed-wing aircraft under Exxon control at the Valdez airport. We already have 180 flights under our belt. We have six smaller skimmers that will be used when we begin the cleanup, and we've got another eight or ten coming. . . . We have twenty-six fishing boats, eight tugs or utility-type vessels, and two large barges in our flotilla."

While Iarossi felt this intensive effort showed progress, it was DEC Commissioner Dennis Kelso's view that Exxon's mobilization obscured the real issue—the actual condition of the beaches. "Exxon should get credit for having mobilized a lot of equipment, but they weren't using it effectively. Very early in the response, Exxon started its list of lists. Their daily reports list all of the equipment that has been procured and every employee—a flurry of numbers which is becoming a full-blown blizzard. We've got drifts of these numbers obscuring the shape of the beaches. Instead of looking at the condition of the shoreline, we're getting numbers of vessels, numbers of people, claims about numbers of barrels of oil recovered."

Out on Prince William Sound, globs of oil-soaked debris, barely recognizable as birds, began washing ashore. Cormorants, auklets, and ducks became coated when they dove into the sea to feed. Eagles ingested oil as they fed upon weakened creatures and contaminated carrion. Spring migrations of geese, swans, and shorebirds had just begun.

Sea otters were suddenly finding the clear waters of their marine world black, thick, and deadly. A strange substance they could not comprehend burned their eyes and lungs and soaked into their fur as they struggled to stay afloat. Many otters swam to exhaustion and drowned. Some managed to crawl ashore, where they died of exposure.

Along the poisoned shorelines, deer grazed on oil-stained seaweed and grass. Bears coming out of hibernation were seen scavenging blackened birds and otters washed up on the beaches.

"This is only the tip of the iceberg," said Frank Rue, director of habitat for Alaska's Department of Fish and Game. "We are finding only a small fraction of the birds and sea otters that have been lost to the spill."[4]

The storm had churned much of the oil into the frothy sludge called mousse. In this emulsified state, the oil was too weathered to be treated with either controlled burning or dispersants. Skimmers, which had proved ineffective under ideal conditions, were now the sole means of recovering oil before it washed ashore.

Those fighting the spill found themselves in a vacuum of authority. Alyeska, which the state had relied on for spill response, had disappeared. Exxon was trying to respond but needed authorization. Most of Exxon's people, having flown up from other parts of the country, had little knowledge of Alaska and virtually no connection to the land and to Prince William Sound. They didn't know Alaska's weather, Alaska's waters, Alaska's shorelines, or Alaska's people. But the state and the Coast Guard, which could have provided the needed direction, strained against the limits placed on their own authority. All three parties wanted to move quickly to clean up the spill, but lacked a clear chain of command, a clear-cut process for making urgent decisions. Where should the skimming boats go? How should the boom be placed? What were the most important bays and islands to safeguard?

Faced with such critical questions and caught in its passive role of monitoring spill response, the state was limited to observing and then assessing the damage. It frustrated Commissioner Kelso and other Alaskans to watch Exxon, so lacking in knowledge of and experience in Alaska, try to manage the spill.

The state wanted to direct Exxon, to draw up and enforce priorities of where to go, what to do. However, as Governor Cowper acknowledged, "It is not by any means clear that we have the authority to direct Exxon to do anything."[5] Commissioner Kelso clarified: "We have enforcement sanctions we can impose if a spiller fails to do something. But there is no sanction we can use . . . to make sure spillers do what they say they are going to do, or what the law requires them to do. You can hammer them after the fact, but not before the fact."

Here was a weakness in the entire response process. Under both state and federal law, a spiller has the right to initiate spill response, to clean up its mess. The government is not allowed to intervene unless the spiller either refuses to take responsibility or its response is obviously inadequate. Only then can the state or Coast Guard step in and take over.

"We are in the position of having to wait and see if the spiller is successful. That's backwards," Kelso fumed. "This loses valuable time, and you can't lose time if you're going to effectively contain and recover oil from the water."

The problem results in part from federal pollution legislation, a web of regulations so confusing that lawyers build whole careers arguing its meaning. One principal law, the Clean Water Act of 1972, requires the spiller to pay for its spill but lacks clear guidelines for governmental intervention. Admiral Nelson echoed Kelso's frustration with the resulting harness on federal authority. "The rules of the game are that unless the spiller is irresponsible or unresponsive we don't take over," said Nelson. "This is wrong. We start out from a losing position. Without relieving the spiller of financial responsibility, we have to be in charge at the beginning, not after things have gone to pot."

By Monday, the spill response had already done just that—gone to pot. The oil that Alyeska and Exxon had recovered, still fewer than 3,000 barrels, represented little more than one percent of the spilled oil. The wind had torn and scattered the boom that Exxon had positioned on the leading edge of the slick. Governor Cowper wanted the Coast Guard to call Exxon's response inadequate and federalize the spill, but Admiral Nelson resisted, explaining that it would take weeks for the Coast Guard to set up the government's cumbersome contractual procedures. He argued that it would be "a logistical and contractual nightmare" to try to take over from Exxon.

Nevertheless, Frank Iarossi himself encouraged Admiral Nelson to take charge amidst the confusion. "Oil was running loose, and instead of being able to act decisively we were caught up in committee activity," Iarossi recalled. "It seemed to me that Admiral Nelson wanted to step in and take charge, and at one point I actually encouraged him to do that. I told him I'd work directly for him. We would continue doing everything we were doing, but we would follow his direction. We would support him with our streamlined logistic and procurement system to get around his problems with procurement. We really needed to get things done in a timely way. I nominated him to head our committee so he could use his authority to decide what had to be done and when. I think he really wanted to, but he had to check with Admiral Yost first."

However, Coast Guard Commandant Admiral Paul Yost did not federalize the spill, which meant that Admiral Nelson could not take command. "As long as we weren't going to federalize," said Nelson, "we could only stand back and watch and let Exxon do it. They just didn't have the equipment up there. It wasn't because Frank Iarossi wasn't trying—he certainly was. But all the needed equipment—all the pads, absorbent materials, boom, skimmers, barges, etc.—just wasn't around. The worst part was, nobody knew where to get it all. I can't fault Exxon for not trying to order everything that was needed—they tried. Their fault lay in not being organized."

At the same time, some of Commissioner Kelso's staff were becoming frustrated with the state's response. "When the spill happened we weren't prepared," recalled one DEC official, who asked to remain anonymous. "We weren't handling it at all well. We had no state contingency plan, no crisis response plan to help us set up emergency services, hire crews, direct helicopters, and bring in supplies. There was real confusion within DEC as we tried to establish direction, purpose, goals, and objectives. It was a time of soul-searching, because none of us knew what to do. And since we didn't know how to use our authority, we were powerless and just stood around watching it all happen."

To bring some sense of order and direction to the chaotic spill response, Iarossi, Nelson, and Kelso structured a three-party command. Seeking to create a decision-making process that would accommodate all of their interests, they set up two working groups. One was a steering committee comprised of three equals, no chairman—Iarossi, Nelson, and Kelso. The other was an operations committee, composed of key operations people from the state, Exxon, and the Coast Guard. The operations group was to meet at 8:00 A.M. and 8:00 P.M. each day and then report to the steering committee, which would pass judgment on its plans for the next day. However, Kelso, Iarossi, and Nelson found they had to attend the operations meetings. This working group soon swelled to forty-six members, and its meetings began lasting proportionally longer.

"The intent was noble—we were trying to get everybody to work together," Iarossi said. "But in fact it turned out to be a disaster, because there was no way to control the agenda or the participation. We'd be crammed into this room. One night, there were two Exxon people, five Coast Guard officers, and thirty-nine representatives from the state and a whole bunch of local community groups. There wasn't a lot of arguing, just endless discussions by the same people who were supposed to be out co-ordinating the spill activities. They got ground up in committee activity, which took an average of five hours a day. This went on and on. Two meetings a day was ridiculous, because the evening meeting would go from eight to eleven or twelve, when everyone was exhausted, and then we'd meet again at eight in the morning. Of course, nothing had transpired between those two meetings, because you had total darkness. It really turned into a disaster, a hopeless situation."

It was a disaster that the world was watching, and regardless of the problems Exxon faced, the public would hold the oil industry accountable for what was quickly becoming the nation's most devastating oil spill. "Exxon is a representative of its industry. It is your spill, your problem, and everyone is watching," California Congressman George Miller admonished Exxon. "We have a world-class demonstration of failure. . . . I don't point a finger just at Exxon, because you have assembled everything available in the world. Your competitors would have had the same problem."

With the failure in Prince William Sound, Miller asked, "How can the public feel comfortable with how you would handle a spill off the coast of California, South Carolina, Florida, or any other coastal state? If the industry can't respond to this spill on a timely and effective basis, I don't think the public is going to buy into new offshore development that expands the risk and expands the opportunity for failure. . . . Unless some dramatic changes take place, I just can't ask my constituents and the constituents of other states to run the risk of this kind of disaster."[6]

Chapter 6

"It Can't Happen to Me"

As oil surged through Prince William Sound, suspicions, allegations, and unanswered questions abounded in the general confusion. But one central question rang through it all: How could such an accident have happened? The world's largest oil company, the "jewel of the fleet," an experienced captain, open waters, and yet. . . .

"You'd think the *Exxon Valdez* would have been the least likely tanker to have an accident," remarked Harvard's Dr. James Butler. "This tanker was only three years old: no violations, no accidents. Clean. Other vessels involved in big spills were in all kinds of trouble—getting old, being run independently by people cutting corners because they are going broke and can't afford the best navigational equipment."

Many Exxon officials, particularly liability-conscious lawyers, had a vested interest in depicting the accident as an anomaly and in dismissing the wreck of the *Exxon Valdez* as a tragic but unpredictable and virtually unpreventable incident. However, reports began to surface of watered-down regulations, oil company budget cuts, Coast Guard cutbacks, rule violations, alcohol abuse, fatigued tanker crews, and governmental negligence, and it soon became clear that many factors besides chance had contributed to the accident's cause.

Bob LeResche, appointed by Governor Cowper after the spill to be Alaska's oil spill coordinator, traced the roots of the *Exxon Valdez* incident back ten years to "a thousand little mistakes and inattentions." While others were quick to blast Exxon as the black sheep of the oil industry, LeResche, a former state commissioner of natural resources who had a Ph.D. in ecology, systematically analyzed the spill. He thought Exxon Shipping was probably in the ninetieth percentile in terms of competently managed shipping companies. "What scares me is that Exxon Shipping is one of the best-managed oil shipping companies. It even happened to them. That ought to give all of us pause. I'm afraid the deepest thread is the 'random event theory': when 10 or 15 or 100 small things come together you've got the wreck of the *Exxon Valdez*."

One of those who tried to fit the multitude of pieces together was Andy Santos, British Petroleum's port captain and the most experienced mariner in Valdez at the time of the wreck. "We're destroying one of the most pristine parts of this planet. There are people out there whose lifestyles could be ruined," said Santos, visibly shaken. "All of us in the industry had this horror in the back of our minds that this might happen as a result of some mechanical failure. But this was a human thing. I don't want to use the word *complacency*, but in twelve years this has become an extremely routine operation. Here it was, midnight, twelve years of successful operation—ho-hum. It was a normal situation: some ice, some elements of hazard. But it hadn't harmed anyone in twelve years.

"The fatal mistake was Hazelwood leaving the bridge," Santos continued. "Cousins knew the ship, knew how to run it. Unless he was a complete chowderhead, Cousins should have known they were heading into the reef. But the ultimate responsibilty lies with the captain of the ship. When Hazelwood went below deck, something fell between the cracks that was godawful."

Hazelwood was an accomplished captain within the ranks of a company that had a reputation of employing the most capable seamen. "Exxon was the cream," said the American Petroleum Institute's Sean Connaughton. "Exxon was the sought-after company. . . . They take care of their ships. They hire the best people."[1]

Joseph Hazelwood's character and sailing abilities emerged in his youth. Richard Behar reported in *Time* that, as a teenager, Hazelwood and some companions were sailing a 65-foot schooner across Long Island Sound when a violent storm came up and a gust of wind blew out the mainsail. While some of the boys cried and vomited, Hazelwood volunteered to climb the 50-foot mast to haul in the sail and its hardware.[2]

Hazelwood excelled at New York Maritime College, a rigorous school with a 60-percent dropout rate. He was capable enough to earn good grades and party on weekends. A former roommate, W. Bryce Laraway, recalls the time he and Hazelwood got so drunk they pretended their convertible Volkswagen was a skateboard. Driving down a steep road, they turned off the engine, jumped into the back seat, and shifted their weight to try to steer the vehicle. "On a scale of 1 to 10, we were probably a 14 in terms of drinking," Laraway said. "We made the movie *Animal House* look like amateur work."

Nevertheless, Hazelwood breezed through maritime college with honors. The motto printed next to his yearbook picture read, "It can't happen to me."

Later, in the merchant marine, Hazelwood's seafaring instincts made an impression on his superiors. "Joe had what we old-timers refer to as a seaman's eye," recalls Steve Brelsford, a retired Exxon captain and Hazelwood's first boss. "He had that sixth sense about seafaring that enables you to smell a storm on the horizon or watch the barometer and figure how to outmaneuver it."

"Joe didn't have *Exxon* tattooed under his eyelids," said an Exxon engineer. "He'd make his own judgments and act accordingly. That's why those at sea respected him and those on land thought he wasn't a company man."

A 1985 incident offshore from Atlantic City, New Jersey, highlighted Hazelwood's seamanship. On a trip south from New York, Hazelwood's ship encountered a freak storm. High winds snapped the ship's mast and it toppled, along with the ship's radar and electronic gear. With 30-foot waves and 50-knot winds overpowering the vessel, several sailors grabbed life jackets and prepared to abandon ship. Yet Hazelwood calmed the crew and rigged a makeshift antenna. Then, with the safety of his crew and cargo in mind, Hazelwood turned the ship and followed the storm back to New York.

However, Hazelwood's reputation as a drinker developed along with that as a capable seaman. "Ever since I had known of Joe, I heard he had alcohol problems," said James Shiminski, a former Exxon chief mate. "He had a reputation for partying ashore and on the ship."

One Exxon crewman recalled that, on a voyage with Hazelwood just two months before the wreck, the captain asked the crewman into his cabin "to destroy a bottle."

"It was almost like Joe was trying to get caught," said another seaman who knew Hazelwood well. "He'd close his door, but everyone knew what went on. He always said that everything was fine, but then why was he drinking? The guy was begging for help, but he kept it all inside."

The wreck of the *Exxon Valdez* abruptly threw Hazelwood's drinking into the open. The state of Alaska's lab report revealed that Joseph Hazelwood's blood alcohol level had registered .06 nine hours after the grounding. A toxicologist calculated that Hazelwood's alcohol level could have been .20 at the time of grounding, well over the limit for driving automobiles and five times the legal limit for vessel masters. What wasn't clear was precisely when Hazelwood consumed the alcohol, before or after the crash.

One fact remained indisputable: at the time of the accident Hazelwood's driver's license had been invalid, revoked as a result of a drunk driving incident the previous fall. In all, the license had been suspended for drunk driving violations three times since 1984.

One piece of the accident puzzle had to do with the renewal of Hazelwood's master's certification. Why had the Coast Guard made the renewal without checking Hazelwood's motor vehicle driving record for driving-while-intoxicated citations? Exxon denied knowledge of the fall incident and of the earlier license suspensions, but the company was well aware of Hazelwood's past drinking problem. In April 1985, Captain Hazelwood had voluntarily entered a private alcohol treatment program. A year later, former Exxon employee Bruce Amero had sued Exxon for $2 million, claiming that from 1980 through 1982 Hazelwood had been abusive while drinking aboard ship. "I smelled liquor on him on a number of occasions," Amero said. "I was asleep, and he was jumping up and down on his floor one evening screaming at me to come up and drink with him. There's a bad joke in the fleet that it's Captain Hazelwood and his chief mate, Jack Daniels, that run the ship."[3]

After the grounding on Bligh Reef, Exxon Shipping president Frank Iarossi addressed Hazelwood's drinking: "We are all outraged that an officer in such a critical position would have jeopardized his ship, crew, and the environment through such actions."[4] Yet before the accident Exxon had not only failed to examine Joseph Hazelwood's driving record, but had also evidently disregarded Amero's allegations. Iarossi pointed out that company officials had observed Hazelwood whenever he checked into port or attended company meetings. "We all spoke up about what we had seen him do, how he was reacting, how he was interacting, what he was drinking. And it was all iced tea and Perrier."

Since no one in Exxon's management had actually witnessed Joseph Hazelwood drink alcohol, he was allowed to command the company's largest tanker. After the accident, Hazelwood's employment with Exxon was terminated. Frank Iarossi recalled that "I fired Hazelwood for not being on the bridge during a critical passage and after test results showed that he had more than the maximum permissible blood alcohol level. It wasn't clear to me when he drank, whether it was preincident or postincident drinking, but it didn't make any difference."

The state of Alaska charged Joseph Hazelwood with misdemeanors for operating a ship while intoxicated, reckless endangerment, and negligent discharge of petroleum. The misdemeanor charges carried combined maximum penalties of two and a half years in prison and $11,000 in fines. Hazelwood also faced one felony charge of criminal mischief: maximum penalty of 5 years in prison and a $5,000 fine.

When the National Transportation Safety Board (NTSB) analyzed the *Exxon Valdez* accident in May, it came to view Hazelwood's drinking in light of a larger issue: oil industry control of substance abuse. The NTSB, comprised of transportation experts from around the country, held hearings in Anchorage, Alaska, for five days in mid-May. The board's mission was not to put individuals on trial, but to learn what the *Exxon Valdez* grounding could teach. As NTSB investigators compiled detailed reports, alcohol use and abuse emerged as problems in the shipping industry.

At these NTSB hearings, *Exxon Valdez* crew member Maureen Jones was asked if she had ever been checked for alcohol when reboarding a tanker. "No, I have never been searched," she answered, adding that prior to 1987 "Exxon used to give you little pint bottles of wine for your holiday meals, but they have discontinued that."[5]

When asked at the NTSB hearings how strictly alcohol was controlled on the *Exxon Valdez*, the tanker's helmsman Harry Claar said, "It's probably not any different than any others . . . stricter than some and looser than others."

Harbor pilot Ed Murphy had twice smelled alcohol on Hazelwood's breath during the tanker's departure from Valdez. The NTSB asked if this was a common occurrence—that is, how often had Murphy smelled alcohol on a master's breath? Murphy replied, "I haven't counted. It happens once in a while." Was he surprised when it happened? "Not particularly."

Murphy was then asked whether it had occurred to him that, having smelled alcohol on a captain's breath, "you might have to take some action in the interest of the vessel's safety?" Murphy replied, "Absolutely not."

A harbor pilot such as Murphy could conceivably serve as a final check on a captain's sobriety. Yet when asked what he would do about an obviously drunk master reassuming command of a tanker, Murphy said, "I really don't know what I'd do."

Katie Hite, a Valdez bartender for thirteen years, recalled instances in which she would have to stop serving drinks to tanker crewmen and put them in cabs to get them back to their ship. "I've seen guys come in and drink and drink and drink—and they complain about how they have to go back on watch," she said. "I wonder that these guys can get through the gate and be so drunk."[6]

According to Ed Kiml, head of security at the Alyeska terminal, tanker crew members who have been drinking can pass through security "as long as they've got their faculties to walk and get back on the ship."

Exxon's alcohol policy states that employees may be required to submit to drug and alcohol testing, and some surprise checks had been done on a number of tankers. However, when Iarossi was asked if Captain Hazelwood had ever been tested to follow up his rehabilitation, Iarossi replied, "Not to my knowledge."

After the wreck of the *Exxon Valdez*, Exxon announced that vessel officers who volunteered for rehabilitation would not be permitted to return to their original positions. With this decision, Exxon confronted a dilemma that faces many corporations. Confidentiality encourages employees to voluntarily enter rehabilitation but also shields them from being moved to less critical positions. However, Exxon's prohibition, which dismantled the shield of confidentiality, "may just drive [the alcohol problem] underground," said Frank Iarossi. "So at this point, I'm not sure what is the best policy."[7]

In fact, in Exxon's 1982–1983 review of officer performance, the appraisal of Joseph Hazelwood recommended that he be reassigned to shore duty. However, this appraisal was never signed or forwarded to Exxon headquarters for review. Hazelwood was assigned to the *Exxon Valdez* in April of 1987 because, as Iarossi put it, "supervisors, who hadn't seen the negative appraisal, felt that he was our most experienced master in terms of operating in and out of Valdez." Exxon CEO Lawrence Rawl described Joseph Hazelwood as "the most scrutinized employee in the company," yet the seriousness of his drinking problem escaped management's attention until the night of March 23, 1989.[8]

"Lots of the captains are alcoholic. It's just that Joe Hazelwood crashed," observed Bob Pudwill, a Cordova fisherman who worked for Exxon in Valdez in the early 1980s. "It's a lonely life out there. I think all that time away from families and friends may drive some of them to drink.

"But alcohol isn't the only problem," Pudwill continued. "Crewmen work together and become like a family. Sometimes they get too protective of each other, and then you start to lose an important system of checks and balances. They start to cover up for each other, not say anything if someone drinks or makes a mistake.

"Exxon is among the best in tanker maintenance and professional crews, but like other oil companies they try to save money wherever they can," observed Pudwill. After the tanker *Prince William Sound* lost power and almost ran aground near Knight Island in 1980, the Coast Guard had recommended installing reinforced tow lines on the tankers and requiring a tugboat to escort oil-loaded tankers out to Hinchinbrook Island at the edge of the sound. "The oil companies fought these safety measures because they cost more money," Pudwill continued. At the state of Alaska's insistence, the tow lines were incorporated, but the tug escorts, which would have prevented incidents such as the grounding of the *Exxon Valdez*, were not required.

As technology was improved, oil companies also reduced tanker crew sizes to save money. New, automated tankers require fewer crewmen, which "in some ways is good," Pudwill said. "The digital plotting and collision-avoiding systems are safer. But in a way they are less safe. With smaller crews, people work more overtime. They get less sleep. Their judgment is impaired. Accidents are more likely to happen."

"After the wreck," said Valdez mayor John Devens, "a couple of tanker captains who were feeling bad about Hazelwood called me. They told me, 'Sure, Hazelwood did something wrong, but he's not the biggest culprit in this whole affair. When we get into port we often have to work for twenty-four hours straight. We're dead tired. There's pressure to turn the ship around. Time is money. The deed is done, but don't make Hazelwood the scapegoat.'"

Others who appeared before the NTSB also cited crew fatigue. Helmsman Harry Claar reported that he sometimes felt so tired his performance was impaired. Asked if mates or engineers ever complained about being tired or overworked, Claar responded, "Sure."

Exxon Valdez chief mate James Kunkel testified that ablebodied seamen were allowed to work up to eight hours of overtime per day, up to 140 hours of overtime per month. When asked whether crew members worked the maximum amount,

Kunkel said, "Some of them do and some of them don't. . . . You're talking to a person who is just used to this. This is normal to me. . . . If you want to be a chief mate, this is how you will work. If you want to be a second mate or a third mate, this is how you will work. If you want to be a captain, this is what is expected of you."

In order to ensure that crew members are well rested while on duty, the U.S. Congress established guidelines for regulating overtime hours and required periods of rest. While seamen may choose to work overtime, they cannot be required to work more than eight hours per day except when "performing work necessary for the safety of the vessel, its crew or cargo." Review of the *Exxon Valdez* work records reveals that Seaman Maureen Jones worked eleven hours on March 23, the day the tanker departed Valdez.

Another rule issued by Congress prohibits an officer from active duty unless he or she has had at least six hours of rest during the previous twelve hours. When the NTSB asked Exxon marine expert William Deppe how Exxon Shipping ensures adherence to this rule, he replied, "We don't have any program to give six hours of rest to any deck officer before we get under way."

Third Mate Cousins's work schedule prior to the grounding was perhaps the most critical. Cousins, scheduled to go off duty at midnight, was working overtime when the tanker crashed. In his first report to the NTSB on the accident, the state's Bob LeResche wrote, "Cousins had only three and a half hours of rest in the twelve hours prior to departing Valdez—a violation of Coast Guard regulations. . . . It is difficult for the state to understand how Exxon Shipping Company can dispatch its tanker fleet with so little regard for the law or for the alertness and readiness of its crews."[9]

However, Frank Iarossi countered, "When we get into answering LeResche, we'll certainly wipe away that comment. By our count, Cousins had six hours off duty in the previous twelve hours, and he had ten hours of sleep in the twenty-four hours prior to the grounding. We're quite comfortable with Cousins's work schedule, and he was too. He even decided to take an extra hour of watch. I'm sure he now wishes he hadn't. We do too."

Exxon Shipping Company records show that the "workday"

aboard tankers is eleven hours long. "I would call an eleven-hour workday not too long," Frank Iarossi said. "That gives somebody thirteen hours with nothing to do. The biggest problem on ship is not fatigue but boredom. If you work eleven hours a day, you have thirteen hours a day with nothing to do but stare at the ocean. Most of our ocean-going people ask for extra work. It gives them something to do."

Nevertheless, LeResche thought he detected an attempt by Exxon to obscure the number of overtime hours crew members worked. According to LeResche, Exxon Shipping Company, aware of the weight the Coast Guard places on vessel-crew overtime levels, instructed its masters to minimize overtime hours in its records to justify Coast Guard–authorized crew-size reductions. LeResche said, "This heavy-handed attempt to manipulate the facts regarding manning levels is indicative of Exxon Shipping Company's cavalier approach to those levels."[10]

Representatives of a seamen's union, which had an interest in both safety and putting seamen to work, also testified to the NTSB that the *Exxon Valdez* was undermanned. However, Coast Guard certification of the *Exxon Valdez* required a crew of fifteen, and Exxon maintained a crew of twenty. So, to the extent that fatigue from undermanning was a contributing factor, the Coast Guard had to share responsibility for it.

The Coast Guard is responsible for ensuring tanker compliance with transit rules. Violations aboard the *Exxon Valdez*, such as having only one officer on the bridge while exiting Prince William Sound, raised the question of how well the Coast Guard was enforcing its regulations. Under query by the NTSB, Commander McCall acknowledged that the Coast Guard's capability to monitor tankers was limited. "We don't have radar coverage throughout Prince William Sound. We have no radio communications throughout the sound and beyond. . . .[We] have to rely on the integrity of the vessel operators to adhere to the traffic separation scheme."

One safety regulation that was both inconvenient for industry to comply with and difficult for the Coast Guard to enforce was modified in stages until it was effectively eliminated. This federal statute requires that tankers moving between the open sea and a port be commanded by someone with the proper "pilotage endorsement." Where the ship's officers lack the necessary experience and licensing, a harbor pilot is required to guide the ship. This regulation, where it is in place, is designed to prevent accidents in coastal areas with unusually strong currents, islands, reefs, or congested traffic lanes. When tankers first came to Prince William Sound, these pilotage regulations were active between Hinchinbrook Island and the port of Valdez. However, pilot boats that returned harbor pilots to Valdez struggled on the rough seas, especially in winter, when 90-knot gales can throw up 30-foot waves, freezing sea spray to decks. One pilot boat sank; its crew narrowly escaped.

In such cases, the Valdez Coast Guard might either have required tankers to hold offshore until weather conditions improved or required oil companies to upgrade the pilotage certification of their crews. Instead, the Coast Guard acquiesced to reductions of pilotage requirements in the sound, reasoning that the seas were too stormy for pilot boats to venture out as far as Hinchinbrook Island. The Coast Guard did not explain why it deemed it safe for tankers to run through these same rough waters without the guidance of harbor pilots. Beginning in 1986, the Coast Guard issued a series of temporary and conditional directives that made pilotage requirements so complicated that at the time of the accident many people were uncertain as to just what those requirements were.

Shortly after the accident, Coast Guard Admiral Paul Yost, Jr., announced that *Exxon Valdez* third mate Gregory Cousins had been "fully qualified" to pilot the tanker at the time of the accident. Later, in an interview with *Time* magazine, Yost shifted his position, saying that Cousins "was competent, but he was not technically qualified." Whatever the gray areas, there is no doubt that the cloud of uncertainty hanging over pilotage requirements played a part in the confusion on the night of March 23.

An inadequate Valdez radar system also hindered the Coast Guard's ability to prevent tanker accidents. The additional radar site strongly advocated in 1981 by Commander James Woodle was never installed near Bligh Reef, and at the time of the accident a cost-saving 50,000-watt radar system had replaced the old 100,000-watt system. In 1984, a radar technician had warned Alaska's congressional delegation that "this is not an upgrade of an existing system, but a downgrade with a new system. I can't help but feel that this is a tremendous waste of taxpayers' money and is also bringing an oil tanker disaster closer to reality."[11] The technician's warning went unheeded, and the Coast Guard testified to Congress that the new system would be capable of tracking both tankers and icebergs in the shipping lanes.

Budget constraints were at the root of these radar problems and of other Coast Guard cutbacks. "The Coast Guard is in bad shape financially," said Lee Crockett, a former Coast Guard officer now working for the U.S. House of Representatives. "We used to go to the navy to salvage their junk. We'd try to get old vessels that they were giving away or scrapping. Congress and the President said, 'Stop the drug smuggling,' and the Coast Guard got increased responsibilities. Yet they also got decreased funding. The Coast Guard tries to take everything on as best it can, but when it comes right down to it, you end up having to economize in areas you don't really want to."

Another casualty of budget cuts was a Coast Guard program to monitor ice conditions, long recognized as a hazard on the Valdez route. During one week in 1984, ice conditions had forced eighteen tankers to reduce speed or divert from designated traffic lanes, passing as close as 500 yards to Bligh Reef. When the Trans-Alaska Pipeline permit was issued, oil industry and federal officials assured the public that ice conditions would be carefully monitored with state-of-the-art equipment. They were not. "There is no observation system in place," said Commander Steve McCall, acknowledging that "any ice is a hazard to navigation." The Coast Guard was forced to rely on observations made by tankers. Such a subjective report remains valid, McCall said, "until the next vessel comes along and either substantiates it or . . . mitigates it."

An accurate ice report on the night of March 23 may have averted the grounding of the *Exxon Valdez*. Moments before impact, Third Mate Gregory Cousins had been studying the sketchy outline of ice on the ship's radar. Cousins may simply have become mesmerized as he stared into the radar screen, losing track of precious time while trying to figure out the ship's position in relation to the ice.

Hindsight revealed another contributing factor to the accident: tanker crew reliance on Coast Guard monitoring. Tanker crews believed that the Coast Guard plotted their progress at six-minute intervals out to Bligh Reef—this was a requirement detailed in the Coast Guard operations manual. And at the time of the accident, the Coast Guard manual explicitly required the plotting of tanker passage beyond the Narrows. However, the Coast Guard had discontinued plotting vessels as far as Bligh Reef without informing tanker crews. When the safety board asked why tankers were no longer tracked beyond the Narrows, Commander McCall replied that it was "no longer necessary." When the NTSB pressed, asking why the Coast Guard had not complied with its own manual, McCall hedged: "It's a living document—that's how I refer to it. It is and should be under constant evaluation, constant flux."

When the NTSB asked Cousins if he thought he was being plotted by the Coast Guard's vessel traffic service, he responded, "I assumed that was what they were doing."

If, on the night of March 23, the Coast Guard had been plotting the course of the *Exxon Valdez*, the radar man in Valdez would have been able to warn Cousins of the tanker's imminent collision with the reef.

Since the quality of radar coverage used to track tankers varies with weather conditions, a Coast Guard directive had been issued earlier to improve radar coverage. At the time of the accident, the equipment necessary to make this radar improvement had been sitting in Valdez for more than a year and a half without being used. No one had bothered putting it into operation.

When pressed to explain the Coast Guard's failure to warn the *Exxon Valdez* of its impending collision with Bligh Reef, McCall said, "A warning wouldn't have done any good. . . . All we can do is advise. . . . We can't direct a vessel to make a course change." This response reflected the Coast Guard's deference to an ancient mariner's rule that is one of the basics of modern maritime law—the master of a ship holds the ultimate responsibility for his ship's safe passage.

However, the Coast Guard's own manual on vessel traffic control states that in critical situations the Coast Guard should actually "direct or prohibit vessel movement." To emphasize the importance of actually directing ships in times of danger, the manual provides an example of what a traffic controller should say: "This is Valdez traffic. Our radar shows you 100 yards to the left of traffic lane, inside the separation zone. You are DIRECTED to take corrective action."

Some federal, state, and private investigators who pored over evidence of the *Exxon Valdez* grounding came to the conclusion that the event was not really an accident. They cast blame in many directions. A few even raised the possibility of an out-and-out conspiracy to account for the myriad things that shouldn't have gone wrong but did. That suggestion aside, it is certain that a conspiracy of sorts *was* at work—an unconscious conspiracy of denial. A tanker captain denied his drinking problem. A harbor pilot and tanker crew members denied their responsibility to report breaches of safety regulations. Company officials denied the potential consequences of crew fatigue and of placing an alcoholic captain in command of an oil tanker. Coast Guard officers denied the necessity of following their own safety procedures.

In retrospect, the wreck of the *Exxon Valdez* appeared to be less an accident than a widespread denial that such an incident could happen at all. It seemed as if everyone involved had adopted Joe Hazelwood's yearbook motto: "It can't happen to me."

Meanwhile dark, oil-laden waves surged out across Prince William Sound. The world's oil spill experts, many of whom had gathered by then in Valdez, had more specific ideas about who was to blame than how to save the coves and beaches, the otters and flocks of birds, that lay in the path of the oil. As gale-force winds blew on through the sound across the Kenai Peninsula to Kodiak and the Aleutian Islands, no one knew how far those winds, the tides, and the currents would carry the oil. And no one knew to what extent denial would impede efforts to safeguard the people and wildlife along those wild coasts.

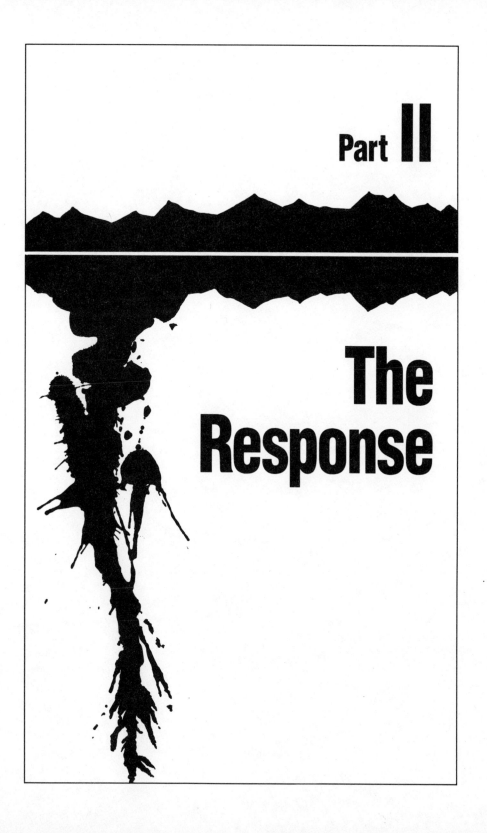

Part II

The Response

Chapter 7

The Great Promise

T he thing that is hardest for a development-minded individual is this tremendous sense of betrayal," said one longtime Alaskan. "I believed our state officials when they said they were taking care of things. And I believed the oil companies when they said we could have both a pristine environment and oil."

The grounding of the *Exxon Valdez* was precipitated by individual, industry, and government errors and the underlying denial that such an event could occur. But once the oil was loose, where did responsibility lie for the failure to contain and recover it before it killed wildlife and spread along Alaska's beaches?

During the first hectic days of the spill, most of the blame fell on Exxon, which was trying to mount a response virtually from scratch. "There's no doubt that all these contingency plans and all this planning and everything did not anticipate ever having to respond to a spill this big," Iarossi said. "I don't know why it didn't. I wasn't involved in the plan. But clearly, no one ever anticipated trying to handle 250,000 barrels of oil on the water. This spill just overwhelmed everybody. No one was organized to control a spill of this magnitude."

Nevertheless, while Iarossi may not have been personally involved and responsible for the failed response plan, Exxon was a major partner in the Alyeska consortium, and from its inception Alyeska had reassured the public that it was prepared for a major oil spill.

"Alyeska's contingency plan is the greatest work of maritime fiction since *Moby Dick*," said Alaska's Department of Environmental Conservation commissioner, Dennis Kelso, after the wreck of the *Exxon Valdez*. He was incensed that after claiming it could recover at least 100,000 barrels of oil in seventy-two hours, Alyeska actually recovered barely 3,000 barrels within that time span.

"Alyeska stands as a monument to a powerful and rich industry's fundamental failure to keep its commitments," Kelso said. "The oil companies have operated as if they were a sovereign state, with terrible consequences. As a nation we have to ask ourselves, 'Can we trust them anymore?'"

However, Kelso's comments raised questions that would come back to haunt him. If Alyeska's contingency plan was a great work of fiction, why had he approved it on behalf of DEC? And why, as the state's chief environmental regulator, had he evidently trusted the oil industry in the first place? To what extent did DEC, along with other state and federal agencies, share responsibility for the devastation being wrought by the oil spill?

One thing was clear. Both the state and Exxon had counted on Alyeska as the first line of defense in an oil spill. An oil spill contingency plan had, in fact, been required when the seven oil companies that formed Alyeska applied for a permit to build the Trans-Alaska Pipeline in 1970. When lobbying Congress for the permit, British Petroleum, with a 50.01-percent share of Alyeska, ARCO and Exxon, with about 20 percent each, and Mobil, Amerada Hess, Unocal, and Phillips Petroleum, with minor shares, all made promises to protect the environment. All the companies committed themselves to ensuring air and water quality with state-of-the-art pollution technology, and all undertook to prepare and commit themselves to a contingency plan that would take every possible measure to protect the environment.

With the pipeline right-of-way permit in limbo in 1971, British Petroleum's top pollution specialist, L. R. Beynon, testified at Department of Interior hearings that Alyeska's contingency plan "will detail methods for dealing promptly and effectively with any oil spill which may occur, so that its effects on the environment will be minimal. We have adequate knowledge for dealing with oil spills. . . . The best equipment, materials and expertise—which will be made available as part of the oil spill contingency plan—will make operations in Port of Valdez and Prince William Sound the safest in the world."[1]

When the permit to build the Trans-Alaska Pipeline was approved in 1973—over the protests of environmentalists and Cordova fishermen—Alyeska's oil spill contingency plan became both a covenant detailing the oil industry's promises to the American people and a condition of the consortium's extraction and sale of North Slope oil. Mandated in the pipeline-enabling legislation, this agreement was no less than a contract between Alyeska's seven oil companies and the people of the United States to protect and preserve, in all pipeline-related activities, the quality of the air, water, and environment.

The contingency plan was not a general promise of good intentions, but a document that spelled out precisely how Alyeska would respond to a spill: the oil spill equipment that would be available, the names and backgrounds of cleanup personnel, response times, lists of subcontractors, and so on. In an attempt to eliminate confusion, the pipeline permit called for one plan to cover all Alyeska's parent companies.

"It is supposed to be Alyeska who is responsible for a cleanup and no one else, because that was the promise the oil companies made to the people of the United States," said Dan Lawn, DEC's longtime representative in Valdez. "That's why they got a chance to build this pipeline. The people of the United States didn't want 4,700 different oil companies coming in here with 47,000 different cleanup contractors. They wanted one. That was Alyeska. And Alyeska was going to take care of everything. We've got a plan that says that. Where the hell were they?"

Dan Lawn, who describes himself as a "meat and potatoes guy," stands well over six feet tall and weighs around 250 pounds. At forty-nine, he looks like an aging linebacker who has taken too many hits. With his gray beard and long silver hair, Lawn looks more like a maverick than a career bureaucrat. There is still a swagger to his stride, but his eyes look weary. An Alyeska executive once denounced Lawn as "that jerk." Some of his own co-workers have called him a troublemaker. Others have viewed Dan Lawn as a lone voice of caution.

"A lot of people with the state have called me a hard-ass," said

Lawn, who had dealt with Alyeska on a daily basis for more than ten years. "But I'm a realist. I cut through the bullshit. Big oil has to stop dictating to the world what it's going to do. To get the whole flavor of this thing, you have to go back to the very beginning. I was involved with the 'Great Promise' of the pipeline and terminal, the largest private undertaking in the history of mankind. I believed Alyeska was going to live up to its promise: to do it without degrading the environment. I know more now."

One of the promises Dan Lawn meant to see that Alyeska kept was that it meet water quality standards in the port of Valdez. However, according to Tami Thomas, a member of Alyeska's oil spill response team, "We'd have spills daily. We'd put a boom around a tanker, but lots of times our supervisors didn't want us to pick up the oil. They'd order the boom opened to let another ship in. They always seemed to know when Dan Lawn was going to fly over to make an inspection. They'd scurry to make everything look right. It was ridiculous. And instead of fixing equipment, they'd junk it and never replace it."

Thomas described a trick Alyeska workers used when cleaning oily sludge from terminal pilings. A DEC-approved biodegradable detergent took longer to use than another much more toxic solvent, so "we put a bottle of the approved detergent on deck for show, in case someone came around to see what we were doing. We kept the toxic stuff, which we used, hidden under wraps. It would almost take the skin off your arm.

"The ballast water treatment never worked properly either," recalled Thomas, whose observations were eventually confirmed by the Environmental Protection Agency. Ballast water, which tankers carry in empty cargo tanks for stability, always contains oily residue, or mousse, that must be siphoned off before the water is flushed back into the bay. Reported Thomas, "If we didn't suck off the mousse, they'd just let it go. Sometimes they'd have us pump that oily water right into the bay. I got so angry. Everyone else on the crew knew what was going on. But they wouldn't talk to anyone else because they didn't want to lose their jobs. When they figured out I was talking, they started giving me crappy jobs. They had me go into the sludge pit, wading in crude up to my waist. I had to shovel out sludge from the ballast treatment. That stuff corrodes steel. They didn't even give me an air mask. I'd get sick from breathing the fumes. I finally had to quit."

Furthermore, Alyeska manipulated required testing for toxic effluents by sending samples of treated ballast water to Seattle, 1,200 miles away, rather than testing them in Alaska. By the time the samples were tested, enough of the pollutants had decayed to yield results within the legal limits. One Alyeska supervisor later acknowledged that "had we tested them in Valdez, they would have been off the scale."[2]

Another way to circumvent ballast water standards was revealed by Steve Edward, an Alyeska technician from 1977 to 1980, who acknowledged that he had frequently disconnected the meter measuring ballast water discharge into the ocean. He admitted that the federal law limiting ballast discharge was routinely ignored. "The way around it was to shut off the mechanism for gauging how much we dumped. There was no other way for the regulators to check it."[3]

In addition to polluting the port of Valdez, Alyeska created serious air pollution. In a cost-saving measure, Alyeska disconnected equipment in its incinerators that helped burn off toxic vapors from its oil-storage tanks. Tankers coming into Valdez emitted as much as 1,000 tons of hydrocarbons per week during tanker-loading operations. Alyeska argued that refitting the tankers with new, pollution-reducing burners would be too expensive. Yet Jerry Nebel, a former Alyeska supervisor, said, "That was a lie and we knew it was a lie."[4]

In other breaches, Alyeska failed to keep its promise to transport oil without seriously affecting air and water quality, and far from initiating an adequate oil spill response system, Alyeska actively resisted the idea. According to Dan Lawn, the state had never been able to stand up to the fabrications and power of the oil companies. "I've been listening to Alyeska for ten years, and I'm tired of it."

As early as July 1982, Lawn warned his supervisor in the Anchorage regional office that Alyeska's "contingency plan is superficial at best. Technically, their response probably satisfies the regulation requirements on paper; however, Alyeska has never been able to demonstrate that their recovery rates . . . are possible to obtain. In fact, all our experience with Alyeska oil spill recovery rates indicate that the recovery rates listed are 80 percent too high."

Two years later, in a 1984 memo to his supervisor, Lawn wrote, "There has taken place a general disemboweling of the Alyeska Valdez terminal operational plan. Most knowledgeable and competently trained individuals have either quit, been terminated, or transferred up the line. This has left inadequately trained people to maintain the facility and an insufficient number of people to operate it.

"As you know, [we have] been underbudgeted and understaffed to adequately inspect the terminal and keep in touch with Alyeska's day-to-day operations," Lawn's memo continued. "Unfortunately, this has been a signal to Alyeska that the state is no longer interested in the Trans-Alaska Pipeline project. Alyeska has consistently broken promises made to the state of Alaska and the federal government prior to our granting permission to build the terminal. We can no longer ignore the routine monitoring of Alyeska, unless we do not care whether a major catastrophic event occurs."

Lawn's "disembowelment memo" resulted in no significant action. It was filed and forgotten. "Why didn't I fight?" Lawn asked. "I didn't have the time. I had two other investigations. I was just too exhausted."

After the wreck of the *Exxon Valdez*, Lawn pointed out that "three years ago the governor said he agreed that we need twice as many people, but the legislature funded only 10 percent of what we needed. Why is that? We're so goddamned overworked that no one has time to listen to anyone. Well, I'm angry about this. I'm angry about not having enough people here. This mess was preventable."

The state of Alaska hardly lacked the funds to afford better regulatory protection. From 1969 to 1987, the state made $29 billion in oil-related income,[5] an average of more than $1.5 billion per year. Yet the Department of Environmental Conservation received only a fraction of its requested budget. And while the state handed out more than $400 million a year to its residents in the form of permanent fund dividend checks—at least $800 apiece simply for living in Alaska—it funded not one single staff position for oil spill contingency planning.

Meanwhile, the oil industry was making substantial efforts to influence state policy. In 1987, the oil industry's lobbying of the Alaska legislature and state regulatory agencies cost $759,000[6]—more money than in DEC's budget for regulating the oil industry. A review of profits from North Slope oil indicates that maintaining a state-of-the-art oil spill response capability would have made no noticeable dent in the earnings of the Alyeska parent companies. After accounting for all expenses, including exploration, lease acquisition, income taxes, and depreciation, the oil industry realized an estimated $42.6 billion in profit from production and transportation activities in Alaska from 1969 through 1987. On an hourly basis, the parent companies earned after-tax profits at the rate of $463,144 per hour, twenty-four hours a day, every day.[7] Just a single day's profit per year would have gone a long way toward financing the state-of-the-art response capability Alyeska had promised.

"Why the hell does Alyeska fight us on every issue?" asked Dan Lawn, who had watched Alyeska repeatedly cut back environmental safeguards in order to save money. "This contingency plan, this whole thing with Alyeska, was the big lie. We've known for years that they couldn't clean up the damn oil. And they have always had an excuse for one reason or another. Every time we'd raise a red flag, they'd counter, 'It's impractical. It costs too much.' They just lie about everything. They are absolutely immoral. They argue you into the ground.

"It doesn't matter whether it's an oil spill out there or the tons of pollutants they're putting into the air and water—those oil companies have a total disregard for the environment," Lawn said. "They also have a total disregard for the promises they made to the people of the United States when they built this thing. And we've allowed this to happen to us, because it's easier not to resist. No one, including myself, could think big enough. This was an accident that's been waiting to happen for ten years."

Lawn's sense of inevitability was shared by Valdez Coast Guard Commander James Woodle, who had foreseen trouble with Columbia Glacier ice and had urged the Coast Guard to install an additional radar site. Woodle, who had retired from the Coast Guard to become Alyeska's marine superintendent, said of the spill, "Based on my experience with Alyeska, the only surprise is that an accident like the *Exxon Valdez* didn't happen sooner. There was an overall attitude of petty cheapness that severely affected our ability to operate safely. I was shocked at the shabbiness of the operation."[8]

At the time of his resignation from Alyeska in April 1984, Woodle wrote a letter warning Alyeska that "due to reduction in manning, age of equipment, limited training opportunities, and lack of experienced coordination personnel, serious doubt exists that Alyeska would be able to contain and clean up effectively a medium- or large-size oil spill. Recent manning reductions have affected all operating areas, while efforts to cut costs have limited purchase of new oil spill recovery equipment. The present oil spill coordinator lacks both experience and training. Attempts to provide formal training and experience were disapproved due to costs. Response to any spill beyond the limits of Valdez Narrows should not be attempted with present equipment and personnel."[9]

A review of DEC files and Alyeska's track record reveals an overall pattern of denial marked by both the oil industry's tight-fisted resistance to making good on its promises and the state's lack of perseverance in requiring it to do so:

- *December 1976*. The Coast Guard "strongly recommended" that the industry position appropriate cleanup gear in Prince William Sound. Alyeska did not comply with the recommendation.

- *January 1977*. DEC's first commissioner, Ernest Mueller, determined that the cleanup gear Alyeska had on hand was inadequate and urged that it be upgraded to meet actual conditions in Prince William Sound. Alyeska did not comply.

- *March 1977*. The Alaska Department of Fish and Game declared Alyeska's containment boom insufficient, its maximum spill estimate of 74,000 barrels too low, and its cleanup crew too small. Alyeska took no corrective measures.

- *May 1977*. DEC and the Coast Guard urged that Alyeska permanently anchor barges loaded with boom, lightering pumps, skimmers, and dispersant at Bligh Island and Hinchinbrook

Island. Alyeska's parent companies did not want to incur this expense, and the state did not require them to.

• *June 1977.* The federal Alaska pipeline office approved Alyeska's first contingency plan—over the objections of one state official, who said that Alyeska "has maneuvered the government into accepting a shoddy piece of work."

• *March 1978.* The Coast Guard again urged Alyeska to deploy cleanup equipment in Prince William Sound. Alyeska refused.

• *March 1982.* DEC asked Alyeska to address spills larger than 74,000 barrels in its plan. Alyeska appealed DEC's request in court, challenging the agency's jurisdiction in Prince William Sound.

• *May 1984.* State inspectors reported severe personnel cuts in the trained oil spill response teams Alyeska maintained. They also questioned the reliability of Alyeska's cleanup equipment.

• *October 1984.* Alyeska performed a spill drill. State observers reported that "response efforts failed to contain the hypothetical spill." The Environmental Protection Agency concluded that "Alyeska is not prepared."

• *November 1985.* DEC stated that Alyeska "consistently failed to follow up on commitments" made after spill drills.

• *May 1986.* At DEC's insistence, Alyeska finally worked into its contingency plan a scenario for a 200,000-barrel spill. It nevertheless protested that such a spill would happen only once in 241 years.

• *March 1989.* The once-in-241-years spill happened. And Alyeska disappeared.

"The spill should not have come as a surprise," said DEC commissioner Dennis Kelso. "Their projection of 241 years before something like this would happen is imaginary, a way not to take the threat of a spill seriously. They seem to have a belief that this would never happen. Their pattern of behavior is one of denial."[10]

"We wrote that 200,000-barrel scenario with great reluctance," explained Alyeska spokesman Tom Brennan. "There are hundreds of variables, such as wind, temperature, daylight, currents, and ice conditions. There are literally thousands of possible scenarios, but DEC said, 'Do a 200,000-barrel scenario.' In retrospect, it seems unrealistic.

"Sure, there were some lousy estimates on our part as to what we could do with the equipment on hand," Brennan said. "And the state is right. If we'd had high-capacity equipment, it would have made a difference."

Even within Alyeska there were periodic requests for better oil spill response equipment. "Exxon Shipping had always maintained that we needed more oil spill equipment in Valdez," Frank Iarossi said. "We specifically asked that dispersant-spraying equipment be stationed in Alaska, that prior dispersant application arrangements be made with C-130s in Alaska, and that there be a bigger barge for unloading skimmers. Our last official plea was made in September of 1987. I don't know which companies voted against our request. But to get to the scene of this spill and not have that equipment was a real bitter pill."

Although Alyeska guards the secrecy of votes within its owners committee, it is clear that British Petroleum, with 50.01 percent ownership and a controlling vote, vetoed the purchase of much-needed oil spill equipment. While Exxon took all the heat for the failure to control the spill, British Petroleum and the other owner companies quietly faded into the woodwork.

When asked why the necessary equipment was not purchased, Fred Garibaldi, British Petroleum vice president and chairman of Alyeska's owners committee, said he had decided to put off purchasing it in order to force federal and state agencies to develop dispersant use guidelines. He said, "Our only bargaining chip was to say we were prepared to buy the package, but not until the [guidelines] were in place."[11]

To keep their promises to the American people, industry and government officials should have resolved their gamesmanship before placing the environment at risk by bringing tankers to Valdez. But after the spill, Alyeska had trouble getting even its limited equipment mobilized. Pressed to explain why Alyeska was so late in reaching the spill, Alyeska spokesmen described the oil spill scenario in Alyeska's response plan, which the state had relied on, as "a set of conditions that cannot really be extrapolated to the real world."

They even denied that the contingency plan, with its 200,000-barrel scenario, constituted a contractual agreement between the state and Alyeska. They said it was their "understanding that they are guidelines."[12]

"That's like saying the fire code is just a set of guidelines," DEC's Dennis Kelso shot back. "It's just an incredible and appalling fabrication."[13]

When Illinois congressman Richard Durbin grilled Alyeska at a field hearing in Valdez, he asked for an explanation of Alyeska's previous claim that it could recover 50 percent of a 200,000-barrel spill. When Alyeska responded that "recovery means mechanical recovery, burning, or dispersants," Durbin was amazed to hear *recovery* construed to mean dispersal of oil into the ocean and shot back, "I don't see how you can make this representation. We think you made a promise with [your contingency plan]. You abused our basic trust. You promised to deliver if a disaster occurs."[14]

"We have not broken our promises to the people of this state," replied Theo Polasek, Alyeska's vice president of operations. Yet when asked how many barges and skimmers were needed to retrieve the 100,000 barrels of oil Alyeska had claimed it could collect in seventy-two hours, Polasek said, "This question cannot be answered. We never implied or said we could pick up 100,000 barrels in seventy-two hours."

"Well, it says so right here in your letter," retorted his congressional interrogator, waving a copy of a letter from Alyeska to the state of Alaska.

Later, Theo Polasek pointed out that the contingency plan's 200,000-barrel oil spill scenario "says you're going to be looking at a long-term cleanup. It was very, very straightforward." He felt that the process of writing the plan and preparing for a large spill "went well. We worked on it with the state for a year, writing letters, holding meetings, discussing it. . . . It took six months to get tentative approval and another six months to get final approval." Polasek said Alyeska thought it had a "common expectation" with the state as to what could and could not be done if a large spill occurred.[15]

Although the oil industry aroused the public's anger for the failed oil spill response, the state of Alaska was also party to the Great Promise to develop North Slope oil safely, and it also faced some troubling questions. If Alyeska's plan was flawed, why had the state approved it? Why had Exxon, British Petroleum, ARCO, and Alyeska's other owner companies been allowed to continue operating when the oil spill contingency plan proved to be inadequate? Why had Dan Lawn's warnings gone unheeded?

Former DEC commissioner Bill Ross received Dan Lawn's memo the week after taking office in 1985. While commissioner, he never considered rejecting Alyeska's contingency plan, which would have shut down the pipeline. However, after the wreck of the *Exxon Valdez*, Ross acknowledged that "there was no one really keeping track of how well this transportation system was holding together." Realizing in hindsight that he could have more carefully "assessed the factual situation," Ross was troubled by the state's failure to demand an adequate contingency plan. "Was the state responsible at the moment that tanker went up on the rocks?" Ross asked. "That question has caused me some sleepless nights."[16]

Exxon accepted responsibility for the spill, but to what extent was the state responsible for failing to make certain industry could clean up the oil? "The commitment of industry to do things right will always be short-lived unless the government fulfills its role," said Walt Parker, a longtime Alaska transportation planner. Although appointed to represent the state as chairman of its oil spill commission, formed after the spill, Parker said, "I have been completely shocked by the total lack of care for the environment within state government. Oh, there are a few individuals here and there who have some cares. They're the Dan Lawns. Usually, they're the outlaws, the ones who have been singled out to be gotten rid of."

Parker concluded that, while many had to share responsibility for letting the *Exxon Valdez* spill get out of control, "most of the blame lies with state government for not realizing that the Alyeska situation was generating such great peril. DEC was created as a result of major oil discoveries in Alaska. It was supposed to be an environmental watchdog. But DEC was given the job of inspecting barber shops and restaurants, which diluted its ability to watch over major resource development issues. DEC has never played a strong regulatory role from day one.

"DEC's failure was not just a matter of budget," Parker continued. "It was also a matter of will and direction. For example, Denny Kelso admitted he had never been to Valdez until after the spill. What's more important environmentally in the state of Alaska than control of that pipeline and the Valdez terminal? What's a greater environmental threat? But what did DEC do with its permitting authority over Alyeska? Nothing that one can determine.

"The people who run DEC's Valdez office have a primary responsibility, but they are regarded as field grunts and not a part of the Juneau hierarchy," Parker said. "The Juneau hierarchy never went to Valdez to back their man up. Dennis Kelso met Dan Lawn only after the accident. Alyeska and all those tankers were treated as a ho-hum thing. If the local state people don't care very much, you can't expect Alyeska employees and those young Coast Guard officers to get excited about protecting the environment. So the result was the oil spill."

While reviewing Alyeska's contingency plan, former DEC commissioner Bill Ross decided it was important to actually test Alyeska's capabilities through an unannounced spill drill. However, Alyeska was allowed to suggest the day when the spill would take place. To simulate spilled oil, workers threw thousands of oranges into the water near the Alyeska terminal.[17] After watching Alyeska personnel chasing the bobbing oranges over the water with booms and skimmers, DEC field officer Pat Cyr said, "Alyeska's response was acceptable but not by a wide margin." Cyr recommended that the state hold a truly unannounced spill drill and use a chemical that behaved more like oil than oranges.

After becoming commissioner of DEC in December 1986, Dennis Kelso said that, although he didn't know the actual cost of the spill drill, he felt it was too expensive for the state to devise such drills and then evaluate Alyeska's performance. One DEC official estimated the cost of a spill drill at $10,000 and asked, "Can we afford not to do it?"[18]

The neglect of its watchdog role was not something new to DEC in 1989. Dennis Kelso inherited a certain amount of institutional neglect when he became commissioner of environmental conservation in December 1986: DEC was not even funded for oil spill contingency planning. In fact, the agency had to borrow employees from other positions to complete an eighteen-month review and updating of Alyeska's plan just before Kelso arrived. Having no oil spill contingency planning staff and preoccupied with other matters, Kelso accepted the plan in the form approved by his predecessor. In March 1987, three months after Kelso became commissioner, final approval of the contingency plan was sent to Alyeska. Kelso had not personally read the plan, nor would he do so until after the spill.

However, Kelso did detect and help correct an oversight in state statutes: even though Alyeska had a contingency plan, it was not required to use it. The legislature closed this loophole by passing legislation requiring oil companies not only to write contingency plans but also to follow them. Regarding this step, Kelso said, "We still did not have enough money to carry out oil spill contingency planning, but at least now we had stronger authority." And, he explained, "When the contingency plan was written and approved, nobody thought it was fiction. It was only after Alyeska failed to carry it out that it became fiction."

Environmental attorney Patti Saunders disagreed. "We heard the unvarnished truth when Kelso described Alyeska's contingency plan as the biggest piece of maritime fiction since *Moby Dick*. This notion that it only became fiction later is just legal mumbo jumbo designed to obscure DEC's kowtowing to Alyeska. I think DEC has some serious liability problems because it signed off on that worthless contingency plan."

Saunders had worked for the state of Pennsylvania enforcing environmental statutes and had come to Alaska to work for Trustees for Alaska, an independent environmental organization. "Having worked for an agency, I've seen the kind of stuff that industry tries to pull," she said. "I can see DEC's side of the picture. But I think there is real negligence involved here. Actually, DEC is more than negligent, because its actions were deliberate. The upper management in DEC was told everything that was wrong. They were told by citizens. They were told by environmental groups. They were told by fishermen. Told by their own staff. Sure, DEC is understaffed, and that might be a justification for slow work, but it's no excuse for shoddy work.

People at DEC knew just how bad that contingency plan was. And they signed off on it anyway.

"There are good people who work in DEC," Saunders said. "But there is a limit to how far they are going to stick their necks out. Take Dan Lawn. He had a lot of guts just to put his criticism in writing. But did he ever really do anything? He wrote inspections up, and he banged on Alyeska and sent memos, but did he ever send a notice of violation? No, he didn't.

"The root of the problem is that Dan Lawn's superiors just didn't have the guts to stand up to the oil industry," Saunders said. "For example, after the spill, Lawn's supervisor was going to issue Alyeska an air quality permit without having the necessary information. I asked him, 'You don't have the information required under the statute to review this permit properly, but you are going to issue it anyway? What's the deal?' He said, 'Patti, I can't deny that permit. If I don't issue that permit, I'll lose my job.'"

Such lack of resolve in getting necessary information before granting permits had apparently become standard operating procedure within DEC. The state repeatedly approved Alyeska's evolving oil spill contingency plan without really knowing the consequences of a large spill. In fact, the state allowed the pipeline to operate for more than six years before insisting that Alyeska provide a scenario projecting what would happen if 200,00 barrels of oil were spilled. And the state *never* insisted that Alyeska prepare a worst-case scenario, such as a wintertime spill of the entire 1,200,000 barrels carried by the *Exxon Valdez*.

"I think fear has kept us from getting contingency plans for the largest possible spills," said Jim Hayden, a ten-year employee of DEC. "Exxon and Alyeska felt this would never happen. We always had fears of this happening. But it was so frightening to think about that there was a tendency to avoid dealing with it.

"There was apathy, but not totally on DEC's part. Many times the legislature put us in a no-win situation," Hayden continued. "We were told on the one hand to regulate and control environmental degradation. But we didn't have the budget. We have never had a properly staffed oil spill contingency review staff. We are spread too thin. We can't do the detail work that's required. We don't have enough people to handle thirty projects plus the oil and hazardous waste spills. It is not uncommon for us to have our investigations backed up for ten years."

The state was also limited by the penalties it could impose on Alyeska. Other than citations and small fines that amounted to no more than a slap on Alyeska's wrist, there was only the Draconian sanction of shutting down the pipeline. "The state had no legitimately functioning regulatory tools," said Dr. Bob LeResche, appointed as the state's oil spill coordinator after the spill. "I mean, we had the nuke: if we didn't like Alyeska's contingency plan, we could shut down the pipeline, and that would last five or six hours until the National Guard arrived. There was no way in hell we were going to get away with shutting down the pipeline. They knew it and we knew it. Short of that, we had no conventional weapons. We had the nuke but we didn't have the tanks. Shutting down the pipeline was the only thing we could do to Alyeska if its contingency plan was insufficient."

Since shutting down the pipeline would cut off more than 80 percent of the state's income and 25 percent of the nation's domestic oil production, it was highly unlikely that either the state or the federal government would ever do it. Closing the spigot on North Slope oil was supposed to be the ultimate regulatory tool, but in reality it could never be used to compel Alyeska to run a safer tanker operation.

Also, whether the state actually had jurisdiction to require safer tanker operations in Prince William Sound was unclear. In 1982, when Alyeska went to court to challenge DEC's right to request any safeguards in Prince William Sound, a settlement was reached in which Alyeska agreed to do certain things, with the condition that the state temper its requests. "We pushed it just as far as we could," said LeResche. "It is really unclear how much authority the state has to review the contingency plan for Prince William Sound. If we try to force Alyeska to do this or that, they can take us to court, and the interstate commerce laws would push us back to the dock. I think someday the Supreme Court may decide that the state doesn't have a goddamned thing to say about what those tankers do in Prince William Sound."

Thus, a lack of clear authority combined with apathy, fear, and institutionalized neglect to undermine the state's ability to prevent the devastating effects of the spill.

The federal government, the third player along with the oil industry and the state, made its own contribution to the Great Promise. When the proposed Trans-Alaska Pipeline route was criticized in the early 1970s because it involved tanker transport, the federal government promised to require double-bottom tankers. In 1972, Secretary of Interior Rogers B. Morton told Congress that "newly constructed American flag vessels carrying oil from Port Valdez to United States ports will be required to have segregated ballast systems incorporating double bottoms."

This commitment to double-bottom tankers was a key factor in Congress's subsequent approval of the Trans-Alaska Pipeline route. Nevertheless, oil industry officials continued to argue that, in some situations, single-hull tankers are safer. Cost was an underlying motive. Construction of a double bottom can add up to 5 percent to the cost of a new tanker—about an additional $6 million for the *Exxon Valdez*—and a complete double hull runs 1 or 2 percent more. Inefficiency is the highest cost of double-bottom and double-hull tankers. Ships with double hulls can carry only about 60 percent as much oil as the same size tanker with a single hull. Herein lies a cost for environmental protection that the oil industry is loathe to make. After the wreck of the *Exxon Valdez*, Frank Iarossi acknowledged that "Double hulls clearly would protect for both collision and grounding, and in that respect would seem to provide the ultimate solution." He added that requiring double hulls could increase the chance of an accident because it would necessitate 60 percent more tankers to move a given amount of oil.[19] Shipping costs could also increase up to 60 percent.

The double-hull debate reached a crescendo in 1975. In January of that year, a study by Coast Guard naval architect James Card concluded that in thirty tanker groundings from 1969 to 1973 double hulls would have contained 97 percent of the oil that was spilled. Then, in April, a task force set up by the American Petroleum Institute recommended against double hulls. In July, the Congressional Office of Technology Assessment concluded that double hulls offer "a significant degree of pollution protection in the event of a grounding accident."[20] By the end of 1975, the Coast Guard was siding with industry. Coast Guard Rear Admiral William Benkert said, "We collected new data, and we changed our mind. We don't think groundings are as serious a problem as we once thought."

However, one Coast Guard official, who preferred not to be identified, said that safety was not the deciding factor in the double-hull issue: "The bottom line was keeping costs low enough for American vessels to be competitive with foreign tankers." In any event, the federal government did not require more than a single hull. As a consequence, 73 percent of the tankers in the Alaska trade, including the *Exxon Valdez*, are single-hull vessels. After the *Exxon Valdez* grounded on Bligh Reef, the Coast Guard estimated that 25 to 60 percent of the spilled oil—3.1 to 6.8 million gallons—could have been contained if the vessel had had a double hull.[21]

While the federal government could have initiated safer tanker requirements at any time, much of its direct regulatory authority over Alyeska diminished once the first barrel of oil coursed down the pipeline. When that first barrel reached Valdez, it triggered a transfer of ownership of the title to the land under Alyeska's terminal: from the federal government to the state, which in turn deeded the property to Alyeska. Although only a few acres changed hands, the switch in ownership resulted in a highly significant shift of authority and regulatory power. The federal government would no longer be directly involved in watchdogging Alyeska's operations in Prince William Sound. That task now fell to the state, which, for the reasons discussed, proved virtually incapable of regulating the oil industry.

Nevertheless, the federal government is mandated to step in and take over if an oil spiller fails to recover the spilled oil, rescue stricken wildlife, or clean up oiled shorelines. The national contingency plan—formed under the Clean Water Act of 1972 and the Comprehensive Environmental Response, Compensation and Liability Act of 1980—establishes a process for parts or all of a spill response to be handled by the federal government. Specifically, the plan provides a response system—an oil pollution fund, equipment, regional response teams, on-scene coordinators—to ensure "quick and efficient response to oil and hazardous chemical spills and releases."[22] This national response system is designed to be a final line of defense against a large spill. It is the government's guarantee that, in return for its share of oil royalties and tax income, it will be prepared to protect the environment from an oil spill of any size and at any time.

As long as the spiller is effective in cleaning up its spill, the national response system remains in a monitoring, advisory role. However, the moment a spiller shows signs of not being able to handle the situation, the on-scene coordinator is authorized to federalize the spill—at which point the national response system takes over, cleans up the oil or other hazardous waste, and sends the bill to the spiller. During fiscal year 1988, federal on-scene coordinators federalized more than fifty oil spills. However, there had never been a spill of this magnitude, and the Bush administration was wary of taking over responsibility for it. Apparently, one reason for this reluctance was the cost involved. While the federal treasury had received more than $25 billion from North Slope oil production, the government had allowed oil spill contingency funds to dwindle to less than $5 million— less than the amount spent on the first day of the spill.

"I was pushing to keep the federal government from taking over the spill," Coast Guard Commander Steve McCall acknowledged. "We don't have the money—the pollution fund has dwindled down to nothing. Just the mechanics of setting up a system to contract men and equipment could take two weeks."

While Alyeska was criticized for arriving at the spill nine hours late and Exxon for taking three days to get up to speed, the federal government would have needed at least two weeks to begin mobilizing, and even then it could not have mounted a comparable spill response. Vice Admiral Clyde E. Robbins, who would relieve Commander McCall as the Coast Guard's on-scene coordinator in Valdez, said that "Exxon has been able to spend more money than I could, hire people I couldn't have hired. They brought in equipment I couldn't have brought in. I have never supported federalizing. If it were federalized, I couldn't handle it."

The wreck of the *Exxon Valdez* revealed that the Great Promise represented nothing but the wishful thinking of those who favored oil development. Tragically, the oil industry, the state, and the federal government were all failing to live up to the commitments they had made when the pipeline was built.

Once the storm sent oil from the *Exxon Valdez* racing away from the wreck and throughout Prince William Sound, Exxon's staggering cleanup problems became even more overwhelming while state and federal agencies faced their own challenges. Each of these agencies had its own distinct responsibilities. DEC would monitor Exxon, assess the damage, and make decisions regarding permits. The federal government, via the Coast Guard, would continue to provide an on-scene coordinator, approve Exxon's cleanup plans, and play a key role in setting the standards Exxon would have to meet in cleaning the shorelines. Another federal agency, the National Oceanographic and Atmospheric Administration (NOAA), would provide scientific advice. The National Park Service would attempt to protect the parks caught in the path of the oil. And the U.S. Fish and Wildlife Service, as trustee of the nation's wildlife, would be responsible for protecting birds and animals.

It remained to be seen how well these agencies and the national response system itself would function in a real crisis. Oil from the *Exxon Valdez* was endangering fisheries. Thousands of marine birds were being killed by oil. Hundreds of oil-soaked sea otters were dying a slow death of exposure. Bald eagles were becoming disoriented; many lost their ability to fly and crippled themselves by banging into rocks or trees. Vast stretches of Alaska's coastline were becoming covered with oil. Through the early days of this disaster, state and federal agencies were scrambling to determine what they should do and what authority and resources they had to fight the oil. Like Exxon, each would be tested and each would face its moment of truth.

Chapter 8

The Mosquito Fleet

The people of Cordova reacted as if there had been a death in the family. "It was like a funeral," said Marilyn Leland, director of the fishermen's union. "After the service everyone brings food to the family's home. After the spill everyone came to the union hall. They brought doughnuts, cakes, meat, and cheese. Everyone wanted to do something. They had to come in."

The union hall became so crowded the staff had to go across the street to the Club Bar for a quiet place to meet. Soon after reports of dead otters and birds began appearing on television, letters started arriving from children all over the country. "It seems like this will never end," Marilyn said. "Seeing the dead animals day after day really got to me. I found myself standing in the middle of Main Street crying."

Tension had been mounting for days when Exxon made its first appearance in Cordova. A town meeting was called. The high school gym was packed.[1]

"Do you think the oil is worth the risk?" someone asked Exxon spokesman Don Cornett. "In light of this event, would you reconsider the Canadian pipeline route?" The Cordova fishermen's 1971 lawsuit had unsuccessfully sought to impose that route on the oil companies.

"This [pipeline] has been a phenomenal success," Cornett responded. "It's hell to say that today, but this has been one of the greatest successes and one of the largest projects we've ever been involved with. But I would reconsider it . . . yeah, I would reconsider it."

"Has Exxon considered shutting down the pipeline?" a fisherman asked.

"I don't think that's an option," Cornett said. "Think about it. It's the backbone."

"Shut the sucker down!" someone yelled.

"It's the backbone," Cornett tried to continue, as people jeered. "It's just not an option. The idea of shutting down that port is just not worth discussing. It is not going to happen."

One fisherman reminded those gathered of a much smaller oil spill that had occurred near Anchorage two years before. After that spill, lawyers had tied up the local fishermen's claims. "The shipping company is still fighting the fishermen's class action suit in court, trying to nickel and dime them," he said. "Is Exxon Shipping Company prepared to reimburse commercial fishermen for damage to the fisheries in Prince William Sound?"

"You'll need to have records of what you have earned in the fishing business," Cornett replied, "and demonstrate that you did not earn that this year to some reasonable degree. And . . ."

"Don't give us that 'reasonable' crap," a fisherman interrupted. "To us, fishing's . . ."

"Just a second. Let me get the thought out," Cornett shot back. "Exxon and you won't have a problem. I don't care if you believe that or not. That's the truth. You have had some good luck and you don't realize it. You have Exxon. And we do business straight. But standing and yelling at each other isn't going to get us there."

"How far has the oil gotten down the bay?" asked an older fisherman. "We make our living fishing. We are very, very concerned. We're not drifters; we have property in those sheltered bays. My wife and I are very, very upset."

"I understand that, sir," Cornett interrupted. "If you'll see me after."

"We want to know," the fisherman continued, "what's going to happen to our livelihoods?"

"On the very first day, I had a fisherman call me and say, 'I want you to go out there and protect our fisheries,'" Cornett replied. "All of the boom that was in stock as required by the contingency plan was deployed."

"That is entirely untrue," a man yelled. "*Entirely untrue!*"

"Just a second, folks," Riki Ott broke in. "Let me, if you don't mind. These are my people and I'd like to tell them what happened on the first day. The boom material was offloaded from the barge because the barge was under repair. Okay?"

"That's correct," Cornett said.

"We asked why this boom was not run out on little boats," Ott continued. "And we were told that it was because your little boats could not operate beyond Valdez Arm. Whereupon we said, 'Why isn't that boom material being loaded into our fishing boats and being taken out?'"

"I think that's a real good question," Cornett said.

"Yeah! Right!" responded Ott.

Later, Cornett confided, "The problem those first three days was that we had a bunch of people who'd never seen an oil spill. They were afraid to make a mistake, afraid to act. They were paralyzed and did nothing for three days."

On the first Friday of the spill, Jack Lamb and thirty other fishermen had stood ready with their boats. "We kept trying to contact Alyeska and Exxon in Valdez to offer our help. But call after call went unanswered," Lamb recalled. "In the beginning, I felt no anger. But the anger began to build when our offers to help were totally ignored."

On Saturday, Lamb had chartered a plane to fly over the spill. "It's very hard to imagine the nightmare I saw on the flight to Valdez. More than thirty-four hours after the tanker went aground, there was only a small line of oil spill boom visible, hanging in a straight line downstream from the crippled tanker. The sound was calm, the weather good, but there was no attempt whatsoever to surround the oil."

Lamb had been in Valdez on Sunday when dispersants were being debated. Being a fisherman, he had wanted the oil extracted from the water. "But it's important to keep in mind that we are fishermen, not oil spill experts," Lamb had pointed out. "We are trying to learn a lot in a very short time."

When the wind rose on Monday, March 27, Lamb heard reports of oil rushing through the sound. That night, he attended the strategy session of the three-party spill response steering committee formed out of desperation by Exxon, the Coast Guard, and the state. The parties might soon be suing each other, but for the moment Coast Guard commander Steve McCall, Exxon's Frank Iarossi, and Alaska Department of Environmental Conservation commissioner Dennis Kelso had rolled up their sleeves to work together.

With the Coast Guard held back by its observing/monitoring role and Exxon preoccupied with lightering, extricating the tanker, and recovering oil from the sound, Lamb found DEC commissioner Kelso to be clearly agitated at the lack of palpable results. To provoke action, Kelso asked Lamb to represent the fishermen on the operations committee, the group composed of key people from the state, the Coast Guard, and Exxon. Lamb had no official authority but was unhampered by bureaucratic restraints.

At the first operations meeting Lamb attended, the committee heard the Monday night report on the action out on the sound. The wind was dying down, but the slick now covered more than 300 square miles. Oil was drifting toward Eleanor and Naked islands. No one, including scientists from the National Oceanographic and Atmospheric Association (NOAA), could predict where the oil would spread next. Scattered slicks were drifting aimlessly. Sheen and mousse were swirling into coves, estuaries, and tidal pools and onto rocky shorelines. The lack of containment boom and skimmers was forcing Exxon to begin making difficult decisions: some areas would have to be sacrificed in order to save others.

Lamb found himself thinking about the beautiful Bay of Islands—its deep, clear waters, cliffs, and tidal pools. "It's my favorite spot in the sound, and here I am hoping the oil gets trapped in there, because the hatcheries at Sawmill Bay and Eshamy Lagoon have to be protected at all costs. We gotta save the hatcheries."

The fishermen had built fish hatcheries in the early 1970s, when pink salmon runs, the mainstay of the Prince William Sound fishery, were so small the seasons had to be closed. "It was real tough . . . no money. But fate was not going to ruin us," said Cordova fisherman Ross Mullins. "Armin Koernig came along. Without him, we wouldn't have any hatcheries."

"We either had to give it up or do something," recalled Koernig, in a gravelly voice. "So we did something for our future."

Armin Koernig had immigrated to Cordova from Germany in 1963. He'd been educated in law and economics, but when he found these disciplines different in the United States, he started over. "I like to work with my hands, so I went to work in a steel mill," Koernig said. "To learn the American character, I tended bar for a while. Then I came up to Alaska and went fishing. I looked around and liked the people. I believed the stories that you could fish, make all this money, be independent, be surrounded by all this beauty."

When the wild salmon runs failed, Koernig recalled hatcheries he had seen in Europe and asked, "Why not build one here?" There were streams to supply the fresh water and indigenous salmon to use as stock. Natural food would come from Prince William Sound's highly productive ecosystem, which draws on the phytoplankton and zooplankton plentiful in the Gulf of Alaska. All Koernig and his fellow fishermen lacked was money.

"It was oil revenues that made the hatcheries possible," Koernig recalled. Using their own resources for seed money, the fishermen appealed to Alaska's legislature, which had oil royalties to invest. The fishermen received $18 million in loans to build the Sawmill Bay and Esther Island hatcheries. By 1989, the Koernig Hatchery, once an abandoned cannery on Sawmill Bay, was producing more than $20 million worth of salmon each year. The Esther had become the world's largest salmon hatchery, releasing 200 million pinks, 100 million chum, 4 million kings, and 2 million silvers.

"We didn't base our system strictly on dollar value," Koernig explained. "We're not just producing income. We're producing food, supporting a lifestyle. And we're proud of it. A check from Exxon won't work. It would hurt our hearts. We produce about one pound of seafood for every American. We are not interested in having Exxon just pay us off on a straight dollar-and-cent loss. And we know these same oil companies have safer operations elsewhere in the world. Here in Alaska they have tried to buy us with bullshit, expensive ad campaigns. Neither the state nor federal government had enough poop to stand up to them."

At the time of the spill, the Koernig Hatchery at Sawmill Bay had been about to release 117 million pink salmon fry, which workers had been nurturing since harvesting 160 million eggs the previous summer. When the silvery, inch-long fry had emerged in early March, they were flushed through large transparent hoses into 40-by-40-foot net pens floating in Sawmill Bay. Workers walking on wooden planks between the pens had been feeding the fry a commercial fish food rich in protein, vitamins, and minerals. The fry had been due for release in early April, just as the plankton upon which they feed began to bloom in Prince William Sound.

But Koernig and the hatchery managers knew they couldn't release the fry into the sound this spring. Even if many of the fry skirted around the main front of the slick, oil was likely to pool up in the intertidal zone, where the fingerlings feed over the summer. Some thought that if the oil didn't kill the young salmon outright, it would still knock out their food sources. However, the most immediate threat was to the rearing pens. At this critical time, the fishermen feared, just a few gallons of oil could wipe out an entire generation of pink salmon.

Now the storm was pushing the leading edge of oil toward the hatcheries. At the operations meeting in Valdez, Jack Lamb told Frank Iarossi what Exxon had to do: boom the facilities at Eshamy Lagon, Main Bay, Esther Island, and Sawmill Bay. "Those hatcheries have got to be saved. The fisheries are the most important thing. And we flat are not going to give up."

Frank Iarossi said he'd get the fishermen some boom and asked, "How soon can you have boats available?"

"Immediately," Lamb said, as he started to dial the union hall in Cordova.

"We'll take 'em all in one whack," Iarossi said, committing Exxon financially. Later, at a press conference, he summed up his position on the money. "At this point, I don't have any assessment of the costs. That's somebody's worry, but it's not mine. There is no reason for me to even be concerned about that right now. There's no monetary limit on what I can do to help. It's going to be a helluva bill, but right now I'm not stopping to count."[2]

At 10:00 P.M. that Monday night, Jack Lamb called for five boats to be deployed to each of the four threatened hatcheries. Ten minutes later, four boats were under way. By 2:00 A.M. Tuesday morning, another fourteen fishing boats streamed out of the Cordova harbor. The "Mosquito Fleet," a makeshift armada of seiners, bow-pickers, long-liners, and skiffs, was on its way.

"These guys don't yet have contracts to be paid," Lamb told Kelso and Iarossi. "They don't even have a firm idea of exactly what they are going to do. But they are going to do whatever has to be done, because Prince William Sound is the most special place in the world to us."

Worried about the fate of the hatcheries, Commissioner Kelso lingered after the meeting to speak with his staff. Despite Iarossi's willingness to spend money, Kelso wasn't convinced that Exxon appreciated the full magnitude of the problem. He was concerned that this initial reaction would fall short of what was necessary. "It doesn't look like Exxon's thinking big enough," said Kelso. "What do you guys think?"[3]

"It's frustrating," said one of Kelso's deputies. "I've been listening to these Exxon people from Houston, and they don't have the foggiest idea of how to deal with this spill. They just can't get the oil out of the water. We could respond faster than Exxon."

"Yeah," said another. "Where should we start?"

"We could get a state ferry," Kelso said, realizing that the Mosquito Fleet would need a large supply boat to serve as an operations center. Knowing that he was pushing the limits of his authority, he said, "I think we should change our responsibility from monitoring to actually going out and starting our own recovery operation."

That key decision made, Kelso and his staff targeted a major objective: within forty-eight hours they'd have boats, men, and equipment on the sound recovering oil. They would bring in the state ferry *Bartlett* from Cordova until the much larger *Aurora* could arrive from southeast Alaska. Before returning to their hotel rooms, Kelso and his staff had laid plans to hire workers, purchase boom and skiffs, contract oil spill experts—do whatever had to be done.

Meanwhile, Jack Lamb had been sitting alone, thinking. The state was bringing in a ferry to supply the fishing boats that were already on their way to the hatcheries. Iarossi had promised to send boom out by helicopter, and he had to send over skimmers to scoop up oil, too, and barges to store it in. But there really was no efficient way, Lamb realized, to transfer oil from the small skimming boats to the barges.

Lamb thought about his own boat, designed to transport fish from fishing vessels to processors. Perhaps he could adapt the suction pump on his tender to transfer oil instead of fish. He sketched possible modifications and calculated the capacity of his machinery to handle the thick oil. Still thinking out the problem at 4:00 A.M., he called a friend, a contractor familiar with heavy equipment. "Larry, we've got this problem. We need something big to suck up oil."

Larry told Lamb they had "something like that, trucks kinda like big vacs on wheels, called supersuckers." There were six of them on the North Slope. Lamb asked, "What'll it take to get them here?"

Larry explained that the supersuckers were all under contract to North Slope oil companies. "I don't know if we can get them off the slope. But I'll see if I can get you one."

Larry phoned Prudhoe Bay. A truck driver got out of bed to answer the phone: "You want to do what? You must be crazy." But at 6:00 A.M., the driver snuck one of the supersuckers out of the security yard.

Lamb called a friend in Homer. "Get us a boat to put this baby on."

By 8:00 A.M., the supersucker was a hundred miles down the road, and a barge was on its way to Seward to meet it.

Tuesday morning, after two hours of fitful sleep, Lamb boarded a helicopter. He was accompanied by Rick Steiner, a marine biologist and half owner of a Cordova fishing boat. The two flew over the spill and saw the boats of the Mosquito Fleet speeding toward the hatcheries. And they saw the oil.

"I was shocked at what I saw," Lamb said. "The massive oil slick extended down as far as Herring Bay on Knight Island. The water between Eleanor and Lone islands was pitch black and looked thick enough to walk on."

Steiner had flown over the spill on the first day. "I saw a small group of stellar sea lions then—about five of them—poke their heads up in the oil. They looked bewildered," he said. "They're pretty rugged guys, but I couldn't believe they had survived. There was an enormous pool of oil, but sitting there on those calm waters it almost seemed benign. It was terrible, but you had the feeling it was controllable."

Now, four days later, circling with Jack Lamb in a helicopter 40 miles from Bligh Reef, Steiner saw oil piled up on the beaches of Smith Island. They flew to the small island called Applegate Rock and landed. Oil oozed through the beach grass and lichen growing above the high-tide line. Among the slippery, oil-coated rocks lay dead and dying scoters, auklets, cormorants, and oystercatchers. Sea gulls and an eagle were picking them apart. Steiner saw a cormorant wedged in a crack between two rocks. "I touched it. All it could do was blink."

They spotted twenty harbor seals huddled together 50 feet from shore, heads sticking out of the oil. "They wanted to come ashore," Steiner said. "They kept looking at us with their big brown eyes, staring at us. There was a connection . . . as if they were asking, 'What's happening? Why?' I felt they didn't blame us for it. They had no sense of what had caused the sea to turn black, why their noses and eyes were burning. They were ingesting oil and were going to die slowly."

Steiner and Lamb picked their way toward blobs of oil that were actually sea otters that had managed to crawl ashore before dying. A two-year-old otter was frantically licking oil from its fur. Its eyes were bright red from trying to see in the oily water. Steiner caught it easily and both his and Lamb's first reaction was to bring the young otter back to Valdez to try to save it. "Jack and I looked at the otter," said Steiner. "We looked at each other. We realized he'd be dead very soon. We let him die where he'd lived.

"Jack and I were hit hard," Steiner said. "This emotional trauma was something neither of us had ever gone through in our lives. It was like we'd gone way beyond the bounds of living with nature—way out of control."

After releasing the otter, Steiner and Lamb plodded silently back toward the helicopter. Out of sight of each other, crouched down and separated by a large rock, each man began to cry.

Tom Copeland was another fisherman deeply affected by what was happening to Prince William Sound. Broad shouldered, full bearded, and fiery tempered, Copeland scorned de-

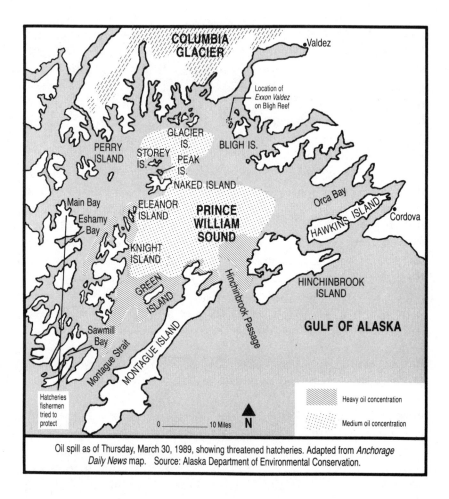

Oil spill as of Thursday, March 30, 1989, showing threatened hatcheries. Adapted from *Anchorage Daily News* map. Source: Alaska Department of Environmental Conservation.

pendence upon others. "After a few days, I realized that no one was going to clean up that oil. Ain't going to be anyone out there. I gotta go."

While other fishermen sped toward the hatcheries in the Mosquito Fleet, Copeland spent $5,000 of his own money on a pump, gas, and 5-gallon buckets. Then he went looking for oil. When he and his crew reached the slick near Knight Island, they just started dipping buckets and pulling out oil, 5 gallons at a time, until their arms felt ready to fall off. The first day of work they scooped up 1,500 gallons of oil, and on their best day 2,500 gallons. Exxon's best skimmer collected just 1,200 gallons a day.

"We're not victims of Exxon," Copeland said scornfully, "we're reluctant participants. Basically, Alaskans are addicted to that oil money. We've got that needle in our arms. We're all a bunch of junkies. We don't deserve another dollar from that pipeline."

Meanwhile, the leading edge of the oil was approaching Sawmill Bay and the hatchery there. "All you could see was black," said Eric Prestegard, manager of the Koernig Hatchery. "I was truly scared. I came back really depressed. I just cried. I knew the boats were coming, but I didn't think they'd make it in time."[4]

But they did—the Mosquito Fleet reached the Koernig Hatchery a full day before the oil. The fishermen's first task was to figure out how to use the boom Exxon had flown out. "It was a joke," said Gerald "Butch" Johnson of the flimsy, fair-weather, harbor boom. "A two-inch chop or a boat driving past could push oil right over it. We were constantly trying to keep this stuff together. It ripped in half all the time. It was junk when we got it."

Butch Johnson—described by an acquaintance as "a regular beer-guzzling guy, a bit of a loud mouth, but a straight-up, hardworking fisherman"—had been one of the first to respond to Jack Lamb's call. Johnson reckoned that during the week after the spill, when he was guarding the hatchery twenty-four hours a day, he slept a total of five hours. His was the only boat outfitted with lights for night work and a winch lock that could pull boom together when it broke. "The boom they sent us was light neoprene-type stuff that was supposed to be stiffened with chains," Johnson said. "But the chains were missing. It was the most incredibly disastrous mess I've ever seen."

Boats with boom stretched between them tried to halt the oil flowing toward the hatchery. Exxon sent out anchors to hold the boom in place, but they were too light and were easily dragged by the current. An Exxon contractor suggested attaching long lines to the boom and tying it to the shoreline. "That was a great idea," Johnson said. "Wonderful. Except the lines broke every hour."

Some fishermen tried to seine up oil using the limp boom the way they would normally draw their nets around a school of salmon. But no matter how the lightweight boom was used— towed like a net, stretched between boats, or anchored to the shore—oil slopped over it. "We tried every way to stop the oil," Johnson said, "but it was unstoppable."

Rick Steiner returned to Valdez to urge Exxon to send better equipment to the Mosquito Fleet. "The disaster was unfolding minute by minute," said Steiner. "None of us had gone through anything like this before, so we were winging it, figuring out what to do as we went along. The fishermen needed stronger boom, more skimmers, and better logistical support. We needed all the help we could get from the state and Exxon.

"Exxon's people were trying, but the company was still our biggest hassle those first few days. We'd say we needed something and they'd say, 'Yes, we've ordered it. Yes, it's on the way.' Then it took days. At first we believed them. Then we realized they were just trying to get us off their backs. There were so many people in the chain of command that if one link goofed, nothing got done. Some of the Exxon people were trying their damnedest, but there simply wasn't enough equipment available."

Steiner kept pressuring Craig Rassinier, Exxon's oil spill response manager, to send skimmers to the Mosquito Fleet. Rassinier, knowing that skimmers were needed in several places at once, took a deep breath, and said, "Okay, we'll send them over."

Steiner pressed for better boom and more of it. "Send us some real containment boom. We need it immediately."

"There just isn't any," Rassinier said.

"Well, find some. Come on, we have to have it," Steiner insisted. "We can't lose that hatchery."

Steiner noticed tears welling up in Rassinier's eyes. "He

wanted to give us what we needed, but he just couldn't do it. He had to leave the room. Later, they shipped him back to Texas. I think he was under too much stress."

Meanwhile, on Saturday morning, April 1, the state ferry *Bartlett* arrived at Sawmill Bay. The supersucker Jack Lamb had called in from the North Slope arrived that afternoon. The makeshift armada that converged at Sawmill Bay was a cooperative effort—some boats were under contract to DEC and others to Exxon, and there was a large skimming boat there from the navy. "The state hired a garbage scow to handle oily debris," said DEC's Jim Hayden. "We hired a barge for a helicopter pad and some smaller fuel-supply boats. We had helicopters and fixed-wing planes."

When Exxon finally located some heavy-duty boom, it was flown out to the Mosquito Fleet at the Koernig Hatchery. Even it was stressed to its limits. Designed to withstand a 1-knot current, it had to be anchored against a 3-knot current. It didn't break as easily as the lightweight boom, but oil still slopped over the edges. Any oil that got through this boom was met by a second and then a third ring of containment boom protecting the cove and its mesh pens full of fingerling salmon. Beyond the barriers of anchored boom, fishing boats towed lengths of boom, using it to encircle patches of oil. They pulled their collected oil to the large navy skimmer, which would suck it up. The fishermen also laid out long strings of absorbent pads to soak up any loose oil.

"Everybody's nerves were raw from getting only two or three hours of sleep a night," said Jim Hayden, who coordinated field operations for DEC. "Tempers were strained, and some of those young fishermen were pretty temperamental anyway. We had some shoving matches. I had to make the rounds several times to settle disputes.

"Most of the fighting was over who was in charge," Hayden explained. "The hatchery people had their oil spill crews and Exxon had theirs. Then, all of a sudden, DEC comes storming in with a ferry boat, a barge, a scow, and a bunch of fishing vessels, and people are wondering if we are going to be a hindrance or a help. So there was some jostling for control. How far out into Sawmill Bay does the hatchery manage? What part does

DEC supervise? What operations does Exxon supervise? What do I manage? What do you manage? Let's not cross paths. But we worked it out. We had to."

"We were all running around like a bunch of nuts," Butch Johnson said. "But even if it looked like a circus, it was working.

"When the so-called experts came through, they said every spill is like this," Johnson continued. "All this, which we thought was pure pandemonium, was just normal oil spill cleanup. The theory among oil companies is that the way to clean up an oil spill is just to throw money at it until it goes away or people forget about it."

Exxon offered to buy more boom and skimming apparatus, but the necessary equipment wasn't available anywhere. With a shortage of skimmers, oil backed up against the boom and some slipped under or washed over the outer barriers. The fishermen's mariner's instincts solved the problem. They cut the current with the boom. Much as a pilot will angle into waves instead of hitting them straight on, they redeployed their boom at an angle to the prevailing waves and current.

"Instead of trying to stop the oil, what we ended up doing was deflecting it," Butch Johnson explained. "We used the boom to keep the oil from entering the hatchery. That was our main goal. In effect, our job was to send the oil on down to Seward. The theory was that it would all break up and never be heard from again. But anybody who lived around here and knew the currents knew that wasn't the way it would happen. Exxon was hoping it would get into the ocean and disappear out of mind, but it didn't."

By mid-April, the main body of the slick had been deflected from the hatcheries. However, patches of oil continued to appear, and the fishermen's hatchery association continued to protect the fingerling salmon with barriers of boom.

"If they were going to continue the defense of Sawmill Bay, they needed money," said Frank Iarossi, recalling the Sunday the association's president came to see him. "We had set up a $10 million fund in an Alaskan bank the previous Friday, but we had no checks. So I pulled out one of my name cards and wrote $1 million on the back. I walked in to meet the hatchery president, shook his hand, and said, 'This is my name card. It's as good as my word.' I turned it over and showed him where I'd written the $1 million and signed my name. I told him to come back and collect it on Monday morning when the bank was open."

"I really feel Frank Iarossi cares," said Jack Lamb, reflecting on the defense of the hatcheries. "He handled everything that had to be dealt with moment by moment, without ever becoming arrogant. Iarossi best summarized those early days of the spill when he said, 'Exxon did everything the fishermen and Jack Lamb asked them to do.' But the problem is that's all Exxon did."

"Jack's right. We didn't have the resources to do much else," Iarossi responded. "And it's because we deployed all our resources, all our experts, and all our energy on those five hatcheries. Once the state and the fishermen decided that Exxon's main objective had to be the five hatcheries, we went all out to save them. We had equipment coming in from all over the world, and as quickly as we could land it and get it to Valdez, it went out to those five hatcheries. Yeah, Jack Lamb's right—we couldn't do anything else at that time because we deployed everything we had at those five hatcheries. There was nothing left as far as boom or skimmers or experts or energy."

With the fishermen working twenty hours a day, the state providing logistical support, and Exxon paying the bills, the Armin Koernig Hatchery at Sawmill Bay and the four other hatcheries in the sound were saved. Exxon paid more than $100 per gallon for the approximately 100,000 hard-won gallons of oil recovered. Meanwhile, however, well over 9 million gallons had swept through the sound. "There was no power on earth that could recover that oil once it had broken loose," Iarossi said.

DEC's Jim Hayden commented on the bittersweet victory the saving of the hatcheries represented. "If we hadn't gone all out, there's no question that oil would have gotten the hatcheries. We made the right decision to try to protect just a few small areas. Saving those hatcheries gave us a feeling of exuberance, but we felt a lot of discouragement and hopelessness looking out and seeing tons of oil pass by. Everyone felt inadequate. We just wondered where it was going to hit next."

Chapter 9

The Lawyers and the Admiral

Saving the salmon hatcheries was a victory not only for the fishermen, but also for the Coast Guard, Exxon, and the state of Alaska in their cooperative efforts. However, that victory marked the end of their cooperation as an ad hoc emergency response committee. Mistrust had begun to hamper the three-party command as it wrestled with complex and controversial decisions. Although the state and Exxon had been trying to work together in some areas, they had been fighting each other elsewhere. Conflict and confusion were inevitable.

While Kelso and Iarossi were trying to help the fishermen save the hatcheries, the state and Exxon were already competing to secure the best lawyers, economists, and scientific witnesses for the legal battles that lay ahead. The state tried to hire attorneys who had represented the oil companies after the 1978 *Amoco Cadiz* spill, which had fouled the coast of France. As one state official said, "We went after those lawyers who did such a good job screwing the French people. This time we wanted them working for us."

Ultimately, the state's legal team comprised half a dozen lawyers from the attorney general's office, half a dozen from one of Alaska's largest firms, and a dozen special-project attorneys. Meanwhile, Exxon contracted two of the largest law firms in the nation as well as two of the best in Alaska. Alyeska also hired two big firms. Literally hundreds of attorneys began preparing to do battle, jockeying for position both with the opposition and within their own ranks. Meanwhile, Exxon tried to assure Alaskans that every reasonable claim would be paid. In Cordova, the company opened a claims office even before cleanup crews were on location.

"It's our very strong desire to settle all of the damage claims . . . without resorting to lawsuits," said Exxon president Bill Stevens. "But we have about 150 lawsuits filed against us by individuals. Fifty-eight of those lawsuits are class-action suits. I'd say twenty or thirty of them are overlapping, primarily fishing interests. We had a preliminary hearing in Anchorage a couple of weeks ago. I'm told sixty-five law firms were represented. So the newspaper article about Alaska covered by a slick of lawyers . . . is certainly true."[1]

Fishermen and fish processors cited losses from fishing seasons closed by the spill that were ruining their credit and putting them out of business. To diffuse the tension, Exxon began making partial claim payments, with the balance of the claims "to be determined later." This arrangement gave fishermen some money to pay immediate bills, and it gave Exxon some time to decide what it defined as a legitimate claim. If a fishing season was lost to a community such as Cordova or Kodiak, it was clear that the fishermen themselves deserved compensation. Exxon recognized a secondary impact among businesses directly related to fishing, such as canneries and marine supply firms. However, the company was reluctant at first to acknowledge that cafes, bakeries, and day care centers were also affected when the primary source of a town's income dried up. With the first hints of delay or dissent, lawyers appeared.

While some potential claimants certainly needed legal counsel, many in the stricken communities were taken aback at the sudden appearance of slickly dressed attorneys, briefcases in hand, stalking the streets and boat harbors in search of victims. "Frankly, I'm appalled at the way many of my colleagues in the legal profession are descending on this spill like vultures," said Anchorage attorney Paul Davis. "I think it is counterproductive for a fisherman, processor, or cafe owner to initiate litigation without trying negotiation first. Suing one of the world's largest corporations won't ever be a picnic, and you're guaranteed years of delay. Since delay costs money, I suggest litigating only as a last resort if Exxon doesn't negotiate in good faith. But I'm afraid a lot of attorneys see Exxon as the big fish to fry, and they are scrambling to see who can get a pan over the fire first."

"It looks like all the bad-lawyer jokes are true," said Dave Walsh, another Anchorage attorney. "My office is getting up to three calls a day from outside firms saying, 'We're specialists. If you have any oil spill victims, we'll cocounsel.'

"Some of these attorneys seem willing to represent almost anyone," Walsh continued. "For example, one potential client asked me to go after Exxon for $40,000 in lost fishing crew wages. It turned out he hadn't fished for seven years but, in order to file for damages, was claiming he had planned to fish this year. I told him he had no claim. He got angry and hung up. The other day, I heard he's being represented by an outside firm."

Melvin Belli, a flamboyant California personal injury attorney, was one of many heavyweight attorneys to enter the fray. Years before, he had participated in Alaska Native claims litigation, inspiring the infamous newspaper headline "Belli Presses Suit." This time around, the colorful Belli pressed the deep pockets. On behalf of fifteen Alaskan residents who depend on Prince William Sound's resources and all others similarly injured, Belli filed a $20 billion class-action suit against Exxon, Alyeska, the Trans-Alaska Pipeline Liability Fund, and the state of Alaska. Belli admitted he hadn't dealt with oil spill litigation before, but said, "You can't beat the king, and I'm the 'King of Torts.'"[2]

Flurries of lawsuits created layers of overlapping litigation. Individuals, such as fishermen, who had suffered direct losses, would stand first in line for compensation. Next came participants in class-action suits such as Melvin Belli's, which represented groups of people such as sport fishermen or tour boat operators. Then there was the umbrella suit pressed by the state of Alaska that sought to cover losses to all Alaskans—and a suit by the federal government that extended that umbrella to cover the interests of all Americans. Many suits sought damages for the same loss. For example, the loss of an area's subsistence hunting and fishing resources might be claimed by individuals, a village, a Native corporation, and the state of Alaska. This set up the possibility that if a judgment was made against Exxon, there might be further rounds of litigation to decide how to divide the spoils.

Virtually all losses that could be quantified were equated to dollars as potential damages. Losses to fisheries and tourism could be based on income generated in previous years and projected for the year of the spill. Secondary losses to businesspeople who depend on the influx of fishing money in the community required detailed documentation. Establishing values for lost wildlife raised debate over the monetary value of a cormorant and what to pay for a puffin. If a sea otter is worth $20, is a seal worth more because it is bigger, or less because seals are more common? What's a sea lion worth? A whale? And how can a dollar value be placed on the loss of wilderness along hundreds of miles of coastal Alaska—the loss of solitude in a vital landscape, marked not by man but the eternal procession of storms and seasons?

"Gathering facts and figures for litigation, . . . the damage assessment process, is massive and very, very unwieldy," said Sheila Nickerson of the Alaska Department of Fish and Game. "Calculating damage claims to be made against Exxon is extremely difficult and complex." In trying to put a price on the mortality of wildlife, state damage assessors struggled with more intangible and reverberating effects, such as genetic disorders and habitat loss. "How do you go back in and replant barnacles, mussels, and tubeworms?" Nickerson said. "We're really up against something unprecedented, and we can't guess what the damage will be based on data from other spills, because there have been no comparable spills."

To help assess the wide-ranging environmental impacts of the oil spill, the Alaska Department of Fish and Game established a new Oil Spill Impact, Assessment, and Restoration Division. Its director, Greg Erickson, a longtime Alaskan and a petroleum economist by training, said, "Exxon seems to be saying, 'Sure, this is a regrettable disaster, but it's only temporary—nature is resilient and self-cleaning.' We expect the damage could be far more long-lasting than Exxon may be willing to accept."

Damage assessment research, sponsored jointly by the state

and federal governments and funded in part by Exxon, ran into problems from the outset. Complicating the assessment process were moves by lawyers to hold environmental data, including wildlife specimens, from the spill as evidence and therefore unavailable to researchers. Another major impasse developed when the state attempted to establish a multiyear research program. The Department of Interior, reportedly under intense lobbying from Exxon, insisted on only a one-year assessment process. Said Erickson, "It is absolutely ridiculous to expect science to tell us in one year what the long-term effects of the spill will be."

The litigation itself revolved around two questions: who had been at fault and whether there had been negligence regarding the spill and attempted cleanup.

"It looks as if Exxon is going to try to pin it all on [Third Mate] Cousins," said one attorney representing the state of Alaska. "We didn't even name Hazelwood and Cousins in our complaint as defendants, on the theory that they really aren't the responsible parties. They made mistakes, both of them, but obviously they can't pay us very much. There is always the chance for human error. However, the state sees the accident as something that was bound to happen because of the way the tankers were being operated. The crews were too small. The crewmen were often overworked and fatigued. Some of them weren't properly trained or licensed."

On the premise that Alyeska is a management shell, the state sued not only Exxon and Alyeska but all the owner companies that form the Alyeska consortium. This reasoning held that companies such as ARCO and British Petroleum were as responsible as Exxon for the failed response, and that British Petroleum, as majority owner, was perhaps most responsible for Alyeska's failure to contain the oil. Lines of defense were quickly drawn. Captain Joseph Hazelwood's attorneys argued that he was immune to prosecution because of an obscure law designed to protect ship captains who report accidents.

As Exxon mounted its defense, the dispersant controversy resurfaced as a key legal issue. State and federal prosecutors were well aware that undue restriction of the use of dispersants had already been used as a successful defense by another oil company. A 1988 U.S. federal court decision awarding damages to victims of the *Amoco Cadiz* oil spill penalized the French government for restricting the use of dispersants to water deeper than 50 meters. In handing down his decision, Judge Frank McGarr said, "Without scientific justification, the 50-meter-limit decision, which so seriously interfered with the success of the dispersant method, seems to have been solely the result of pressure from ecology and nature groups."[3]

During the first week of the spill, Frank Iarossi was asked what had kept him from deploying dispersants before the weather prevented their use. Iarossi replied, "There isn't any way I'm going to engage in fingerpointing or backbiting while I'm still struggling with the biggest disaster I could ever imagine. I know a lot of stones have been thrown, but I'm not gonna throw any. There'll be a time when we'll review the total record, and we have a very careful record of all of our requests, all of our actions, all of our meetings."[4]

Privately, however, Iarossi said there had been a lot of "doublespeak" about dispersants. "The first phrase that's been used to confuse everyone is the term *preapproval*. It's been used by the state to imply that Exxon had authority [to use dispersants], and that's totally untrue. . . . On those first two days, the only authorization we had was one test at a time. See the results of that test, and you get approval for another test. That was very frustrating at the time. . . . There was a lot of shouting going on."

U.S. Secretary of Interior Manuel Lujan helped stir up the dispersant battle in public when he said, "Alaska has to share the blame" for inadequate cleanup efforts. A Lujan assistant said that several sources had given the secretary reliable information that the state had objected to the use of dispersants.

DEC commissioner Dennis Kelso disagreed, claiming that Exxon hadn't been ready to use dispersants. "They didn't have the aircraft loaded and they couldn't make a delivery until many hours after the full go-ahead. So this [reference to the delay for testing] is a litigation strategy, and it's a smokescreen that shouldn't be given any more weight.[5]

"The real issue is that Exxon and Alyeska were not prepared to respond to this oil spill," Kelso continued. "Exxon and Alyeska simply didn't have enough equipment, dispersant, and trained men on hand to handle the spill. They didn't have enough boom.

They didn't have enough skimmers and collection barges. They didn't move quickly enough during nearly three days of flat seas, light wind, and bright sunshine. They didn't think big enough. They didn't produce the results they had promised. They have never been ahead of this spill."

Exxon CEO Lawrence Rawl chose an interview in *Fortune* magazine to stake out his corporation's public defense. He said, "One of the things I feel strongly about—this catching hell for two days' delay—is that I don't think we've gotten a fair shake. The basic problem we ran into was that we had environmentalists advising the Alaska Department of Environmental Conservation that the dispersant would be toxic. Our tests on Saturday and Sunday worked to our satisfaction, and we didn't understand why we were wasting any time testing it. We finally got approval to start applying the dispersant in large quantities at 6:45 P.M. on Sunday. Then gale force winds sprang up."[6]

When asked who prevented Exxon from applying dispersants immediately, Rawl said, "It was the state and the Coast Guard that really wouldn't give us the go-ahead to load those planes, fly those sorties, and get on with it. When you get 240,000 barrels of oil on the water, you cannot get it all up. But we could have kept up to 50 percent of the oil from ending up on the beach somewhere."

Rawl's figure of 50 percent appeared so far-fetched that it further undermined Exxon's already battered credibility. Said Admiral Edward Nelson, "Rawl is way out of the ballpark. I don't know where he gets some of his information, but it's a bunch of bull."

Alaska Oil Spill Commissioner Walt Parker, acknowledging that with free rein to use dispersants Exxon might have dispersed 8 percent of the spill, said, "Exxon officials are simply lying when they claim it was the failure of the state to give them timely authority to use dispersants that was the major reason the spill got away. That's just a blatant lie."

Nevertheless, the state had been less than consistent in its position on dispersants. On March 28, four days after the spill, Governor Cowper had said, "It's been suggested by some that we go into kind of a promiscuous use of those chemical dispersants. The result of those dispersants is very toxic. It's very toxic to marine life. And you should use them only on a very selective basis."[7] However, Cowper now wrote Rawl that blaming the state for delays in Exxon's cleanup was "demonstrably false. . . . Your apparent basic assumption—that the state opposes the use of dispersants—is flawed."[8]

Governor Cowper had initially praised Exxon's response, but after litigious lines began being drawn, he questioned Exxon's ability to respond. "Exxon never had sufficient quantities of dispersant on hand to treat a spill of this size," said Cowper. "Less than 5,000 gallons were in Valdez the day of the spill and only 110,000 gallons were available six days later—one-fifth the amount necessary for a spill of this magnitude. . . . Only after Exxon had trouble hitting the target—and instead sprayed the tanker and Coast Guard personnel—did the state decline to approve the use of chemicals in the most sensitive areas. . . . I urge you to repudiate the inaccurate statements you and other Exxon officials have made regarding the state's actions on dispersant use."

Rawl responded that Cowper's letter "does not set the record straight. In fact, it perpetuates a good many wrong assertions. Repetition of incorrect and misleading statements is helpful to no one. You have repeated once again the incorrect assertion that dispersants increase the oil's toxic effects. There is not a knowledgeable person whom I know of who would support that statement. . . . Your information regarding the application rate and volume of dispersant on hand is also incorrect."[9]

Rawl concluded his communiqué to Governor Cowper with this remark: "It is regrettable that you have chosen to go public on this matter without first discussing these questions directly with us."

An Exxon report substantiating Rawl's assertion stated that "if unconditional authority had been granted to use dispersants beginning with the C-130 plane available early Saturday morning, March 25, the day after the spill, seven C-130 flights could have been made on Saturday and Sunday using 637 drums [of dispersant]. . . . Given the favorable thickness and timing conditions which existed, particularly on Saturday and Sunday, large volumes of oil could have been dispersed."[10]

When the state filed its lawsuit against Exxon and Alyeska,

Exxon countersued, charging that the state should pay much of the oil spill's damage and cleanup costs because it had interfered with the use of dispersants. "The state knew, or should have known, that its vigorous and active opposition to the use of dispersants would cause the Coast Guard to delay granting permission for the use of dispersants," the complaint said. "It was a foreseeable consequence of the state's preventing the timely use of dispersants that much more oil would wash onto beaches, shorelines, and islands and into intertidal and estuarine areas."[11]

"The facts are quite different from Exxon's fabrication," Commissioner Kelso insisted. "Exxon didn't have enough dispersant in Alaska to treat more than about 9 percent of the spill. And they didn't have the equipment on hand to spray the huge amount of dispersant that the Exxon chairman now claims they would have used.

"The most flagrant use of misinformation has been Exxon chairman Lawrence Rawl's repeated untrue statements about the company's supposed efforts to use chemical dispersants during the first four days," Kelso said. "The Exxon Corporation has deliberately attempted to portray the company's response as hampered by state government. These statements are part of a deliberate disinformation campaign. Exxon's apparent strategy is to try and hide from the public the industry's disheveled state of unreadiness.

"It was Alyeska's and Exxon's inertia and incompetence that let the spill get out of control, not government regulation," Kelso continued. "I don't mean to be critical of the many Alyeska and Exxon employees who are trying to do a good job and who have worked hard under difficult conditions. This is tough, sometimes dangerous work. How confusing it must be for Exxon's cleanup staff and midlevel managers when Exxon's chairman and other top executives repeatedly try to blame someone else for their problems with the cleanup. But that's exactly what's happening."[12]

From his office high above the streets of New York City, Lee Raymond, president of Exxon Corporation, argued that even if it hadn't been able to disperse the entire spill, Exxon should have been permitted to do whatever it could to reduce the spill's size. If he had had the chance to go back and do things over again,

Raymond said, "I would order our people on Saturday to spray dispersants. And if they'd say, 'We don't have permission,' I'd say, 'Fly the planes. They're either going to have to shoot us down or get a court injunction.'"[13]

Amidst the crossfire of accusations, it became apparent that both the state and Exxon were partially right, and that both parties had failed the public. The effective use of dispersants was thwarted by two failures: the decision-making process had faltered, and there had been a shortage of dispersants and their application equipment. There were clearly not enough dispersants to handle a spill this size. And it was clear that if Exxon had been given prompt approval, its dispersant stock would have lessened the impact of the oil on otters, birds, and shorelines. The question lay in how much the impact would have been reduced; the answer was probably somewhere between Kelso's estimated 9 percent and Rawl's 50 percent.

"It's a disgrace. And the reason it's a disgrace is because they had a contingency plan which, regardless of the inadequacies, they should have adhered to, and they didn't," said Dr. James Butler in the aftermath of the spill. Butler, a widely respected dispersant expert at Harvard University, assigned responsibility for the failed spill response to all four principal players: Alyeska, Exxon, the state, and the Coast Guard. "They really dropped the ball," he said. "Everybody dropped the ball. Dispersed oil is no more toxic than oil alone, but dispersed in open water in the water column it can be less toxic because its concentration is lower. As soon as the oil was in an area where dispersants were preauthorized, [Exxon] should have started getting planeloads of dispersant out there. This could have greatly diminished the oil's impact on the shorelines."

Butler concluded that, regardless of test results, if dispersants had been used during the early hours of the spill, the oil would have been diluted when the wind came up. Dispersants had never been used on such a large scale, and they certainly would not have prevented all the damage. However, prompt action might have kept some of the oil from hitting the shorelines. This raised the prospect of a painful irony. As with the *Amoco Cadiz* spill, well-intended caution on the part of the state, many fishermen, and some environmentalists with regard to dispersant use may have helped close a window of opportunity within which the toll on wildlife could have been reduced.

All the prevailing conditions—the decision-making paralysis, the infighting within the steering committee, the hordes of scrambling attorneys, the lawsuits and resulting confusion—emphasized the need for strong, clear leadership of the spill response. Birds and otters needed rescuing, shorelines needed cleaning, and the oil was moving out of the sound toward Kenai Fjords National Park. Any hope of mitigating the havoc caused by the spreading oil lay in the emergence of a leader. Someone had to put himself on the line, give orders, direct the players. "What we need," said Frank Iarossi, "is a dictator."

"I'm here to take names and kick butts," said sixty-one-year-old Admiral Paul Yost, commander of the U.S. Coast Guard. He arrived in Valdez three weeks after the grounding and announced, "This spill is a war. And I intend to fight it like a war. When I look at Exxon's operation, it's certainly as intricate and complex as were the many ships, and men, and airplanes, and equipment, and logistics associated with a major battle in Vietnam. No doubt about it.

"The toughest part of this spill is to get everything started from a dead stop," said Admiral Yost, who had commanded a combat unit at the height of the Vietnam War. "There're 10 million gallons of oil in the water. All of Alaska, and frankly all of the country, and beyond that all of the world, is mad at Exxon, mad at the situation, mad at themselves. We have to try to move from ground zero with very little equipment up here. Very little capability. No communications."[14]

Yost proceeded deftly, with a combination of tenacity and diplomacy. When the admiral took over, Exxon and the Department of Environmental Conservation had been haggling for days over a cleanup plan. Yost correctly identified Exxon's central concern: that anything it offered to do at this point might be used against it later in the courtroom. So, ironically, although the state and federal governments saw their role as monitors, not actors, Exxon felt distinct constraints on its freedom to act, not only from the various permits it needed for dispersant use and burning, etc., but also from the legal ramifications down the line

of any decisions it might make now. Commenting on the underlying ambiguity regarding authority, Exxon Corporation president Lee Raymond said, "From the minute this event happened
Exxon did not have unilateral control of anything. Once that oil
was in the water, under the Clean Water Act and under the oil
spill response plan, we no longer had unilateral authority to do
anything. This has been one of the problems all along. There
have been these competing interests of who's got more authority: the state versus federal, are they equal or unequal, all that
kind of stuff. That's an interesting discussion to get into, but it
doesn't help much in getting oil off the water and cleaning up
shorelines. When you're in the middle of a crisis . . . you need a
real iron ass who says: 'Okay, I've heard all that, and here's what
we're going to do—and if you don't like it, stuff it.' Some junior-
level guy in the Coast Guard isn't going to do that. I think you
need somebody who's willing to take the heat and say, 'Hey, man,
I'm calling the shots.'"[15]

Enter Admiral Yost. To reassure Exxon, he set up a short review process by which the company could submit its proposed
cleanup plan to state and federal agencies to get their approval
on the record before proceeding. Less than twenty-four hours
after his arrival in Valdez, Yost held Exxon's first detailed
cleanup plan in his hands. With a showman's sense of timing and
a statesman's respect for the media, he waved the plan in front
of the television cameras. Exxon would have the oil cleaned up
by September 15—nearly six months after the spill.

Given the unpredictable weather, unproven techniques, and
logistical difficulties of supervising crews on remote and unin-
habited islands, however, Yost himself had reservations about
Exxon's cleanup plan and the September 15 completion date.
Since the plan did not address the oil-fouled beaches outside
Prince William Sound, Yost gave Exxon until May 1 to expand
the plan. He realized that by the time Exxon responded, even
more beaches would be oiled.

To progress with the cleanup, Yost faced a gyre of confusion
that turned on the politics of science. Chemists, pathologists, veterinarians, biologists, oceanographers, anthropologists, archaeologists—many of each had set up shop in Valdez. And each had
a different idea of what ought to be done. One biologist won-

126 • THE RESPONSE

dered aloud if anyone had tried tarring a rescued otter with weathered oil to see what would happen. One ornithologist complained that body parts of dead birds were being held hostage until it was decided whose name would appear first on a publication. Some scientists wanted certain sections of the sound to remain untouched, because treatment would foul their experiments. Some wanted to rush heavy equipment to beaches; others insisted on doing surveys to safeguard ancient village sites before making a move to clean beaches.

"There we were, all working on a common goal—to mitigate the spill's effect—but getting tunnel vision, having our own agenda," said Larry Kiester, a NOAA scientist. "Admiral Yost came in and cut right through the crap. He got everyone to wear the same baseball caps."

The days when a fisherman like Jack Lamb could sit down with Exxon's Frank Iarossi and devise a plan of attack were over. Observed Lamb, "Admiral Yost said, 'I'm in charge here.' Nobody had the authority to say that before he arrived."

Rosanne Smith, a young public radio reporter, accompanied Yost's task force to a beach-cleaning demonstration. "He went right to the heart of the problem," she said. "This man was not distracted by dog and pony shows. We were all taken out to Eleanor Island on a Sunday afternoon. Yost was asked if he thought Exxon had enough men and equipment out there. Instead of rattling off the numbers of men, planes, boats, booms, blah, blah, blah—he said, 'Look, all of this equipment is new. It's never been tested under conditions like these before. A lot of this stuff has been jerry-rigged for this operation. I'd like to be able to stand here and tell the American public that this is going to work, but I can't do that.'

"Everybody was asking Admiral Yost all these technical questions about this and that and the other thing. And he just struck me as an interesting guy," Smith recalled. "So I asked him how old he was. And he must have loved a simple little question like that, because he put his arm around my waist, walked me down the way, and, ignoring everyone else, he said, 'I'm sixty-one. How old are you?'

"It touched me," said Smith. "Here's this admiral up to his eyeballs in numbers and men and equipment, and President Bush, and God knows what else—and he was still able to take a moment just to laugh. I mean, just to get us to smile again in the middle of all that madness."

By week five of the spill, Yost had consolidated his command and organized his troops. He left Alaska to oversee the spill's political front in Washington, D.C., turning over the day-to-day supervision of the battle to Coast Guard Vice Admiral Clyde E. Robbins, who would face a daunting task. The spill now covered 6,000 square miles, an area the size of the state of Massachusetts. Oil was spreading in long, reddish-brown fingers far out into the Gulf of Alaska. Oil was heading toward Resurrection Bay and the picturesque town of Seward. Oil was nearing Gore Point and the rich coastal waters of Kachemak Bay. Oil was sighted near Kodiak Island and the outer islands of Kenai Fjords National Park, areas with large populations of seals, sea lions, otters, and seabirds.

The war Admiral Yost had come to fight was now being waged on separate, far-ranging fronts. Public relations battles were being fought in the press and at congressional hearings. Legal skirmishes were pitting fishermen against corporate lawyers and the state of Alaska against Exxon. Boats were rescuing stricken otters, waterfowl, and eagles and retrieving the dead. Shoreline cleanup operations were being organized—and reorganized and reorganized. New equipment was being shipped in, tried, and discarded or modified. Shoreline workers were being dispatched by the hundreds. And the oil was still flowing out of Prince William Sound, forever hitting new waters, beaches, and communities.

As he left Alaska for Washington, Admiral Yost gave his parting assessment: "There will be no miracles here."

Chapter 10

Marine Birds

There are whole populations of birds endangered out there, and I can't save them all," said Jay Holcomb. Alyeska had called Holcomb, of the International Bird Rescue Research Center, to Alaska in the early hours of March 24 to rescue oiled birds. The center was Alyeska's designated bird-cleaning organization. "On the other hand," continued Holcomb, "if we save one little puffin in Alaska, it will represent what people are concerned about, what the whole country is feeling. I try to be real honest about this. Coming to the Alaska oil spill is just my way of contributing. It's important to me that I try to do what I can."

Holcomb had become involved with distressed birds in 1971, when two oil tankers had collided under San Francisco's Golden Gate Bridge. Holcomb, then a twenty-year-old student, had seen pictures of oiled birds on a television newscast and had rushed down to the bay to help save them. "Thirteen thousand live birds were collected," Holcomb remembered. "They were stacked in cages and most of them died."

While struggling through the chaos of that San Francisco Bay spill, Holcomb had met Alice Berkner, who was then beginning to see a need for a worldwide organization to care for birds caught in oil spills. Her dream was eventually realized in the International Bird Rescue Research Center, based in Berkeley, California. Although funded largely by oil companies, the bird rescue center maintains a volunteer spirit and its own sense of purpose. Holcomb became involved. "When we go to a spill, we don't stand there and talk about how horrible the oil company is. We take care of the birds," Holcomb said. "Through the years, we've been on a lot of spills and have developed some pretty good expertise in treating birds."

The center would face the test of its life in Alaska, where the oil was spreading just as spring migrations were about to commence. In the few weeks following the spill, trumpeter and whistling swans and great flights of geese and ducks would be passing through the sound. More than thirty-five varieties of shorebirds—terns, plovers, and sandpipers—would funnel through before spreading out across Alaska. Puffins, cormorants, kittiwakes, auklets, oystercatchers, peregrine falcons, and others would remain in the sound in the path of the oil.

Realizing that the bird rescuers would face great difficulties in Alaska, Holcomb brought along Jessica Porter, a veterinarian with a lifelong passion for helping wild creatures. At the time of the spill, Porter was running the Wolf Hollow Wildlife Rehabilitation Centre, in Friday Harbor, Washington, where she cared for an ever-changing menagerie of injured or orphaned animals—raccoons, seal and sea lion pups, otters, fawns, and birds. On her departure for Alaska, Porter left the care of her Wolf Hollow brood to assistants, thinking she'd be back in a week or two.

"We flew over the spill our first morning in Valdez and were stunned by how much oil was out there," Porter said. "This spill was unlike any we had ever seen." Not only were Porter, Holcomb, and the Alaskans they hired going to have to treat lots of oiled birds, but as soon as they landed in Valdez, Holcomb and Porter faced the problems of authority and responsibility that were plaguing so many aspects of the spill response. On other spills, the U.S. Fish and Wildlife Service had always brought oiled birds to the cleaning centers. The bird rescue center people had always taken birds at the door, cleaned them, and decided when they were ready for release. Now, for the first time ever, Holcomb and Porter were told they would have to find the birds and bring them in.

"It was bizarre. This lady, Pam Bergman, with the Department of the Interior, was calling the shots, telling us we had to go look for the birds," Porter said. "This was crazy! We should concentrate on what we do well—cleaning, feeding, and medical treatment of birds. We can't be out there trying to find birds in places we've never seen. But Bergman kept saying, 'The Fish and Wildlife Service can't do anything. The party that spilled the oil is responsible. Exxon is responsible, period.'"

With the Fish and Wildlife Service assuming a strictly monitoring role, no one had clear authority over Exxon in the area of bird rescue. As Porter said, "We couldn't tell Exxon what to do. Exxon wouldn't listen to us—they'd get ticked off. The Fish and Wildlife Service should have been there telling Exxon to do this and do that. The bird rescue center is not a lead agency. We are not the trustees of America's wildlife. Interior put us in a really bad situation. Bergman dumped all the responsibility on us, but gave us none of the authority. There was nothing we could do but lose."

As the first oiled murres and loons washed ashore near Bligh Reef, the newly created rescue effort became stalled, caught between the priorities of these two women from two different worlds. Porter was used to working long hours caring for wild creatures. In animal pens and operating rooms, she fed baby seals and mended broken wings. Bergman spent her life in interagency meetings, coordinating environmental policy for the Fish and Wildlife Service and other Interior agencies in Alaska.

"Up here it's a completely different ballgame than the bird rescue people have ever dealt with before. I think they felt a little confused," Bergman said. "It's not the Fish and Wildlife Service's mission to mass an army to rescue birds. We have no personnel for rescuing birds. And it really rankles me—why are they called experts if they can't do that sort of thing? The point is, Porter's bird center is contracted to clean birds. Maybe they got a little spoiled, got used to people bringing in birds for them on other spills. Now they have to go out and get them."

Porter said that being forced to capture oiled birds was "totally against" the national contingency plan established under the federal Clean Water Act. "We ended up in the middle, writing contracts, bartering for days. It was wasting our time and raising our frustration level. We needed help from the Fish and Wildlife Service more than ever before."

"We *were* helpful," Bergman countered. "We gave them all the help in the world. We gave them the names of people to call. The bird center's fallback is to blame the Fish and Wildlife Service. They should have been more aware of how things work up here. They said they knew Alaska. But they didn't. They come here and say, 'Golly, why isn't Fish and Wildlife out there collecting birds?'"

The tension and confusion were fueled by the federal government's interagency regional response team's new wildlife guidelines, which had been designed to shift much of Fish and Wildlife's trustee responsibility for wildlife to the oil industry in the event of a spill. The guidelines state that "the Fish and Wildlife Service will assume lead responsibility for capturing oiled birds and transporting them to a cleaning and rehabilitation center(s). Organizations that clean and rehabilitate oiled birds generally will not be responsible for those tasks." This corresponded exactly to the type of assistance Jessica Porter had experienced on other oil spills and had expected in Alaska. However, the guidelines go on to stipulate that the Fish and Wildlife Service would assume this active role *only if* the spiller did not accept responsibility for the spill and respond adequately. This qualifying clause, adopted the previous December, had never been pointed out to anyone at the bird rescue center. Now, in the midst of the spill, Bergman explained that this obscure clause was why Fish and Wildlife wouldn't help rescue oiled birds. As long as Exxon carried out an adequate response, the Fish and Wildlife Service would only observe.

The pivotal question became What constitutes an adequate response? With no guidelines for determining the adequacy of a spiller's response, it fell to Pam Bergman and her supervisor, Paul Gates (who served on the regional response team), to decide when a response was inadequate and federal assistance was needed. Exxon itself didn't have the waterfowl expertise to do the rescue work that the Fish and Wildlife Service had always done. As Alyeska's, and now Exxon's, designated bird cleaners, Porter and Holcomb felt overwhelmed by the difficulty and danger of capturing oiled birds in 10,000 square miles of coastal terrain they had never seen. However, Bergman and Gates determined that Exxon was responding adequately and chose to monitor rather than mitigate Porter and Holcomb's struggles. Said Gates, "I don't think the Fish and Wildlife Service is on the hook in this thing."

Gates cited financial reasons, too, for not asking the Fish and Wildlife Service to take the lead in rescuing oiled birds. He knew the government hadn't set aside enough money for an emergency of this magnitude. During the Reagan administrations, the on-scene coordinator's emergency fund had been allowed to dwindle to less than $5 million. The federal government was not prepared to spend what was needed for wildlife rescue, even though it stood to be reimbursed by Exxon eventually.

However, a lack of funds was only part of the story. As one official, who asked not to be identified, explained, "Back in the early 1980s, the Fish and Wildlife Service decided to get out of the oil spill business. The service basically said, 'We don't want to be a part of that messy business. We are not interested in responding to spills. It's going to be done on a local basis or by contractors.'" This policy shift left the Fish and Wildlife Service unprepared for a large oil spill. Paul Gates acknowledged that "if federalized, the process would be basically the same. We would have hired the bird rescue center. The Fish and Wildlife Service still wouldn't have been out picking up birds."

Dr. Calvin Lensink, who had worked for the U.S. Fish and Wildlife Service for thirty-three years, expressed dismay at Fish and Wildlife's lack of involvement in what he called the biological aspects of the spill—the wildlife rescue efforts. Commenting on what he observed to be a gradual deterioration of the government's ability to protect wildlife, he said, "You'd think we would have been on top of the biological aspects. But we weren't. I was thoroughly disgusted, as were a lot of refuge people. If a problem isn't urgent, the Fish and Wildlife Service tends not to address it. So when a real crisis like this comes along, they aren't ready for it. Fish and Wildlife people were ready to go out to the sound, but they weren't being given the authority to go, so they ended up just sitting around. The advice from Washington was that 'anything you do on the spill, you eat. Basically, it comes out of your own pocket.' And I'll be goddamned if I know why they have this attitude."

Dr. Lensink was far and away the agency's most experienced

biologist on the spill. Among numerous commendations he had received was the Meritorious Service Award from the Department of Interior. However, Dr. Lensink had retired from the service the previous November and after the spill went to Valdez as a volunteer. "I couldn't possibly have sat in Anchorage and done nothing," Lensink said. "I told Fish and Wildlife I'd just as soon not be on salary so I could do what I thought had to be done the most. And I didn't take the nice safe jobs, either. I took some of the nasty jobs. Working with dead animals is a nasty job."

While the struggle went on between the bird rescue and Department of Interior people, oil hit Green, Naked, and Knight islands and currents were drawing oil into coves. With the spring migration imminent, Alaska senator Ted Stevens set biologists to the task of scaring birds away from the oil. The scientists wired propane cannons to automatic oscillators that fired intermittently. Two-man hazing teams armed with rockets and 12-gauge shotguns loaded with cracker shells patrolled the intertidal zone. They planted scarecrows near the high-tide line to stand guard over a tangle of oily kelp, stones, and shells, the mannikins' polyester shirts and Salvation Army jackets flapping in the breeze.

"[Trying to scare off the birds] was the biggest farce you ever saw," Dr. Lensink said. "There wasn't a single biologist who considered it a useful exercise. It was a crash program because the migration was about to start, but the migrants were spread over too big an area. All those scarecrows and cannons were a gut reaction. It was done for one reason and one reason only—because Senator Stevens said we had to damn well scare all these migrant birds away from the oil. It was unnecessary. But, frankly, when Stevens says jump, we're inclined to jump."

While Dr. Lensink set up a makeshift lab to study dead birds, Jessica Porter and Jay Holcomb tried to find a way to rescue those still living. "Interior was forcing us into areas we knew nothing about," Porter said. "All of a sudden, we had to find boats and planes—organize an armada, get equipment, train people to catch birds. We knew nothing about Prince William Sound. Fish and Wildlife knew all the bays and coves, all the estuaries, currents, rivers, rookeries, and marshes. But they wouldn't help us.

"Some Fish and Wildlife people wanted to help, but their

hands were tied by Interior," Porter continued. "We started calling this the 'oil spill from hell'—not because of the dying birds, the long hours of cleaning, the rugged geography, or even the amount of oil, but because of the attitudes of Fish and Wildlife and Exxon. Why weren't they helping? It seemed as if birds were not important to anybody. We felt isolated, on our own—adrift."

At this point, the frustration was so great the bird center considered calling off their rescue efforts altogether. International Bird Rescue founder Alice Berkner, who had been working to set up the Valdez rescue center in cramped quarters shared with another rescue team, said it was too dangerous to send people out. Jay Holcomb replied, "Alice, this spill is killing thousands of birds. We can't just sit back and let this happen. Somebody has to go out there and try to get them."

"But we've never set up a program like this," Alice answered.

"We have to make it up," Holcomb said. "I know how to catch birds. We'll have to find somebody who really knows the sound."

Meanwhile, Kelly Weaverling, a long-haired and bearded Cordova bookseller usually dressed in baggy pants, a camouflage jacket, and a baseball cap, was anxious to put his unusual skills and experience to work. Weaverling was probably the only person who had walked every oil-threatened beach of Prince William Sound. He knew where the winter birds were and where and when the migrants would arrive. When the spill hit, Weaverling had called friends in Valdez to say, "I'm here. I know Prince William Sound. And I want to help. Call me."

Weaverling's love for the mountains and the sea, which had drawn him to the sound, had been nurtured in childhood. "My mother's Cherokee, and she instilled in me her own great love of the outdoors," he said. "When I was a boy we lived in California—out of town a ways at the edge of some hills, surrounded by woods and close to the sea."

Weaverling came to Alaska in 1976. He spent his first summers guiding sea kayakers through Prince William Sound, and after he married, he and his wife, Susan, decided simply to live out there during the summer months. "What we really like to do is camp out in the sound, just be there and kayak from place to place," Weaverling said. "We'll be out there from the first of May until the end of August and always explore places we haven't seen before. I've kept notes and records of every beach I was on, every stretch of coastline I've paddled."

On Wednesday morning, March 29, five days after the grounding, somebody told Jay Holcomb about Kelly Weaverling, and Holcomb called the Cordova bookstore. "Weaverling, can you help us find and collect oiled birds?" he asked.

Weaverling, responding immediately, put out the call for bird-catching equipment. "People started bringing things in lickety-split," he said. "They gave us their plastic dog kennels for cages. If they didn't have plastic kennels, they brought in cardboard boxes. I said, 'I need dip nets,' and they brought me their dip nets. It all came together, just like that."

By nightfall, Weaverling and his companions were headed from Cordova to Valdez with three boats. They arrived at 6:30 the next morning and roused the bird rescue people.

"Weaverling was real defensive toward us at first," Jessica Porter recalled. "He viewed us with suspicion because we were under contract to Exxon. At that time, anyone working with Exxon was the bad guy. And he came from Cordova, where tempers were hot. But he could see that we wanted to save birds as much as he did.

"When he stood there looking at us," Porter mused, "I'm sure he was thinking, 'These people don't know a damn thing about catching birds in Prince William Sound.' And he was right. The Fish and Wildlife Service should have been dealing with him, but he became our main contact with the sound."

The bird rescue center hired Weaverling. One wonders what either the bird center or the Fish and Wildlife Service would have done if Weaverling, with his unique background, hadn't wandered out of the woodwork. Pam Bergman acknowledged that "having a bunch of people in green uniforms running around looking for birds just isn't a reality up here. Those people just don't exist. If the spill had been federalized, we would have worked with Kelly Weaverling ourselves."

In any event, Weaverling arrived in Valdez six days after the spill and went straight to the harbor with Jessica Porter and Jay

Holcomb to check out his boats. Since the boats didn't have enough heated space for bringing back birds, Weaverling began looking for a boat with more enclosed area.

"I glanced around the harbor, and sitting right there in front of us was just the kind of boat we wanted," Weaverling said. "It was one of those halibut charter boats, a sport fishing sort of thing. The bird people said, 'Yeah, maybe we can get that one on contract.'

"We talked to the boat's skipper and found out he was already on contract. I looked at his ship's log and for the last four days all it said was 'standing by for Exxon bird rescue.' The bird rescue people didn't even know that boat was available to them. Anyway, we didn't have to negotiate with the skipper. He was already working for us."

They took off for Knight Island, which had been heavily hit with oil the night of the storm. Jay Holcomb went along to teach Weaverling and his teams how to catch the oiled birds. On the ride out, Weaverling described what he and his wife loved about coming to the sound in spring. "We'd always try to get out there before the bird migration begins in early May," he said. "Twenty million birds go by in a period of about two or three weeks. Sometimes we'd see 150,000 go by in an afternoon—golden plovers, sandpipers, snow geese, swans, all kinds of ducks and small shorebirds.

"And there are lots of little things to discover on the sound, like the little sparrows," Weaverling said. "In early May, we'd watch the songbirds arrive, see them select their territory, court and mate and gather nesting material. Later, we'd come back and peek at their eggs. Then we'd watch their chicks, see them fledge, watch them learning to fly and feed themselves. And toward summer's end, we'd see them fly away."

That's how Weaverling remembered the sound. But on this cold April evening when they tied up in Snug Harbor, oil was a foot and a half deep on the surface of the water. "It was grim," Weaverling said. "Oil was so deep that the water intake on our outboard motors started pumping crude oil through the cooling systems. Those days were horrible. It was cold. It was snowing. There was oil all over the place. Dying animals were floating around. Dead animals. Just the worst. You can't tell what it's like from television, personal accounts, flying over, or from a boat. You have to actually get on a beach and try to walk through the oil. You have to reach down into that oily water and pull out a bird."

"It was so gross," Jay Holcomb added. "No matter where you went it was black. A bird would fly in, it would start to struggle, and then it would go under. Kelly and I went onto this one beach where the oil was almost over the tops of our boots. We heard a noise. It was a loon—big loon. All we could see was its head sticking up out of the oil. Its eyes were red and it made that eerie loon call. I grabbed him and pulled him out of the sludge. He was just covered . . . I mean, I couldn't even hold onto him. The loon was sliding out of my hands and biting me. Kelly just stood there in shock. Then he started to cry."

"We cried a lot," said Weaverling. "All of us did, at least once, maybe twice a day. You'd just have to stop and sit down. People would come up and say, 'We can't catch any more birds,' and they'd break out sobbing. It's just beyond imagination. Oil everywhere. Snow falling. Dead otters. Dead deer. Dead birds."

At first, Weaverling's team of boats consisted of three salmon seiners, the halibut boat, and a bow-picker with a low transom. The three seine boats leap-frogged their way down the shoreline of Knight Island, stopping at each beach to put people ashore. Several team members would cruise close to shore in a skiff or the bow-picker to pull birds from the water. At the end of the day, the crews would raft the boats together, have a hot meal, and then take the charter boat (their fastest vessel) on a night run to Valdez. There they would drop off the collected wildlife and head back out to start again in the morning.

While Weaverling's team began bringing oiled and injured seabirds into the Valdez bird center, Dr. Porter and her coworkers were trying to obtain a supply of soft water, which is vital for removing oil from birds.

"As soon as we hit the ground in Valdez, we told VECO [Exxon's main spill contractor] we needed water softeners," Porter recounted. "They said, 'It's all taken care of.' Then, nothing! We'd hear the same thing the next week. Our orders got lost somewhere in the shuffle of papers between Exxon and VECO. We weren't sure where to turn. It was horribly depressing.

"Finally, we showed VECO the birds that needed cleaning and said, 'See this bird? If we don't have soft water by tomorrow, it's going to die,'" Porter said. "We still didn't get the water softeners for two more weeks. I mean, who is VECO and what do they know about cleaning birds? Birds died because of their delays.

"And those poor little guys were suffering so much. They're victims of something that has nothing to do with them. What they go through must be the most incomprehensible, terrifying, awful thing," Porter recalled. "One of the biggest problems with an oil spill is that you're going to lose about 50 percent of the birds you try to save. After being on a number of oil spills, you almost know which birds are going to make it. Some, well, there's no point in keeping them around and watching them suffer. You euthanize them. And it hurts. It really hurts."

When the water softeners finally arrived—four weeks after they were first ordered—oiled seabirds were put through the cleaning process. Before being cleaned, each bird is force-fed fluids through a tube to counteract dehydration. Then it's placed in a bath of warm water and detergent and gently scrubbed until the water is dirty. Then it's moved to another tub of warm water and detergent and scrubbed until that water is dirty. So it goes, bath after bath, sometimes for more than ten washings, depending on how oily the bird is. The last step is rinsing the feathers with a high-pressure hose.

"Actually, we rinse them until they look dry, which sounds funny, but it's true," Porter explained. "When rinsing, you've got to have enough pressure in the hose to lift the feathers. Once they are well rinsed, they won't look wet—they'll look dry."

Part of the birds' vulnerability to oil relates to their layers of feathers. An insulating layer of downy feathers next to a bird's skin is protected by an interconnecting network of outer feathers that lock out water. If the outer feathers become oiled, they mat together, allowing water to leak through to the down, which then loses its ability to keep the bird warm.

"If you don't get all the soap out, you can have a very clean bird but one that won't float," Porter explained. "A bird floats because its feathers form a basket around its body. It's like a wet suit. Once dry, we put the birds into a pool to see if they can float. We're not going to let a bird go if it can't float."

To begin their recovery, many birds had to overcome their instinctive urge to escape. Volunteers, talking quietly and moving slowly, placed injured birds in settings where visual stimuli had been minimized. "No matter how upset they are, if you put them in a dark, quiet place they calm down," Porter explained. "Unlike dogs or cats, birds can't be cuddled into submission. The only thing you can do for birds is to get away from them—that's what they want.

"A few of the birds lie on their backs while we clean them," said Porter. "They're so relaxed it's almost as if they know it's going to be all right. But the common loons, which are huge birds with rapiers for beaks, always fight. They take the approach that a good offense is their best defense. I have wounds all over my hands."

After repeated washings and, in some cases, just forty-eight hours of intensive care, birds appeared ready to return to the sound. However, to release the birds was to risk their getting reoiled. Cormorants, puffins, and murres would not only stay in the vicinity, but often return to the very beach where they had first been oiled. Common sense suggested holding these birds in captivity until their environment was clean. But that might be a very long time, and every day the birds remained penned up increased their risk of dying from contagious diseases. One night, ten of the fifty murres being held at the Valdez bird center suddenly died of a latent fungal disease, which had apparently been activated by the stress of captivity.

"It had the potential of becoming an epidemic at the bird center," said Gary Sonnevil, a Fish and Wildlife officer assigned to monitor bird rescue efforts in Valdez. "Rather than risking all the murres dying, and, worse, risking an epidemic among other species in the center, we decided to release the surviving birds. If nothing else, it was a real morale booster for the staff. The birds chirped on their way out into the sound, and the staff cheered 'em on."

As oil spread beyond the sound, the surface of the sea swirled with an iridescent sheen. The main front of oil missed some seacliff rookeries and beaches but hit others. In many places, frothy, ankle-deep mousse washed ashore, coating and recoating the intertidal zone with each change of the tide.

Reports of dead seabirds and eagles began coming in from beyond the sound like news of fatalities from some distant war. A pile of bald eagles on a dock. Bags of murres. Stacks of birds too mutilated to identify. The diving birds—particularly cormorants, murres, grebes, puffins, and auklets—died quickly if they plunged into thick patches of oil, more slowly if they ingested oil while trying to preen their feathers. One cormorant was so frantic to clean itself that it broke a hole in its own breast skin.

"It's absolutely wrenching in some of those heavily oiled areas," said a biologist documenting the oil's impact on birds. "Once, I set a tape cassette on a black beach rock, and the rock began to crawl away. It was a seabird caked with oil."

Harlequin ducks, white-winged scoters, and old-squaws may have ingested less oil because they preen less than the sharp-billed diving birds. But many died when the oil fanned out, leaving them nowhere to go—nowhere to land, or swim, or feed. The small, brightly plumed harlequins, not nearly as common as scoters and other ducks, suffered high mortality. They winter around rocky headlands in the sound, and in spring they spread out across Alaska, nesting a pair or two to a stream. Birds killed by the oil would have summered along streams as far away as Denali National Park. Since harlequins tend to return to the streams where they were hatched, it is likely that many years will pass before some mountain streams see nesting harlequins again.

Sheets of oil reached Montague Island, and the leading edge of the spill approached the murre and puffin rookeries on the seawalls of the Chiswells, at the outer reaches of Kenai Fjords National Park. To cope with the spread, Kelly Weaverling took out his map and sectioned off seven bird-capture areas. Each area was larger than the state of Delaware, and he felt that each one needed its own team of bird search-and-capture boats.

In addition to finding vessels and crews, Weaverling had to broker their contracts with Exxon, a process that often tested his patience. "I feel like I've been jacked around," he said. "We've had eight different people in charge of Exxon operations in Cordova alone. They come up here in cowboy boots with names like Skeeter and Bubba, and work here for a week or two, and then they're gone. We never see them again. I don't know whether that's a plan to avoid accountability or not. But it certainly works that way."

Jessica Porter shared Weaverling's frustration with Exxon. She said, "We didn't feel Exxon really wanted us here. Oh, some of their people were helpful, but the thing that was missing from most of them was remorse. It's understandable that they didn't want to be so far away from their families. But they just didn't seem to care about Alaska or the birds or other people trying to help.

"Personally, I've never been treated so rudely by an oil company in my life," she said. "At one public meeting, we were ridiculed when an Exxon manager said, 'We have to deal with birds, so we've got these tree huggers taking care of them. But we'll keep them in line. . . . I'll kick their butts.'

"But the local people and fishermen were absolutely fantastic to us," Porter added. "They came in and gave, even if it was just encouragement. They were caring. And kids in schools wrote us letters: 'Don't worry. We know you are sad. Save as many birds as you can.'"

Meanwhile, Jay Holcomb left Valdez with his assistant to follow the oil out of Prince William Sound and organize another bird rescue center in Seward. As oil moved out of the sound, it began hitting the outer coast of the Kenai Peninsula, which made Seward the logical place to receive oiled birds. On the way, Holcomb would stop at Cordova and Whittier to contract boats.

Holcomb flew to Cordova with Exxon's Tom Monahan, whose task it was to deal with the fishermen. "Tom's a nice young guy," Holcomb said. "He has a family in Texas where he works in a nice air-conditioned oil lab. Now all of a sudden he's thousands of miles from home, bouncing along in a single-engine plane, heading for a town full of fishermen who hate Exxon. On the way over to Cordova I notice Tom going 'uhhnnnn . . . uhnnn.' He was taking deep breaths, stressed out already.

"We got there and the fishermen came at us with death in their eyes," Holcomb said. "I tell you, it was scary. The way they were glaring at us, I wanted them to know I wasn't with Exxon. I told them, 'I'm the bird man. I save birds.' They let up on me, but really bore down on Tom, hitting him with a lot of pent-up anger. I kept saying, 'He's Exxon, but for God's sake he didn't cause the spill. Guys, he's here to try to do his job. Okay?' But Tom couldn't even get a word out of his mouth without somebody yelling at him."

With Jay Holcomb running interference, Tom Monahan signed up a number of fishing boats to rescue birds with Kelly Weaverling. Then Holcomb and Monahan headed for Whittier, where another group of fishermen was waiting for them. Holcomb recalled that as soon as their helicopter landed in Whittier, a policeman showed up and said, "I'm giving you a ride. There's a guy in town who's got a gun and is screaming about Exxon. We want to protect you."

"This was so crazy," Holcomb said. "Tom didn't know what to say—the poor guy was in shock. A part of me was saying, 'All right, let's go.' Another part wanted to get out of there. I don't like threats. Anyway, the cop rushed us into this meeting, and it was really weird, like being in a movie. Everyone was scared, had despair in their eyes. They all thought the sound was gone forever. These people rely on fishing, and all of a sudden they can't fish. They thought they had to kiss off their way of life.

"When they found out Exxon was hiring people to catch birds, they wanted a part of it," Holcomb explained. "At one point, the big, burly guy who was leading the meeting leaned over and asked me, 'Did you know Crazy Joe's in town?' So I asked if the guy was really dangerous.

"'Well, I'll tell you,' the big man said, 'while he's around, I ain't going out of this building with you guys.'

"At this point, the mayor came in," Holcomb said. "She's kind of a rugged type who could obviously handle these guys. She said, 'Stay away from Crazy Joe. There's nothing we can do about him.'

"'Well, if he has a gun, I guess I could arrest him,' the policeman said. 'But I don't know, he's kind of hard to deal with. You never know with Joe.'

"The police took us back to the helicopter," Holcomb said. "I thought for sure we were going to get a bullet, but we got out of there without running into Joe."

Monahan returned to the relative safety of Valdez, and Holcomb went on to Seward with his assistant to set up a bird rescue center similar to the one in Valdez.

"We knew the minute we landed in Seward that something was wrong," Holcomb said. "Exxon had sent us here, but no one met our plane. We walked into town with our suitcases and no idea where to go. Then we heard the most godawful screaming. A little spaniel pup was caught on a lure at the end of a fishing pole. The hook went through his lips. It was horrible, blood everywhere. The dog was dangling from the lure, swinging in circles, screaming its head off.

"We dropped our suitcases. My assistant rushed to help the pup, and I ran into the nearby bar to find its owner. All these Alaskan guys were drinking, and I yelled, 'Whoever owns the dog out front, it's caught on your fishing lure.'

"They all stopped talking. Then this huge man stood up. He looked at me for a moment and said real slow, 'The dog's mine. I knew this would happen someday.'

"And it struck me," Holcomb said, "that this was just what Alaskans were saying about the oil spill: 'We knew this would happen someday.'

"When we saw that dog, we should have known it was an omen telling us we should go back, get out while we had the chance. And things just went downhill from there."

Holcomb found it much easier to hire rescue boats and crews in Seward than to find a place to clean birds. The military offered a warehouse big enough for bathing the birds, but two days after Holcomb started cleaning it up, a young officer told Holcomb's workers to "cease and desist."

"You don't tell us to cease and desist," Holcomb told him. "I've talked to three of your superiors and they've all given us their word that we can use this place. They gave me the keys. Birds are dying and we need to get them in here."

"Well, I just heard your work is supposed to cease, because you can't use this building," the young officer told him.

"I finally just snapped," Holcomb recounted. "I yelled at that officer, 'Okay, we're out of here. If we have to, we'll wash birds in the street.'"

After days of looking, Holcomb found an empty warehouse on the outskirts of town. It was large but needed some work.

Exxon was willing to pay for renovations and the rent. The electricity and water had to be hooked up. However, in order to hook up the electricity, the building had to pass a code inspection, which the building's owner and the city had been fighting over for years.

"Guess who gets caught in the middle of it?" Holcomb said. "The birds. When oiled birds started showing up, we put them in boxes in our apartment. They were covered with oil, but we had no place to wash them. Our kitchen smelled horrible. Their crap stinks—digested herring is really smelly. We packed birds into the garage until it overflowed."

Holcomb pleaded with city officials to approve the code inspection, but to no avail. Then he told the Exxon supervisors that he was going to move some oily birds into *their* apartments— and the code problems cleared up. Work began on the new warehouse.

"The carpenters were great. They'd do anything to help," Holcomb said. "But the plumbers had no sense of urgency. They were always ordering parts from out of town that they could have gotten in Seward. We told them birds were dying, but they really didn't care. Now, I don't expect the whole world to fall to its knees to save birds, but that's our job and it matters to us. It didn't to them. The plumbers stretched out their hours. They did everything they could to slow down completion of the bird facility so they could make more money. That sounds so low, but it's the truth. All these guys wanted to do was make money. And the Exxon people just wanted the whole thing to go away."

By April 16, though, Holcomb was feeling somewhat optimistic. The plumbers had finally completed their work, the warehouse was ready to receive birds, and a group of volunteers was ready to help clean them. By now the rescue boats were bringing in up to a hundred birds a day and the Seward bird center began running smoothly. Then Rex Colter came to town. Colter was Exxon's new man in Seward, and before meeting Holcomb or even returning his phone calls, Colter asserted his authority by cutting off food and water for the bird rescue center. "We're three days into this," Holcom told Exxon's Seward office. "Our supplies have been stopped. We can't get any food for the birds. Tell Colter I'm looking for him."

That afternoon Holcomb saw a stranger on the street, a short man wearing cowboy boots. It was Rex Colter, and he demanded that Holcomb give him an organizational chart of his employees immediately. "I've been looking for you," Holcomb said. "You've been avoiding me for three days. You're our representative. Our people can't eat. We don't have food for the birds. The water has been turned off. Our building's been shut down. Birds are dying. And you're telling me you want a goddamned list?"

Colter responded that Holcomb's job was at stake. Since Holcomb was on contract he wasn't worried, "but I felt so horrible," Holcomb said. "I was ready to cry. I didn't know what to do with these people. They wouldn't listen to me. I thought of going to the press, but I didn't really want a front page headline saying, 'The Birds are Dying.' On the other hand, I needed Exxon's help. So I told Rex Colter I'd tell the whole nasty story to the press. But it didn't faze him. Exxon had gotten so much bad press they probably thought, 'We're never going to look good up here, so why bother.' "

Holcomb got an organizational chart to Colter, who then restored food and water to the bird center. But next Colter went after the rescue fleet, which was headed by fisherwoman Linda Herrington. Since most of the birds were found in tidal rifts floating with oily kelp and driftwood, rescue crews were gathering up the oily debris along with the birds. Colter ordered them not to pick up the oily kelp. Holcomb spoke up for the rescuers. "These people out there have a conscience," he told Colter. "They can't pull a bird out of this oily crap and leave that stuff floating around to get another bird."

Holcomb then received a memo from Colter directing the rescue team not to pick up oily debris, only oiled birds.

"Go ahead and pick up the oily debris when you find a bird," Holcomb told the rescue fleet in defiance of Colter's order. "Don't go out of your way looking for oily debris. Look for birds. That's your job. But don't leave oily kelp out there to kill more birds."

When Colter observed that the bird boats were still bringing in oily debris, he sent an assistant to see Holcomb. As Holcomb recalled, "This man handed me a letter and said, 'I want you to take care of this for me, okay, Bubba?' When he called me Bubba,

I almost puked. His letter directed me to fire Linda Herrington immediately, to remove her from directing the boats because they had numerous complaints about her work.

"How can I fire Linda?" Holcomb asked Exxon's man. "She's great. She hasn't done anything wrong."

"Well, Bubba, just do it for me, will you?" said Exxon's man.

When Holcomb learned that Exxon was blaming Herrington for the fact that the fleet was still picking up oily debris, he made sure Exxon knew that it was he, not Herrington, who directed the fleet to defy Colter on the debris issue. But Exxon still persisted, and Holcomb began to suspect an underlying motive. "Then I realized that if they got rid of her, the whole fleet would fall apart," Holcomb said. "Exxon knew I didn't have time to direct the boats. And they knew Linda's constant attention was needed to keep the crews picking up birds. They knew the key was to get rid of her." Without Herrington, the fleet would be inoperative, Exxon would save money, fewer birds would be found, and the spill would appear less devastating.

Holcomb turned to his boss and confidante, Alice Berkner. "I won't fire Linda," he said. "You'd have to do it. I'd quit before firing someone who has done such a wonderful job with the fleet. She hasn't done anything wrong."

"Send her out to an island and have her sit there for a while," Berkner told Holcomb.

The next day, an Exxon man delivered a message to Holcomb. "Linda Herrington is to be removed immediately from the fleet and from your employment. She is not to set foot on a boat."

"I'm not going to do it," Holcomb answered. He stood his ground. Eventually, the order to fire Linda Herrington was rescinded, and she remained in command of the rescue fleet.

Holcomb reflected on how Exxon went to great lengths to fire or otherwise control some people while lavishing money on others. "I didn't believe it at first, but now I think Exxon is using its money to divide and conquer these communities. At least, that's the effect of its actions," Holcomb said. "The problem is how Exxon deals with people. I've watched the company buy people off in Valdez, Homer, Kodiak, and here in Seward. Exxon goes into a town where everybody is mad and says, 'We're going to give you $5,000 per day for a boat.' And people start thinking,

'Well, we're mad, but give us some of that money and we won't be quite as mad.' Exxon does that with everybody. When they have everyone confused and fighting with each other, they take over.

"They put out big bucks to get everybody to shut up for a while," Holcomb said, "and there's a lot of spoiled people around here now. I can't believe how rich some of these people got. One guy took a chance and bought a charter boat for $150,000. Exxon hired him. In four months he had made enough money to pay that boat off and buy another one.

"I've heard people say it's dirty money," Holcomb continued. "But you have to understand that people *want* to be bought off sometimes. People love that money. It's not like everybody's complaining about it. I just notice that it creates a lot of selfishness, jealousy, and backbiting. I've really learned a lot about greed up here, and it's been a rude awakening for me. I think this is probably how Alaska was built—they call it being opportunistic. This oil spill is just another gold rush."

Holcomb was also running into the same kind of posturing among Fish and Wildlife Service people that had stymied Jessica Porter in Valdez. "We had relied on them. They were the agency we went to for help in saving birds," Holcomb said. "But up here they're basically a monitoring agency. We needed them to take a more active role—to help organize the bird rescue fleet and help treat sick birds. We needed professionals taking tissue samples to determine the long-term effects of this spill. I don't think Fish and Wildlife really helped with these things. Particularly at the beginning, they just watched.

"Now, there are some wonderful individuals in the Fish and Wildlife Service who have been supportive," Holcomb said, "but they've been limited by their agency, which is very concerned about its image. It worries about making inappropriate decisions, and this mentality creates a real paralysis. The birds are not waiting to be rescued. They are dying. They have different ways of dying, but they don't survive. Meanwhile, back in their offices, Fish and Wildlife officials are asking, 'What shall we do? What's the policy? Is there a memo on this?' It gets to me. I've told them many times—'You're making such a joke of it. Why even bother? By the time we get the birds they're all dead or dying. Why not just let the poor things die—turn your back and go home?'"

"I feel depression more than anything else," Dr. Calvin Lensink reflected. "But it could have been a whole lot worse. If the spill had hit a month later, the affected populations of marine birds would have been much higher. In fact, some species got away almost scot-free. For example, the tufted and horned puffins winter at sea and don't start coming back to shore until early May. By that time, the oil would be a less effective killer. However, wherever the diving birds got tangled up in the oil, they got nailed. And some of the sea ducks took it quite hard."

Of the hundreds of thousands of birds lost to the oil Dr. Lensink said, "It's bad. There's no question about it. The loss of birds in this spill is substantially higher than in any other spill we know about—anywhere, anytime," Lensink continued. "It is terribly depressing seeing all these birds. There's a feeling of insult when a bird comes in just sopping with oil. Unrecognizable. You know, the only way we could identify a lot of the birds was by their beaks. With the cormorants, just the size of their beaks is all we had to go on. I thought that if we had a spill like this, everybody would be out right off the bat busting their butts. I was sort of surprised that they weren't.

"We never hear anybody in the Department of Environmental Conservation say it was partially their fault, because of poor monitoring of Alyeska. All the blame is laid on Exxon. . . . Both the state and federal government should have been riding herd on the oil companies. But they weren't," Lensink concluded. "I'd call it a case of deliberate neglect, because no one wants to disturb the goose that's laying the golden egg."

Chapter 11

Sea Otters

K night and Latouche islands are an eerie death zone," said Dr. Ken Hill, a young veterinarian who concentrated his efforts on otters while others rescued birds. "You see these gorgeous mountains in sunlight, but there is this silence. Just like a silent spring."

From his home in Cordova, Hill made frequent trips to the otter center being set up in Valdez and sometimes paused to walk the beaches of the sound. "One of the worst things is hearing the geese and shorebirds coming in. You know it's going to hit some of them. You don't even want to hear them coming in. The otters have already been devastated. Oh, there are a few little niches out there where otters haven't been hit by oil. But the toxic effects go far beyond the slick. There are fumes, and there's oil in the food chain.

"The otters I found dead on the beaches were all curled up. You'd see a glob of oil out their other end, by the anus," Hill said. "Some of those still alive are blind. They swim around bumping into rocks. Sometimes their central nervous systems seemed to be gone: they'd swim right up to us and knock their heads on our boat. They were either blind or brain damaged."

When otters arrived at the Valdez shelter, which was sharing space with Porter and Berkner's bird operation, volunteers immediately scrubbed oil from the otters' fur. After an initial examination the otters were put into small plastic airline kennel cages, makeshift intensive-care units where handlers could watch over them twenty-four hours a day. Many otters died within a few days. From colleagues who performed autopsies on dead otters, Dr. Hill learned that many otters were suffering internal injuries.

"We found that their lungs are burned out. They have liver and kidney damage. Some have ulcers in their digestive tracts from ingesting oil," Hill said. "Only a few of the hundreds brought in here are going to make it. And we are finding only a fraction of those that are dying. A body count of a couple hundred doesn't even begin to reflect the thousands of sea otters that have died."

The widespread death of sea otters occurred shortly after the species had staged a remarkable comeback from the edge of extinction. When Vitus Bering sailed to Alaska in 1741, otters had rolled in the waves from the Aleutian Islands down through the Gulf of Alaska and the Pacific Northwest to Baja, California. Then Russian fur traders had coerced Aleut natives into hunting the otters, which then numbered an estimated 200,000 in Alaska alone. At first the Aleuts had hunted only in the Aleutian Islands, but as otters became scarce, the hunters had been sent as far south as California. By the time the Fur Seal Treaty afforded sea otters protection in 1911, only about 400 otters had remained in Alaska. Strictly enforced hunting bans and the reintroduction of otters into their original habitats had enabled the species to recover in many areas. Before Good Friday 1989, an estimated 10,000 otters had lived in Prince William Sound.

In the wake of the *Exxon Valdez* spill, otters in the sound were once again rendered vulnerable by their luxurious fur coats. Unlike whales, seals, sea lions, and other marine mammals that have insulating layers of fat, sea otters rely on their fur—long, brown guard hairs and dense, silvery underfur hairs—to keep them warm in the frigid waters of the North Pacific. For every guard hair, there are approximately 70 underfur hairs, up to 650,000 per square inch.

When otters encountered crude oil from the *Exxon Valdez*, their fur acted like a sponge, soaking up the oil. The otters' finely regulated buoyancy, which enables them to both float and dive, became imbalanced. Struggling to stay afloat, many otters crawled ashore, where they were caught in a Catch-22. To keep from freezing to death, they needed to burn more calories, which meant they had to eat two to three times their usual amount of food. However, to eat, the otters had to return to the sea, where they would be further chilled and were likely to be reoiled.

During those first frantic days after the *Exxon Valdez* wreck, Cordova resident John Thomas volunteered his boat, his gas money, and his time to search for oiled birds and sea otters. Four days after the grounding, Thomas found oil 6 to 8 inches deep backed up against many of the beaches.

"It was like molasses. It hit everything," Thomas said. "I saw lots of dead birds and animals. Nothing alive. Right now there is nothing out there. It's a real wasteland. You have to go to the edge of the slick to find anything alive."

John Thomas is a stocky, quiet man, his red hair and beard threaded with gray. His soft voice and horn-rimmed glasses lend him a reflective, almost philosophical air. Yet dressed in raingear, shirtsleeves rolled up over his thick forearms, John looks like the Cordova fisherman he is. Normally, at the end of March he would have been readying his nets for the first salmon run.

"My wife and two girls fish with me. We fish as a family at our camp out on the sound," Thomas said. "About a hundred yards off our beach we'd watch the big grays come through. We'd just sit in the skiff and watch the whales come by, as close as you could want. There's an eagles' nest up on the point. We used to go watch the young eagles in their nest. That was our recreation, going to see how they were doing."

When Thomas went out to check his set-net site after the spill, he found an 8-inch ring of oil scum at the high-tide line on rock faces. Oil one-quarter inch thick oozed over the beach and spread down the full 15-foot range of the tide. "I've never seen anything like it," he said, "except maybe a zone that's been napalmed. Everything was dead."

Thomas left his family fishing site. "I had too many memories . . . got too depressed. I can't go back there now." He volunteered for wildlife rescue and was soon picking up otters stricken at the edges of the slick. When the floating oil reached a coastline, some of it would wash ashore, coating cobbles and splattering the sea cliffs. Thick, sludgy froth bunched up in the coves and along the narrow, offshore zone where otters live. Almost all the oil floated near the surface, where otters rest when not diving for food. Once they've caught something to eat, they'll tuck it under a front paw and pop back up to the surface. Then they'll lie on their backs, cracking open crab shells with nimble fingers. After eating, they may nap on the surface of the water, wrapping their bodies in kelp for mooring if the water is rough or the tides and currents strong. Sometimes they swim ashore to doze on rocks or sandbars near the water's edge. Otters spend most of their time in the very places where the oil gathered.

In their weakened condition, otters were easily captured by rescuers such as John Thomas, who quickly scooped up the 20- to 30-pound animals with a long-handled dip net. Despite their cute and seemingly curious expressions, sea otters are wild creatures. In the wild they are usually harmless. However, cornered or captive they will bite and scratch at anything within reach. To avoid losing a chunk of his hand, Thomas gave the otters a stick to clamp their powerful jaws around while he cleaned oil from their ears and nostrils before sending them to the Valdez center.

"We were getting a lot of them just before they died of hypothermia," he said. "Some of them had trouble breathing. They were sort of wheezing. I guess their lungs were shot. In that first week more than half the otters we brought in died."

As the oil spread, new groups of otters and birds were affected. Working with suffering creatures day after day strained the rescue workers. "We picked up a dead bald eagle, a young one that didn't look too bad. It was just dead. We assumed it had ingested oil," Thomas said. "Then we began finding quite a few eagles under their nests, where they had fallen after getting sick from eating oiled birds. And there were dead loons, water birds, all kinds of murres, auklets, and cormorants. The guys who knew all the birds couldn't identify a lot of them because they were so black you couldn't see their identifying marks. Just so many dead things.

"The otters were really suffering. You could see their eyes were irritated. Some of them were chewing on their paws to get the oil off," he continued. "Oil was coating the insides of their stomachs and they were dehydrating. But it's the dead stuff, all the dead stuff, that gets you."

Thomas's voice dropped. He continued in a hushed tone. "After a while you don't get angry. Anger is way in the back. You have moved far beyond being angry, because everything around you is dead. Before I went out I was mad. Mad at the bumbling. Then you get out there. You hope it's going to be limited, not so bad. As time goes on, the oil keeps spreading. More death. You just keep going into deeper depression. Finally, I had to get out of it for my own sanity."

Kelly Weaverling, in his rescue work for Exxon, also encountered stricken otters. "As soon as we began collecting birds, we came across our first distressed otter. We had been sent out to get birds, but couldn't just let that otter die. So we captured it. Pretty soon we got another one. We reasoned that it would be best if the bird people also collected otters, and the otter people also collected birds."

Weaverling found that the otters were easy to catch on shore because they were so preoccupied with trying to lick the oil from their fur. Normally, otters groom themselves for hours each day to maintain the air that provides their fur both warmth and buoyancy. As they lick their fur and comb the longer hairs with their fingers, they align the hair shafts to maintain loft and, in the process, stimulate the production of natural oils in their fur. These unusually fastidious animals became frantic when oil clogged their fur, matting it into sticky clumps. In their obsession to clean themselves, they invariably ingested toxic oil.

Weaverling had been instructed by the Fish and Wildlife Service, which had management jurisdiction over sea otters, to place each otter in its own cage. However, his one cage was soon occupied, and he was finding lots of oiled otters. "When we caught our second otter, we opened up the hatch over the empty fish hold and turned the otter loose in there," Weaverling said. "Then we caught a third otter and were really stuck. We didn't have any more separate areas, so we had to put otters together in the fish hold. They immediately bared their teeth and screeched. But after a few minutes they huddled together and began grooming each other. By the end of the day, we had six otters huddled up together."

Weaverling and his crews began sending their oiled otters to Valdez along with the birds they had rescued. But after three days he was told not to send any more otters, that the otter facility was full. "I didn't think that was a very good reason not to collect the distressed otters," Weaverling said. "All radio and phone communication with Valdez was jammed with callers, so to communicate with the otter people in Valdez I had to go there. I commandeered a guy and his float plane to fly me in. Something had to be done.

"It was nuts. It was just crazy," Weaverling said of the Valdez otter center. "They had no place to receive the otters. They were just stacking them up in cages and kennels. Boxes of otters lined the hallways."

Since the bird and otter rescue operations were sharing the same quarters, every bit of space was stacked with crates and makeshift bins of screeching birds and otters. Jessica Porter and her colleagues from the International Bird Rescue Research Center were familiar with working together under the round-the-clock stress of an oil spill, and they knew how to comfort and support each other when overwhelmed by the sight and smell of dying creatures. "We are a family as well as an organization," Porter said. "We know how to pull together." However, this was a new experience for Dr. Randall Davis, the physiologist whom Exxon had called up from Sea World Research Institute near San Diego to direct otter rehabilitation. It was his first oil spill. He had no seasoned team and would work with local veterinarians such as Ken Hill.

"I think Randy Davis knew he was in serious trouble the moment he got up here," Porter said. "Here he was, a research person, thrown onto the battlefield. With no oil spill experience, it must have been mind-boggling for him. He spent hours talking with us about basic procedures. Then he started bringing up every otter expert he could find. He ended up with fifteen vets, and none of them agreed on anything. They all had huge egos. Each wanted to be *the* one to figure out *the* problem with otters. I mean, there was some nasty all-out, free-for-all backbiting. Some of them were even stealing carcasses from each other."

"I never want to face anything like that again," Dr. Davis said. "We were in a desperate situation—trying to build a facility, organize people, and save suffering otters. Basically, none of us had ever experienced anything like this before. We had done research, but there was no precedent for what we faced in Prince

William Sound. No one had ever had to capture and clean a large number of oiled sea otters before."

Kelly Weaverling found Davis as he was trying to talk with an assistant and two television newspeople at the same time. Commotion, ringing phones, reporters, and onlookers prevented them from talking, so Davis said, "Come on, I know a quiet place," and steered Weaverling into the men's restroom.

"He closed the door and locked it," Weaverling said. "This was the only way we could talk. When people knocked, Davis would say, 'Go away, we're busy.'"

Closeted in the men's room, Davis and Weaverling tried to figure out what to do with the growing number of oiled otters collecting at the center. Davis mentioned that one of the major shortcomings of Aleyska's oil spill contingency plan was its lack of attention to animal rescue operations. A rehabilitation center, he asserted, should have been in place when tankers first came to Valdez. Now the only facilities were makeshift, which meant that the already frightened otters were being heavily traumatized after being rescued. Davis told Weaverling about the new Exxon-funded otter center workers were scrambling to open in Valdez. There would be larger pens and a less hectic atmosphere. The Valdez center would be operational in a week and would be able to handle three times as many otters as the present site now being shared with the bird rescue team.

But Weaverling wasn't reassured. He explained that he had been sending in otters from just one team of three boats. Seven more teams of boats were now heading into the sound. In a few days, his boats would be sending in *seven* times as many otters as they had been previously. By the time the new center opened, there would already be too many otters for it to handle. Davis agreed that another otter facility was needed, but said that he was swamped in Valdez and far too busy to set one up. He urged Weaverling to start a new otter center, if he could.

"I think Davis might have encouraged me because he underestimated me," Weaverling said. "To some people I may not appear very capable. I look kind of goofy, you know. I wear my hair long. I've got a beard. I don't have any business cards to pass out."

Nevertheless, with Davis's backing Weaverling sought out

Exxon spokesman Don Cornett for financial support. "I'll say this in Cornett's behalf," Weaverling said. "Once he found out there was a legitimate need, he was all for it."

But when Dr. Alan Maki, Exxon's chief environmental scientist, walked in on Weaverling's meeting with Cornett, he suggested they reconsider opening the new otter center. The otter population had been healthy before the spill, he said, and the oil wasn't going to extinguish the species. Otters had recovered before. Given enough time, they would come back again. Why spend a lot of money to save a relative handful of individual animals? Cornett told Dr. Maki, "Well, we're going to do it anyhow," and turning to Weaverling, he said, "You can use as much money and as much power and influence as Exxon has to get the job done. Just get it done fast."

As an afterthought, Cornett said, "Weaverling, you've got a great opportunity to screw us over."

"Look, I don't want to screw anybody over," Weaverling replied. "I want to take care of a problem. I want to save some animals." Weaverling noted how ironic it was that "Exxon's head public relations man had just overruled Exxon's top environmental scientist."

A week earlier, Kelly Weaverling had been running his bookstore, the Orca, on Cordova's main street, talking fish and philosophy over cups of coffee, selling an occasional book, and planning his next kayak trip across the sound. Now, his navy training and extensive knowledge of the sound had thrust him into a position of leadership. "I might be more effective than some agency," Weaverling mused. "Bureaucracies can't move with much speed. Too many people have to be consulted. They have to fill out purchase orders and requisition forms, go through committees, do studies and tests. I'm one individual, totally non-aligned. I don't belong to a single organization. I can just walk next door and say, 'I need some lumber and this many guys with hammers. Let's meet two hours from now and start pounding nails.'"

After establishing the need for a new otter center in Cordova, Weaverling lined up a location, carpenters, and building materials in less than thirty-six hours. He instructed his foreman to "build an otter facility so we can get a couple of washing stations and holding pens operational right away. When all the otters are cared for, we can store the modules for the next oil spill."

Weaverling was assured by the builders that the Cordova otter center would be operational in five days. However, before construction commenced, he had to attend to a formality. Since sea otters fell under the jurisdiction of the U.S. Fish and Wildlife Service, the agency had to approve the project. "The only Fish and Wildlife officials I could find to talk to were a couple of lower echelon people," Weaverling said. "I told them the whole story. They took a few notes, and then they said, 'Wait here, we'll be right back.'"

When the Fish and Wildlife officials returned four hours later, they agreed that a new otter facility was needed but stated that if one were to be built, it had to be in Seward. "This went against the advice of otter experts out there in the field, the veterinarians, and my own experience," Weaverling said. "Maybe a center would be needed in Seward later, but we needed a second center in the sound right away.

"Then they dropped the sledgehammer," Weaverling said. "These Fish and Wildlife guys told me that my fleet of wildlife rescue boats had to 'cease and desist' from capturing otters. They said we were unauthorized, untrained, and not inspected by the Fish and Wildlife Service.

"I didn't know what to make of it," he continued. "I was so low. I had worked so hard to get things moving so we could save some more otters. And all of a sudden everything came to a screeching halt. This new otter facility didn't fall apart because some oil company was too cheap. It got squashed by these guys who are supposed to be stewards of our wildlife.

"Here it was the height of the otter rescue, and they had only four boats out there to cover more than a thousand square miles," Weaverling said. "I had another forty-four boats that could have been bringing in oiled otters. If we'd had all forty-eight boats collecting otters, a lot more would have been collected and a lot more would have been rehabilitated.

"Fish and Wildlife said their ban would protect both otters and the people collecting them. But the animals were so easy to capture. And there were so many stuck in that oil that needed help. It was just horrible, and I was powerless to change it.

"I don't know why they cut off the otter rescue," Weaverling said. "But the result has been self-fulfilling. By limiting the number of people bringing in otters, the Valdez facility wasn't going to overflow, and Fish and Wildlife could get some good publicity. And if they didn't bring in thousands of sick otters, the spill and what little they were doing for wildlife didn't look so bad. Maybe they figured, like Maki had, 'Well, the otters would survive as a species, so why worry about saving a few individuals?'"

In response, one Fish and Wildlife Service official, who asked not to be identified, said, "At the time, we thought the rescue operation might be stressing more otters than it was helping. But, in retrospect, we shouldn't have shut down Weaverling. We created a public relations disaster for ourselves. Here was a guy trying to save otters, and we stopped him."

Chuck Monnett and Lisa Rotterman, wildlife biologists who had studied sea otters exclusively for years, were also angry at the Fish and Wildlife Service for "the unnecessary death of thousands of otters due to political and bureaucratic machinations." On March 25, the first Saturday after the spill, Monnett and Rotterman asked government officials to save at least a minimum number of animals. Aware that the spreading oil would be lethal to otters, they suggested two countermeasures: protecting key bays and coves with containment boom and granting emergency approval for the transport of 500 to 1,000 animals in the path of the oil. However, neither boom nor approval to transport was forthcoming.

"We may see 10,000 otters threatened," Monnett said. "We could save a lot of them. But we need a permit to save otters, and the Fish and Wildlife Service has put us on hold."

Monnett and Rotterman were not just concerned about individual animals; they were worried about the viability of the species as well. They knew from their studies that hunting in the North Pacific had previously wiped out all but thirteen isolated groups of otters. Two of those populations had weakened and subsequently disappeared. Of the surviving eleven groups, four were studied for genetic diversity. Loss of diversity makes species more vulnerable to disease and less adaptable to change in the environment. In blood-protein comparisons, the Prince William Sound otters had shown the greatest genetic variability of the eleven groups.

"Nevertheless," Monnett said, "Fish and Wildlife Service's management took the position that there wouldn't be any significant biological consequences, so no action was taken. It's as if the Fish and Wildlife Service's guideline for emergencies was to deny there *was* an emergency."

"We do have plans and guidelines to deal with emergencies, but this oil spill overwhelmed us," said Wally Soroka, a Fish and Wildlife enforcement officer in Anchorage. "We have more work than we can do on a regular basis, so when we have an oil spill, something has to slide. We got two agents out there wading through the oil to collect evidence. But we simply didn't have the personnel or equipment to handle a situation like this."

Yet another Fish and Wildlife Service official, who requested anonymity, said that "a lot of people were asking where we were when this oil hit. And that's a good question. There were volunteers out there trying to save otters and birds before our people got out of their offices. We're supposed to protect the fish and wildlife. Our field people want to get the job done, but sometimes they're held back by budget cuts and directives from Washington, D.C. Here we have the biggest wildlife crime in the history of our country, and what have we done?

"When this spill first hit, there was some denial going on," the official continued. "There was a tendency for some of our people to pretend there wasn't that much oil out there. 'Maybe it'll just go away. If a lot of Fish and Wildlife people run out there, it will just look like a bigger problem.'

"I can tell you that a lot of Fish and Wildlife Service people are disgusted with this kind of attitude within their own agency," he continued. "But if they speak up, they get shipped out to some place like Miami. I've seen it happen. No one ever says, 'You're being transferred because you talked.' They just say, 'Adios.'"

Funding for regulation enforcement is part of the problem. While the addition of new Alaska refuges since 1980 has more than doubled the size of the national refuge system, the Fish and Wildlife Service's enforcement budgets have not been increased. There are more areas to protect, more recreational hunters, and more industrial activity, but the agency's enforcement capability remains geared to the "homesteader-shoots-a-moose-out-of-season" days.

Under the Bald Eagle Act and the Marine Mammal Act, anyone causing the death of eagles or otters is subject to seizure of their vessel and/or cargo. However, enforcing these laws is impossible without well-equipped enforcement officers. Fish and Wildlife Service enforcement vessels in Alaska consist of one 12-foot inflatable raft and one canoe. "Imagine us paddling up to the *Exxon Valdez* and calling out, 'Hey, Hazelwood! Your boat's killed a lot of eagles and otters. So hand over the tanker and the rest of your oil,'" Soroka said.

Although not apprehended for killing otters, as a hunter might have been, Exxon paid for those needing treatment. To replicate their natural diet, Exxon shipped fresh oysters, clams, mussels, and crab—at a cost of $60 per day for each otter. In all, Exxon spent $20 million to treat 350 otters. The 220 otters that were saved cost Exxon $89,000 apiece, a considerable price, when one considers that zoos can purchase sea otters for less than $5,000 apiece.

These high costs raised the question of what an animal's life is worth. To some, every individual life was precious, and saving an otter's life was worth virtually any cost; it was their judgment that a polluting company should spare no expense. On the other hand, some, such as Dr. Calvin Lensink, who had directed many otter relocation projects, questioned the amount of money spent on the 200 otters saved. "From my point of view, it's a waste of money," Lensink said. "I tend to think more in terms of populations than individuals. We have only so many resources we can expend. If we start thinking in terms of individuals, we can waste all of our resources."

Nevertheless, as millions of American television viewers watched the cuddly-looking creatures struggle against the oil, sea otters became a symbol of the spill. Exxon, well aware that their investment in otters would generate good publicity, continued to pay for otter centers and tons of fresh seafood. "Exxon told me to do whatever was necessary to save sea otters," said Dr. Randall Davis. "There was never a question about having enough money. But even the vast resources of Exxon could not buy the precious time we needed for advance planning. Before the spill, there was a lack of preparation for rescuing otters, and a lot of people have to share the responsibility for it. Alyeska and the Department of Interior should have been ready; they weren't. The general public, particularly Alaskans, also have to share the blame. Alaskans have been in bed with the oil industry for a long time; as a whole, they never pressed for stronger environmental safeguards."

Tom McCloskey, operations manager for the Seward otter center, was particularly frustrated with the federal government. "People shouldn't be focusing on Exxon alone. We need to look at our agencies for improvement as well. The Fish and Wildlife Service is the federal trustee of wildlife under the Marine Mammal Act, and it has done nothing. You can't make it up as you go along. We need to ask, What does it mean to be the trustee of a resource?"

One result of Exxon's otter centers was a unique collaborative effort between one of the world's largest corporations and a group of volunteers. At the height of the oil spill, the Alaska governor's office received up to 2,000 calls per day from people wanting to volunteer. The state referred these people to the Valdez-based Prince William Sound Conservation Alliance and the Oil Spill Volunteer Response Hotline in Anchorage. "Literally thousands of people were calling from all over the world," said Sue Libenson, who helped organize the volunteer hotline. "Not all of them could come to Alaska, but each wanted to do something, whatever they could, to help. We were able to put several hundred volunteers in the field; many of them helped rescue birds and otters."

One of the first to volunteer was Tami Thomas, a young woman who had been a member of Alyeska's oil spill response team until she spoke out against what she saw as corrupt practices—whereupon she was assigned to the sludge pit at Alyeska's ballast water treatment facility. Thomas became the volunteer coordinator for the Seward otter center, which opened in late May.

"People were calling from all over the country," Thomas said. "They all wanted to help. We could only use a few of them. For everyone we accepted there were a hundred more—gosh, maybe a thousand—who wanted to pay their way up here to help the otters. . . . These people wanted to do whatever they could."

One volunteer at the Seward otter center was Suzanne Marinelli, who flew in from Hawaii in late May, two months after the wreck of the *Exxon Valdez*. "When we got to Alaska we saw so much heartbreak, so many angry people," she said. "The lucky ones were able to do something—to work with their hands, to help in some way. This hastened their healing process."

In her home on the island of Kauai, Marinelli had seen the television images of dying birds and otters day after day. She and her friends had discussed the spill at Sierra Club meetings. Then she saw the Sierra Club ad in the *New York Times* that read, "If you can help on the spill, then we need your help."

"I thought maybe I could make just a little difference," Marinelli said. "I decided I had to go. Sometimes you've just got to take a leap of faith.

"I love Hawaii, and we have so many beautiful birds that could die in an oil spill. I felt that going to Alaska could teach me how to care for our birds in case we had an oil spill in the islands," Marinelli said, her voice soft and reflective. "And by coming to Alaska, I thought I might learn some things in terms of awareness."

Marinelli, forty-four, had grown up in the Southern Appalachian mountains, in the coal fields of North Carolina. "I saw the coal being shipped out to the steel mills. My home was destroyed," she said. "Northern industrialists had come down in the twenties and offered fifty cents an acre for our land. The mountain people sold. Then the mining companies strip-mined the tops of our mountains and tossed the rubble in the valleys. Floods came; streams were destroyed. I saw the spirit of my people destroyed. My people's spirit was gone because the land was destroyed. And that's what makes me so fiercely determined to protect places like Alaska.

"My grandfather was a preacher," she went on. "He loved those mountains. And when we were little kids, he instilled in us a commitment to take care of the land. He taught us that you can't hope to turn everything around all by yourself and right away. But if you do what you can and work hard, you'll make a difference in the long run."

When Marinelli and several friends from Kauai arrived in Alaska, they were assigned to Seward to clean otters brought in from the sound. The oil had already hit more than 400 miles of beaches—"more than four times our entire coastline in Hawaii," noted Marinelli. "Volunteers had come from all over the country—Minnesota, Colorado, New York, Texas, Florida . . . lots of them from the West Coast states. We worked alongside people from Australia, Germany, Switzerland, and China too."

Many of the volunteers lived in tents down by the beach. Marinelli and her companions from Hawaii, who had gone into debt in order to help the otters, received some help themselves from schoolchildren in Nottingham, New Hampshire, who raised several hundred dollars from bake sales and washing cars to help the volunteers. Marinelli said, "I don't know if I could have handled the cold down on the beach. Some of the volunteers were sleeping in little tents on the cold rocks. All these people gave and gave and gave, and their only recompense was the satisfaction of helping the otters.

"My job was taking care of twelve otters in six pens," Marinelli said. "I fed them and cleaned their pens. I watched them grooming, splashing in the water. Being a mom, I wanted to make each of these little hurt beings feel better. You know, they are a lot like kids. Some liked squid. Others wanted shrimp and clams. Some wouldn't eat their haddock. Some ate out of their bowls and some dipped their food in the water."

The otters were fed five times a day in a carefully prescribed manner. Volunteers meticulously recorded the type and amount of all food consumed. Water dishes were always filled with fresh water. All otter food had to be lightly iced and kept for no more than four hours. Crushed ice or snow had to be available at all times. While feeding the otters, volunteers noted the color and consistency of the otter feces and monitored such behavior as appetite, sleeping, grooming, vocalization, and swimming.

Marinelli was particularly interested in one mother and baby otter in her care. "When they first came to me, the baby was very bothered by people. It hissed when anyone came near. By the third day, when they saw me, they saw food. It was a little disconcerting to see how quickly they became tame," she said. "But I could watch the mother teach her baby. She'd be grooming and he'd mimic her. She would show him all the little ways to spin and flip in the water, rolling and pinwheeling forward. It was a riot to watch the pup try. When he just couldn't do it, he'd flop forward on his face. And at times he'd just lie on his mother's belly and sleep while she sang and cooed."

Tom McCloskey and other otter experts cautioned volunteers not to form close attachments. "When looking into a cage, move slowly and avoid direct eye contact. Do everything you can to avoid 'imprinting' between you and the otters. The otters are wild animals and must remain so. If they place too much trust in us, it will reduce their chance to return to the wild successfully."

Some otters died at the center for no apparent reason. Marinelli had been caring for one male otter for several weeks. It looked fit and had a voracious appetite. Then one afternoon, at feeding time, she found him dead. "He was just lying there in the water," she said. "'It made us fearful. All those otters we had helped—maybe they'd die too from internal damage. If not now, then maybe months later."

By summer's end, controversy was raging around the release of rehabilitated otters. Some biologists urged that the otters be returned to the sound as soon as possible. Others, fearing that the otters might have picked up domestic diseases that could infect other wild otters, wanted to send the rescued otters to zoos. Several biologists wanted to attach tracking devices to indicate where the otters went and whether they survived. This idea incited the wrath of animal-rights activists, who argued that the otters should not be subjected to the further stress of having transmitters sewn under their skin. While these controversies held the otters in limbo, someone sneaked into the Valdez center and cut the nets of the floating seawater pens. Twelve otters escaped. Five of them lingered close to their pens, perhaps expecting their next meal, and were recaptured.

By October, young otters that had not learned how to survive in the wild were sent to zoos. Most of the other otters were returned to the sound, where the otter population was expected to restore itself in five to ten years.

The wildlife rescue effort was the beginning of the healing process for many of the humans involved. Individuals who took part were both restoring the sound and reaffirming that wild creatures had to be protected. But day-to-day interactions with the otters as well as participation in the overall rescue effort yielded new insight and a deepened commitment as well. Marinelli recalled the day "when they brought in some orphaned seal pups. The vets told us they were black seals. Then, as we began washing them, we realized they were silver and white harbor seals. They had been so dark that even the vets had been fooled. They looked so helpless. They had these enormous eyes and just sat there on the floor, looking up at us through the slats of their cage.

"One day I heard a young man singing, 'Forgiving won't come easy in Prince William Sound,' and that line really stayed with me, because if we are going to heal ourselves we must forgive," Marinelli said. "I've seen a lot of heartbroken people. But our memories are short. Everyone's hurting over the spilled oil now. But in a year, five years? We forget. It's the limit of our memory that frightens me. If we don't remember what happened in Prince William Sound, it will happen again."

Chapter 12

Bald Eagles

When the spill first happened, nobody was thinking about eagles. Everybody was talking seabirds and otters. Then all of a sudden, we started to find dead eagles," said Anchorage veterinarian Jim Scott. "Some of them were lying stiff on the beach, covered with oil. Others were just wounded, dazed, or flopping about with broken wings. Some were in convulsions from eating oiled carrion. People started saying, 'Something has to be done. This is our national symbol.'"

With more than 2,000 bald eagles, Prince William Sound is one of the few places where the outstretched wings of these great birds gliding on the wind have remained a common sight. One often sees a bald eagle high in a weathered tree waiting for the tide to turn. The bird slowly spreads those huge wings, lifts lightly into the air, and floats over the beach. It glides along the tide line, wheels, and then circles over the sea. Wings suddenly fold. The eagle dives and hits the water. With a fish clutched in its powerful talons, the bird rises slowly into the sky.

To many Native Americans, an eagle rising into the sky, soaring up over mountains and into the clouds, links heaven and earth. "Seeing an eagle lying in that oil makes me physically ill," said Maria Williams, a Tlingit woman whose father is a member of the Eagle Clan. A young eagle lay dead on the beach, its powerful wings outstretched and stiff. "Some people say, 'Oh, don't worry, they're not all dead, they'll come back.' That makes me furious," Williams said. "The death of an eagle is like the death of a friend. A part of me dies with each one of those birds."

While for some each death is personal, others view the demise of an individual eagle in relation to the larger population and the health of the species. As large numbers of bald eagles were stricken in Prince William Sound, these different perspectives led to controversies. Should oiled adult eagles be rehabilitated? Should they be studied for the effects of the oil? Should young eagles be rescued from their nests and transplanted to other states where the species is beginning to reestablish itself? And who should decide these questions?

Eagles whose feathers were oiled lost their ability to fly and often crippled themselves lurching into rocks or trees. Ones that became completely flightless were easy prey for bears and foxes. Those escaping that fate eventually starved to death or were poisoned by contaminated carrion. Ingested oil burned their vital organs, particularly the liver, kidneys, and intestines. When the kidneys fail, an eagle is no longer able to filter waste products from its blood. When an eagle's intestine is immobilized by oil, its body can no longer absorb nutrients. Some eagles may have been starving even as they gorged themselves on oiled seabirds.

Eagles, particularly nesting pairs, have a low tolerance for human activity. Thus, Exxon's beach-cleaning operations, which would proliferate and intensify throughout the summer, posed a trade-off: clean beaches—perhaps—versus additional stress for eagles.

Jules Tileston, an environmental consultant who had worked for VECO, Exxon's main spill contractor, talked about the overall effect of the planned cleanup. "I brought VECO a map covered with hundreds of dots showing all the eagle nests in Prince William Sound," Tileston said, his voice rising in anger. "I told them they should send out a memo cautioning the crews to be careful around the eagle nests. But VECO didn't want to hear about it. Their attitude was, 'Hey, don't tell us any more. If we don't know, we can't be blamed.' They wanted to proceed unimpeded. They never warned the cleanup crews to be careful around the eagle nests."

The combined effects of oil and cleanup activities accumulated over the spring. By June, fifty-three dead bald eagles had been recovered from Prince William Sound. While some of these deaths were attributed to natural mortality at the end of winter,

biologists believed that many oiled eagles would never be seen
because, even under normal circumstances, dead eagles are
hard to find. When eagles are ill or injured, they usually seek
refuge in the woods, often roosting in the branches of a high
tree. If they die, they fall into underbrush, out of sight.

"The loss of adult bald eagles is a greater tragedy than poor
reproduction in a season," said Dr. James Scott, who treats eagles
and other wild creatures at his Anchorage veterinary clinic.
"Only 5 to 7 percent of young eagles make it to adulthood. When
adult eagles are killed, it takes many years for the population to
reestablish itself. The survivors face an uncertain future. Many
are now weakened with oil-related injuries. Eagles face a very
hard winter every year, and after going through a summer like
this, a lot of them aren't going to make it."

Scott organized eagle rescue efforts from his Arctic Animal
Hospital in Anchorage, where books, letters, reports, tools, and
bones spill over every shelf and counter in his office. Children
hugging sick puppies and cats wait in the reception room. Young
assistants dart from room to room tending the clinic's patients.
A young woman feeds a trio of abandoned baby thrushes with a
syringe full of chopped bugs; another feeds a fishy mixture to
an orphaned Bonaparte gull.

In twenty-nine years of practice in Alaska, Scott has treated
moose, bear cubs, seals, otters, owls, hawks, and a host of other
wild creatures, in addition to the regular flow of puppies, cats,
parrots, rabbits, and guinea pigs. "We've treated everything wild
that's come through the door and never charged a dime," Scott
said. "Falcons, ravens, tiny little songbirds—we've had them all.
We once raised a baby moose in the back yard. And when our
kids were little, they had a bear cub in their bedroom."

Over the years, Scott had treated many bald eagles, but he had
never lived through anything like the summer of 1989. By early
May, the first eagles had arrived at his clinic for treatment—Big
Female and One-Wing, who hobbled across the floor of a large
raptor cage. In their brilliant yellow eyes, the thin, dark pupils
remained attentive to every movement near their pen. Three
weeks before, they had peered down at the sea from high over
Prince William Sound.

"Old One-Wing, what an eagle!" Scott said admiringly. "He
ate some oiled birds and became disoriented. He flew into a rock

and broke a wing. It had to be amputated. But what a fighter—the epitome of what we want for a symbol and the kind of eagle we want out there breeding. Now he's going to spend the rest of his life in captivity."

In the operating room adjacent to Scott's office, lights were dimmed to calm an immature bald eagle lying on the table. With its head hooded in plastic, the young eagle was fighting the anesthesia-induced drowsiness. Its wings were wrapped in layers of red gauze, and its long flight feathers were sticky and tarred with oil. As Dr. Scott painstakingly cut away layers of gauze, the eagle clenched its talons tightly. The doctor used tweezers to clean the raw skin on a wing. Then he lifted and flexed the bird's toes. "There's plenty of blood in there," he said. "His feet are stiff, but warm. He's got some swelling."

A young assistant took the eagle's foot in her hand and massaged each toe, carefully rubbing it between her thumb and forefinger. "This is only the second time I've worked with him," she said. "He's doing much better."

Scott drew a blood sample to determine if the eagle had ingested oil. If it had, it would require six weeks of chemical cleanup. "The capture effort is going to determine how many eagles we can save," Scott said. "When the eagles are sitting in trees they may look good, but once they flip their tails you can see oil. Sometimes you will see them fly from a kill and their oil-caked feathers will be noisy. They sort of rattle."

As the number of oiled eagles increased, Exxon asked Dr. Scott for advice on setting up an eagle rescue center. "I told them about the raptor center in Sitka," Scott said. "It's good, but it's 500 miles from the oil spill and has only one vet. Judging by the number of injured and oiled eagles reported, we were going to have to handle 200 to 300 eagles. We needed a new treatment center. Exxon said, 'Get us a proposal.'

"So I figured out what was needed," Scott said. "We would have to have a long-term-care facility, both to heal the eagles and to hold them until their habitat was safe for their return. These eagles are philopatric, which means they return to their homes—to their bays, their beaches, the very trees they used to roost in. If they return too soon, they'll get reoiled or eat contaminated food again."

Scott believed that badly oiled eagles needed to be held in captivity until they molted and grew new feathers, which usually takes a year. The annual cost of raptor care in Alaska is approximately $7,500 per year per bird for food, care, fly pens, warehouse space, lighting, and plumbing. Just 200 eagles, at $7,500 each, would amount to $1,500,000 a year. Exxon offered $102,000 to launch the effort.

Scott hoped that any facilities built near Anchorage for the oiled eagles might become part of a nonprofit bird treatment and research center. But first he had to deal with the crisis at hand. To stretch available funding, he sought volunteer help to build fly pens for the injured eagles. "The pens were built by the most wonderful set of volunteers you've ever seen in your life," he said. "Tim Sell, a master falconer and master carpenter, sat down and designed the whole thing from scratch. With a dozen volunteers, we built the best raptor holding facility I've ever seen. It took 4,000 hours. . . . We had a young woman attorney working on doors. Housewives had paintbrushes in their hands, and a colonel from the air force base was pounding nails.

"But we ran into a wall," Scott said. "I think Exxon was willing to pay whatever it had to. But when it comes to eagles, Exxon is going to do what the Fish and Wildlife Service says. And Fish and Wildlife said, 'We don't want a facility for any more than twenty eagles.'

"I told them that wasn't enough. Everyone coming back from the sound said it wasn't enough. Even Fish and Wildlife staff members were saying we were going to have a lot of eagles. But I think word came down from Washington, D.C., that twenty eagles were the maximum number of oiled eagles expected, and that's all we had to be prepared for. It was outrageous."

Dr. Scott was mystified at how agency people sitting in their Washington, D.C., offices could predetermine how many eagles would need treatment. He felt they were denying the magnitude of the problem. Nevertheless, under his agreement with the Fish and Wildlife Service and his contract with Exxon, he readied his clinic and new eagle facility to receive oiled and injured birds. Then the Fish and Wildlife Service informed him that they had decided it was best to do just an initial exam in the field, take a blood sample or two, and turn the eagles loose.

"Exxon thought that was wonderful. It was just what they

wanted to hear," Scott fumed. "It would cost less. And if the eagles died out in the sound, they would be out of sight and out of
mind. I knew it was the wrong decision, and I've paid a trusted
friend to periodically fly the sound for me. I get regular reports
directly from him, and I guarantee that there are eagles dying
out there. Oil had gotten down in the rocks and sand. When the
tide comes in, the oil rises. It's killing the ecosystem, just as if you
poured poison out there."

Through most of May and June, the Fish and Wildlife Service
assigned just one search boat to an area with more coastline than
the entire East Coast of the United States. At a meeting in Valdez, Scott pushed the agency for more capture teams. "Each
team needs a boat, a fixed-wing plane, a helicopter, and a vet,"
he said. "I can't understand why the Fish and Wildlife Service
isn't pushing for more eagle-capture teams. I agree with other
animal rehab people that wild animals are better off in their own
environment, but only if that environment is healthy. The sound
isn't safe for eagles—it's not clean. Beaches are still being oiled.
Eagles are scavengers, and turning them loose in an area with
that much oil is just sending them out to die.

"We started having meetings—so many godawful meetings
with the bureaucracy," Scott recalled. "I told them I was dead set
against their new policy of briefly examining and releasing oiled
eagles. If they insisted on this quick release, they should at least
have the eagles examined by a veterinarian. We had more than
200 young veterinarians volunteering to fly to Alaska at their
own expense to help. I mailed the list to Fish and Wildlife and it
was 'lost.' I sent it again and it was misplaced a second time. The
third time, I hand-delivered the names of vets who wanted to
help along with a list of absolutely essential things to be done.

"Before you turn an eagle loose, you need to know if it is fit,"
Scott said. "Are its eyes clear? Is its skin color good? Its wings?
You ought to know if an eagle is about to die before releasing it.
Remember, we're not talking mallards. We are talking about our
national symbol. There are people in the lower forty-eight who
drive hundreds of miles to see an eagle."

As court cases began to appear after the spill, dead eagles became evidence substantiating claims of environmental loss. Scott
explained that "it became a pissing contest between Exxon and

the Fish and Wildlife Service over who had the legal rights to evidence. Both sides were fighting over the eagles—a match-off, where attorneys get rich and everyone else gets angry. Fish and Wildlife was saying that they were responsible for all birds and animals. And Exxon was saying, 'We're paying, so we feel the information is ours.' Maybe we can't really blame Exxon for not wanting to supply information that would crucify them in court cases for the next twenty years.

"But while people are squabbling and protecting their turf, eagles are dying," Scott said. "And we're losing a chance to learn a lot about eagles. The Fish and Wildlife Service is releasing eagles without even attaching tracking devices to let us know if the birds return to oiled areas or survive at all. They won't even let us hold the oiled eagles long enough to do blood tests, which can indicate kidney damage from oil. Dr. Pat Redig is standing by to do the blood work at his raptor center in Minnesota, but he isn't getting the samples."

Dr. Redig, widely respected as the most knowledgeable raptor biologist in the world, echoed Scott's frustration. "I think Scott's treatment program is a sound one, and I'm disappointed it wasn't used more." After surveying Prince William Sound, Redig said, "We are dealing with a lot of unknowns. I expected a couple hundred oiled eagles to come in. We don't know how oil is going to affect these eagles over the long term. So I don't agree with catching eagles with a little oil on them and just letting them go. Trapped birds should have been kept so we could study them for future reference. There are going to be more oil spills, and we need to know as much as we can about the effects of oil on eagles. Basically, we have been deprived of this opportunity.

"It's hard to know what's gone on in people's minds over these eagles," Redig continued. "But I think when people outside the medical area didn't see a mass of dead eagles, they assumed it wasn't necessary to bring oiled birds in for treatment. They said, 'Let's save ourselves the trouble.'

"The damage is going to be insidious. Initially, in almost all cases, the oiled eagles have had organ damage," Dr. Redig explained. "With just one blood sample, at one point in time, we can't determine if there are any trends. Finding out what's going on with these eagles is a long-term project, an endeavor that would take the better part of a year. This is where the Fish and Wildlife Service and Exxon got cold feet. I think their mind set was to deal with the birds for a week or so, which is too much of a short-term affair."

By the first of October, the Fish and Wildlife Service's count of dead bald eagles stood at 146. "We are not sure how many died," said Phil Schimph, a Fish and Wildlife Service biologist specializing in eagles and other raptors in Alaska. "It's hard to substantiate the number of dead eagles. People who estimate are just grabbing numbers out of the air.

"In the context of all the eagles in Alaska, the loss to the oil spill is not devastating," Schimph said. "On the other hand, we know of more dead eagles here than many states have eagles altogether. We've made a mess, and it's going to take a long time to set it right, if we ever can. I expect it will take five years or more for the Prince William Sound eagles to rebound. Of course, the high mortality of this year's young will increase the time needed to repopulate."

The problems and considerations involving the young eagles of Prince William Sound differed from those involving adults. A June survey revealed that most eagle nests had been abandoned. In 118 nests on Knight Island, only eleven eaglets were found alive. Sometimes an adult bird had fallen dead below its nesting tree. There were no young eagles at all on the hardest-hit islands. At the edges of the impact area, more baby eagles had hatched but they were in danger of dying from oil-contaminated food carried to the nest by their parents. In lightly oiled areas, 50 percent of the nests failed to produce young. In heavily oiled areas, more than 80 percent failed.

Before the spill, Prince William Sound had had such a healthy population of bald eagles that the loss of an entire season's young birds might not have undermined it. However, some observers thought the unnecessary death of eaglets should be avoided no matter how large the state's eagle population was. They proposed transferring the young to healthier areas in regions of the country where bald eagles had once been numerous but were now all but gone.

"How can eaglets learn to survive with oil around? Why not get them out of the disaster area, help repopulate other areas?"

asked Al Cecera, president of the National Foundation to Protect America's Eagles. Cecera, who lives in Tennessee, describes himself "as just the average person who loves wildlife. Like a lot of people, I figured government agencies were taking good care of our wild birds and animals, so I could go on about my life." Then one day Cecera read about a bald eagle that had been shot. He asked his state Fish and Wildlife officials about protection programs and was stunned to learn that not only were protection funds for bald eagles scarce, but programs to reintroduce them to states where they once flourished were stalled for lack of money. He noticed individuals and corporations chipping in to restore the Statue of Liberty and thought, "Why not raise some support to help restore our country's living symbol, the bald eagle?"

As soon as he heard that the oil spill was killing eagles and contaminating Prince William Sound, Al Cecera proposed gathering eggs or newborn chicks that might otherwise perish and transporting them to Tennessee, which had received Alaska eagles in the past, wanted more, and had the technical support to handle them. "In my heart of hearts, I knew this was the right thing to do," Cecera said. However, before proceeding, he asked Dr. Pat Redig whether his plan was sound.

"I wholeheartedly endorse your proposal to remove up to 100 eagle chicks and rear them for hacking [transplanting] in states in the south where eagle restoration projects are under way," wrote Dr. Redig, who had surveyed Prince William Sound eagles in mid-May. "I expect that the eagles will continue to select prey washed up on shore which is contaminated by oil, and feed this to their youngsters whose nutritional requirements are very exacting and demanding in the early stages. I would expect high nestling mortality in this environment. Since there is great potential for poisoning of young eagles reared in the sound this year, removal of young eagles may, in fact, save the lives of those removed, and certainly won't adversely impact the population beyond what the oil is doing to them already. And the eagle restoration projects will clearly benefit."

Bolstered by Dr. Redig's encouragement, Cecera turned to Steve Sherrod, director of the Sutton Avian Research Center in Bartlesville, Oklahoma, to implement his plan to save the young

eagles. Over the past fifteen years, Sherrod had pioneered techniques for hatching and raising birds of prey in captivity—for
example, feeding young eaglets with an eagle-shaped puppet to
prevent them from bonding with humans. Later, young eagles
are placed in an isolated tower from which they can fly out, gradually gaining more freedom until they are fending for themselves. Sherrod, who runs the world's largest eagle-hatching and
-rearing facility, was the most qualified person to rescue and
transplant eagles threatened by the spill.

"After talking with Dr. Scott and checking with Dr. Redig, I
contacted Exxon," Sherrod said. "Initially, Exxon hoped we
could remove eggs and hatch them artificially. But we decided
against that. Eaglets are difficult enough to hatch and raise under ideal circumstances." Sherrod proposed, instead, that eaglets be removed from their nests as soon after hatching as possible, because the first few weeks of a young eagle's life are
critical. While adult eagles can eat almost anything, young ones
have very particular nutritional requirements. Most of the
young eagles, whose parents were bringing oiled waterfowl to
the nests, were not expected to survive. Sherrod agreed with
Cecera that capturing the nestlings, rearing them in captivity,
and then releasing them in states where eagles are scarce would
accomplish two objectives—save young eagles from dying and
boost the eagle populations in states where they had been
dwindling.

"It was going to take a lot of work to catch, raise, and release
the eaglets," Sherrod said. "We'd have to charter planes, work
sixteen-hour days in the field, watch the chicks twenty-four
hours a day at the center, and eventually teach the young birds
how to fend for themselves. But that's what we know how to do.
So why not save some eagles and help repopulate other areas at
the same time? Exxon was willing to pay the bills, and Alaska's
governor, who wanted to save as many young eagles as possible,
was all for it.

"But the Fish and Wildlife Service pretty much ignored our
proposal. They didn't want anyone involved in any large transplant of young eagles from Alaska," Sherrod said. "We were
shocked. We thought the Fish and Wildlife Service would be
driven to save birds. We urged them to let us bring some young

eagles to Tennessee, which needs more eagles. Alaskan eagles have gone to Tennessee for years, but now they said it would be a mistake."

"I'm happy that some of the people up there in Alaska would like to send us some young eagles, rather than have them die from contaminated food," said Bob Hatcher, who runs Tennessee's eagle-recovery program. Hatcher said, "We have received eagles from Alaska over the last four years, and we would have liked to have some more. But the Fish and Wildlife Service decided against it. And we have to respect their opinion."

According to Phil Schimph, the Fish and Wildlife Service "felt that most of the mortality had occurred by the time the transplant proposal could have been acted on. We thought that removing production from an impacted area would add insult to injury."

A week after denying the transfer of a large number of endangered young eagles, the Fish and Wildlife Service asked Sherrod if he wanted to capture half a dozen birds in the sound, raise them, and bring them back to Alaska. "Unbelievable!" Sherrod said. "Hundreds of young eagles are dying, and they ask if we want to save six. It costs too much to mount a massive effort for just six birds. And if we did raise some of the Prince William Sound eaglets, it would be unwise to bring them back to contaminated areas. But that's what Fish and Wildlife wanted."

Al Cecera was perplexed. "We were holding the money to transplant young eagles," he said. "I went back to the Fish and Wildlife Service and said, 'Why can't we take a handful for another state? Please give us the opportunity.' We were denied. They just weren't going to allow those eagles out of Alaska. It was their lack of approval that stopped us. I don't understand, but I'm sure some politics were involved."

Political considerations were apparently prompting the Department of Interior to downgrade bald eagles from their endangered status. Dan James, national bald eagle coordinator for the Fish and Wildlife Service, has said, "We are very optimistic about the recovery of bald eagles in America. Recovery is not a return to historic levels. But we know bald eagles are becoming secure by the number of nesting pairs and their distribution. Their productivity and survival rate is improving. We thought it prudent to initiate the process of downgrading the status of bald eagles."

However, many eagle experts disagree. While bald eagles are indeed making a comeback in the Pacific Northwest, the Great Lakes region, and in the vicinity of Chesapeake Bay, they remain scarce in many areas where they were once numerous. In 1988, all three Fish and Wildlife Service regional coordinators for the southeastern states told James it was too early to remove bald eagles from the endangered species list. But according to one observer, James told them that they needed to reconsider. Some biologists heard that the Department of Interior was motivated to downgrade the status of bald eagles because they wanted good environmental news to publicize.

One biologist reported that he was told that eagles were coming off the endangered status list and that he would have to go along with it even though he didn't believe in it. "We are being ordered by a superior to start downlisting a species as part of the political process rather than on the basis of biological information," he said. "Here is something that needs to be said, but please don't quote me as the source. Fish and Wildlife Service permits are necessary to work on raptors. However, these permits can be made very difficult to obtain for those who have openly confronted the agency. It's sad, but sometimes politics seems to have more to do with bald eagle policy than the health of the eagles themselves."

In Alaska, Dr. James Scott was incensed that political considerations could influence the endangered status of bald eagles and, at least indirectly, hamper the rescue of bald eagles threatened by the oil spill. Steve Sherrod's plans to capture and transplant young eagles were never approved, and Scott's eagle rehabilitation center remained almost empty. "What gets you is the bind of being honest," said Scott, who relies on Fish and Wildlife permits to do his medical work with eagles and other raptors. "You are asked to compromise your principles to maintain your ability to continue doing what you've spent your life doing. A society gets into trouble when too many people are afraid to say what they know.

"The professionals think it's poor biology to downgrade the endangered status of bald eagles. Some of these biological experts have thirty years of service on the line. They are at the top of their professions. Their principles are being compromised, but they've got to survive. Yet they know that their heads are going to roll if they speak out. This brings us to an underlying tragedy of this oil spill: while people are afraid to talk, adult eagles are dying unnecessarily out in Prince William Sound. And young eagles, which could have been sent to other states, are dying.

"At first, I expected the Fish and Wildlife people to do everything in their power to protect wildlife, but I came to realize that they have other priorities," Scott concluded. "But they are mandated to take care of wildlife. *That's their job, to perform to the best of their ability.* It's easy enough for them to say, 'Well, we have a whole lot of eagles, so losing a few won't hurt that much.' But eagles died. And a lot of those birds died because of bureaucracy."

Chapter 13

Shorelines

As the wildlife rescue efforts were mounted, oil continued to stream through Prince William Sound and along the outer Kenai coast toward Katmai and Kodiak. The death of otters and birds was only one of many effects of the oil on the coastline, each stretch of which had its own distinct physical characteristics and ecosystems.

"We have all seen the heartbreaking images of dead or dying wildlife. But oil contamination also affects fish and wildlife in other less obvious ways," cautioned Frank Rue, director of habitat for Alaska's Department of Fish and Game.[1] Oil's toxicity lowers organisms' resistance to disease, reduces reproductive success, inhibits normal growth and development, and interrupts normal biochemical processes and behavioral patterns. Long after most of the obvious signs of the spill have disappeared, these subtle, complex effects can prove lethal to animals.

"Beaches are being recontaminated as tides and wind resuspend oil and transport it along sensitive coastal areas," Rue said. "Shoreline cleanup is not an easy task. As time goes by the oil will weather and harden, which means it will be more difficult to remove by high-pressure washing. In places, oil has penetrated 4 feet into beach sediments. It will go deeper, becoming more inaccessible to surface cleaning methods.

"We're in a terrible double bind. We have to remove as much oil as possible. But we can't throw manpower and equipment at it without regard for wildlife and its habitat," Rue continued. "Cleanup techniques must be thoroughly tested to avoid additional mortalities and to avoid rendering habitats unsuitable for repopulation. Cleanup crews must minimize their disturbance of animals."

Wildlife considerations were one of many variables that turned shoreline cleanup efforts into a complex puzzle. The ever-changing conditions along the coastline comprised another set of factors. As the oil thickened from mixing with water, seaweed, and debris, and as its lighter components evaporated, in effect the *Exxon Valdez* oil spill became many spills. The days when Frank Iarossi could concentrate Exxon's efforts on defending the hatcheries were over. Exxon now faced two daunting tasks: recovering the widely scattered oil before it contaminated a variety of shoreline ecosystems, and removing oil that did reach the shore.

To recover oil from the water, Exxon relied primarily on skimmers, such as those inherited from Alyeska that had proved ineffective even under the ideal conditions of the first seventy-two hours. Ironically, in the January before the spill, Alyeska had decided to purchase a $5 million, high-tech, 122-foot-long oil-skimming vessel, but at the time of the spill it was not ready for service. The Norwegian government had large skimming vessels, but since they were on the other side of the world, no one would ever know how much oil such boats might have recovered in Prince William Sound. However, an envoy of Norwegians offered to come to Alaska to share their experience with oil spills in Norway's rocky fjords, which resemble parts of Prince William Sound. The Coast Guard declined their offer. Only after state officials extended an invitation did the Norwegians travel to Valdez to share their expertise. By the time they arrived, it was too late for them to be of much help—the oil was already spreading out of control.

Another offer of assistance came from John Wiechart, manager of Clean Sound Cooperative in the state of Washington. On the first day of the spill, he offered Exxon a 73-foot skimming vessel, the largest of its kind in North America, plus a barge and other equipment that could have reached Valdez in five days. Wiechart said his offer was declined by an Exxon official who indicated Exxon was "putting more reliance on chemical dispersants and burning at the time." Wiechart said that he was puzzled by Exxon's lack of interest in his equipment and personnel. He knew that his cooperative's vessel was not a complete solution to the spill, but said "it certainly would have helped. We're somewhat chagrined because we would at least like to have them inquire about the details."[2] A week later, an Exxon official, acknowledging there had been a lot of confusion, asked for Wiechart's equipment, but by then the oil had spread too far for the skimmer to be very effective.

Another option came from Russia, which offered Exxon the use of the world's largest skimming vessel, the *Vaydaghubsky*, a 435-foot combination harbor dredge/fire-fighting boat/oil skimmer. When the *Exxon Valdez* went aground, this multipurpose vessel was dredging a harbor off the east coast of Siberia, less than a week's voyage from Prince William Sound. The per diem price of the *Vaydaghubsky*, $15,000, struck Iarossi as "surprisingly cheap compared to what we were getting skimmed up with the other units. I guess the Russians didn't catch on to how desperate we were."

Iarossi wanted to charter the *Vaydaghubsky*, but both the Coast Guard and Alaska's Department of Environmental Conservation (DEC) wanted to inspect it first. However, the only quick way for them to get from Anchorage to Russia was to charter a plane—at $90,000. Iarossi protested. "The ship costs only $15,000 per day, so why the hell don't we get it under way and when it gets to Alaska we can take a look at it?"

Complicating the issue even further was a notice sent to Iarossi that U.S. Customs was objecting to a Russian ship entering American waters. Iarossi said, 'Look, get word to the Customs Department that that ship is coming to Prince William Sound. If the customs agents want to stand at the entrance to the sound and say it can't enter, be my guest.'"

On April 19, the *Vaydaghubsky*—flying the flags of both the United States and the Soviet Union—steamed past the snow-covered peaks of Resurrection Bay toward Seward. The vessel's decks were piled with hoses, winches, enormous pulleys, cables, and rope. With an oil-storage capacity of 670,000 gallons and a recovery rate of 200,000 gallons per hour, the Russian ship was designed to be the world's most effective skimmer as well as the world's largest.

"I'm kind of glad the Russian skimmer came over and showed us up," said a high-ranking U.S. Coast Guard officer. "It's an embarrassment. They have a boat like this and we get our budget cut and cut and cut."

The *Vaydaghubsky* might have recovered a significant amount of oil during the first seventy-two hours of calm weather, but by the time it arrived in Prince William Sound, the oil had become heavily emulsified and had broken up into scattered slicks, greatly reducing the Russian skimmer's efficiency. Too big to maneuver in confined waters, the *Vaydaghubsky* was reduced to chasing patches of oil on the open seas and picked up very little.

The best American skimmer may have been Tom Copeland, the Cordova fisherman whose bucket brigade outperformed Alyeska's best mechanical skimmer. If Copeland had had his way, Exxon would have put the fishermen in charge of cleanup. "If Exxon had placed a $5 per gallon bounty on the oil," he asserted, "the fishing fleet would have collected 75 percent of it. We have 100 fish pumps capable of pumping a 10-inch column of oil and filling a 40-thousand-gallon tank in three minutes. Our tender boats have the capacity to store 10 million gallons of oil—they could have done that right away, from day one. Hell, we pump 10 million gallons of fish and sea water every day during the season. All we needed was some boom, and it would've been child's play. But they told us to stay the hell out of the way."

Exxon's extended shoreline cleanup program began on April 4. That morning, at 5:30 A.M. Australian time, Otto Harrison, then managing production for Exxon-affiliated Esso, received a phone call from Exxon. "They asked would I come to Alaska, and I said, 'Yes.' I did my income taxes that night and flew out the next day," Harrison recalled. "They didn't tell me how they selected me. It's got me beat. They haven't told me since."[3]

When Harrison arrived in Alaska, Coast Guard Admiral Edward Nelson and Frank Iarossi were trying to rescue the spill response from the morass of indecision and committee meetings. To that end, the two discussed investing the Coast Guard with authority to direct the cleanup. "We had an agreement drawn up and we were going to sign it," Nelson said. "At this point Frank thought he was going to be relieved, so he and I hashed out [the agreement] until we were pretty happy with it.

We were ready to sign the thing, but then these other guys from Exxon came in. Otto Harrison looked at [the agreement] and went running into another room. When he came back, he wanted to change a word here, a little bit there. I thought they were petty, but I said, 'Let them slide. Let's do something. We need to formalize it. Let's do it.'"

By this time, Ulysses LeGrange, senior vice president of Exxon U.S.A. and Iarossi's boss, had flown to Valdez, and he too reviewed the agreement. Remarked Admiral Nelson, "That's when I saw why the little people worry about the big companies closing you off. They were playing a game with me. As mixed up as things were, I couldn't get this doggone agreement from LeGrange. He was checking with his attorneys to see if they had any objections to the way it was worded. They were playing Mickey Mouse. LeGrange said their attorneys back there on the East Coast had to make sure they approved of the Coast Guard and Exxon working together. They were clearly playing games.

"I never lost my respect for Frank Iarossi, who did a marvelous job under an extreme amount of pressure," Admiral Nelson continued. "He stayed with that doggone ship and kept the other million barrels of oil from getting in the water. I thought moving that ship without spilling more oil was a rather remarkable feat. My problem was that I didn't think Exxon was bringing in the right people to run this thing. There was no coherent direction. It was an absolute zoo."

In April, Admiral Nelson survived an apparently stress-induced heart attack and retired from active military service. It was then that Coast Guard Admiral Paul Yost came to Valdez to hammer out the first of many cleanup agreements and designated Vice Admiral Clyde E. Robbins the on-scene coordinator. And it was then, after the lightering and refloating of the *Exxon Valdez*, that Frank Iarossi was sent back to Houston. "I felt bad about leaving," Iarossi said. "I had become so emotionally involved. I didn't want to walk away because the job wasn't finished and we were just starting some cooperative efforts." This changing of the guard was reportedly to give Iarossi relief from the high-stress situation and time to prepare for hearings about the spill. However, Exxon may have made the change in order to bring in someone who had not experienced the painful early days of the spill and who would, therefore, be less emotionally committed and more disposed to take a tough company stand during the long, liability-laden cleanup that lay ahead.

When Iarossi left Alaska in mid-April, Otto Harrison settled into his job of directing Exxon's cleanup. In his Valdez office Harrison, a large man, sat behind a desk strewn with field reports and several half-empty bottles of Tabasco and hot picante sauce. On one wall hung a clock in the shape of Texas. Harrison had been raised 30 miles southeast of Houston and had attended the University of Texas. He spoke with a good-old-boy Texas drawl in a manner that suggested he could play his cards close to the vest. He had been with Exxon for thirty years.

Two things struck Harrison when he took charge of the cleanup—the extent of the spill and the anger surrounding it. "I was surprised at the animosity. It made the committee system very difficult, and it soaked up a large amount of time and energy of all parties involved."

By April 14, three weeks after the spill, the Coast Guard had approved Exxon's initial cleanup plan. However, as oil spread through the sound from beach to beach, down the Kenai Peninsula and toward Kodiak and Katmai National Park, the task at hand grew more and more complex and larger in scope. As would happen time and again, the spill itself was rendering Exxon's cleanup plan obsolete, and Harrison found himself continually revising to catch up.

Exxon's first step in executing the plan was to dispatch a Shoreline Cleanup Assessment Team (SCAT). There were two members of this original SCAT team: an archaeologist and a biologist. According to plan, they landed on Naked Island three hours before the first cleanup crews and hurriedly divided the beach into segments, noting significant amounts of oil. Then they developed cleaning guidelines based on their observations for the cleanup crews. The SCAT team's improvised but systematic approach was to become the prototype for Exxon's cleanup effort. As one of the members said, "We didn't realize it at the time, but SCAT would become the driving force of the cleanup."

Exxon added a geomorphologist to the SCAT team model and eventually contracted enough professionals to form seven teams of three. As the elaborate system of surveys, recommendations, and procedures that was Exxon's approach to cleanup evolved, the SCAT team's field findings were no longer passed directly on to crews on the beaches. Instead, they were sent to Exxon's Valdez command center, where they were shaped into recommendations. These, in turn, were passed to interagency shoreline cleanup committees in Seward and Homer. These multiagency committees (MACs)—composed of representatives from such agencies as DEC, state parks, and the U.S. Forest Service—reviewed and modified the site-specific recommendations and passed them on to the Coast Guard. After Coast Guard review, the recommendations were returned to Exxon as approved plans of action. The review process that Iarossi and Nelson had conceived of had evolved into this complicated loop.

By the end of April, all of Exxon's crews and equipment had cleaned less than two miles of beach. A revised cleanup plan issued on May 8 called for the cleaning of 364 miles of shoreline. In this new plan, four types of oil-affected shorelines were assigned priorities on the basis of urgency. Beaches given first priority were those on five islands where seals were about to give birth to their pups. Ranked second were 85 miles of "heavily oiled" shoreline—there pools of thick, sludgy oil were sloshing back and forth and reoiling the beaches with every change of the tide. Third in line was the cleanup of 85 miles of shoreline that had been "moderately" affected. The fourth priority was 191 miles of "lightly oiled" shoreline. Not included in the plan were beaches marked with a bathtub ring of oil 3 feet wide or less; they were considered clean.

Tension developed between Harrison and DEC over Exxon's objective "to environmentally stabilize" beaches rather than actually clean them. Harrison clarified the goal: "We are not removing all the oil, but removing enough so the environment can stabilize and restore itself. We want to leave the beaches not damaging to wildlife." He glanced at an oil-coated stone sitting in his office: "While that rock doesn't look good, the fact is that [its oil] isn't going to rub off on anything."

DEC continued to argue for a more thorough cleanup. Meanwhile Exxon worked with the Coast Guard to refine and update the May 8 cleanup plan that called for surface treatment of beaches only. Exxon U.S.A. president Bill Stevens said, "Specific milestones have been set for shoreline cleanup, which has commenced and is expected to be completed by mid-September."[4] By June, a revision of the May 8 plan expanded the cleanup to more than 700 miles of shoreline, a significant increase over the 364 miles covered initially. The new plan divided the spill into sectors: Valdez-Cordova, Seward, Homer, and Kodiak.

The oil's path now extended over more than 10,000 square miles, an area so large that flying around it in a small plane would take all day and crossing it in a skiff would take several days. Coast Guard Vice Admiral Robbins later testified as to the spill's size. "Seeing the fouled beaches and the devastating effect on wildlife removes any doubt of the severity of this spill." He explained that "during daily operations the Coast Guard was itself deploying seven major vessels, more than twenty aircraft, a variety of small support vessels, and more than 1,000 personnel." In addition, Robbins stated, Exxon had "deployed approximately 70 miles of boom, 55 skimmers, 460 support vessels, and over 3,000 personnel."[5]

In accordance with its revised plan, Exxon delegated much of the shoreline cleaning to VECO, a private contractor that had served the oil industry in Alaska for years and had earned a reputation for fighting environmental regulations. In fact, while Alaskans reeled from the initial shock of the spill, VECO president Pete Lethard urged state legislators against passing tougher environmental laws. Such laws, he said, would "do nothing but eliminate the industry upon which this state depends. . . . We mustn't throw the baby out with the dirty bath water."[6]

"VECO is basically a construction outfit servicing the oil and gas industry," said Bill Luria, a former planning director for the city of Anchorage who helped VECO organize an environmental monitoring program to guide their cleanup efforts. "That's how they got rich and famous." Now VECO was running an intensive, high-tech cleanup along hundreds of miles of the nation's most remote and ecologically rich shoreline. "They're having to deal with sensitive environmental situations that they had never considered before," Luria said. "What do you do with oily waste? Do you incinerate it? How do you store the dead birds and debris? How do you keep thousands of laborers from messing up eagle nests, spawning streams, estuaries, and tidal pools?"

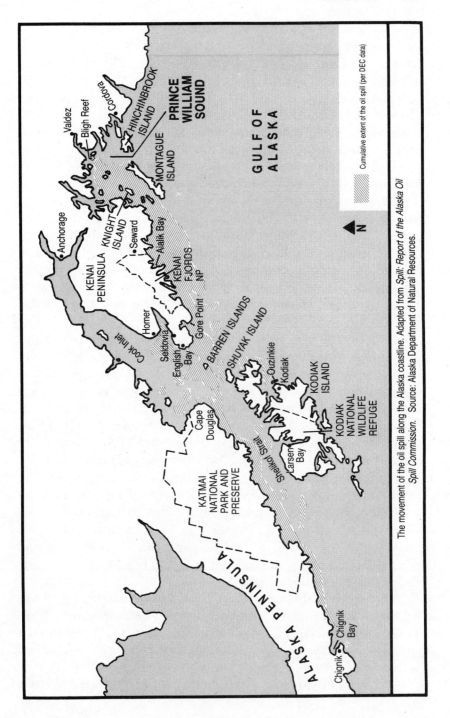

The movement of the oil spill along the Alaska coastline. Adapted from *Spill: Report of the Alaska Oil Spill Commission.* Source: Alaska Department of Natural Resources.

"It's a zoo. Of course it is," said a manager for VECO, who asked not to be identified. "This is a cattle operation: round up some workers, load 'em up, ship 'em out. We make up the rules as we go. Nothing like this has been done before."

VECO drew its workers from a core of transient laborers, out-of-work plumbers and carpenters, secretaries, college students, housewives, and people from small Native villages. After running recruits through a two-hour safety course, VECO dispatched workers to scrub oil from rocks with large paper towels, hose down cliffs with high-pressure nozzles, rake beaches, or bag dead animals and debris. Crews worked from a flotilla of skiffs, fishing boats, yachts, and Coast Guard clippers—even an old navy warship. Choppers and float planes carrying supplies droned through the long daylight hours. In effect, VECO had created an instant community of makeshift camps that moved from cove to cove and island to island, along waterways where once the calls of whales and seabirds were the only sounds to be heard.

"We were there to be on-site advisors," said Bill Luria of the participants in the environmental monitoring program he helped create for VECO. "It was our job to say, 'You know this is against the regs,' or 'Do it this way,' or 'Hey, you're screwing up here, how about doing it this way?'

"We hired about eighteen pretty good people [for the monitoring role]. They were biologists, science types, technically trained people," Luria said. "And when they got into the field, they saw a lot of things happen that just weren't right. For example, one day our people saw VECO crews using diesel fuel to wash the rocks. Sure, diesel is a solvent, but it's mighty toxic too. Our field people were telling the VECO supervisors, 'Hey, this ain't right, so don't do it.' And VECO got ticked off. They didn't want to hear any bad news. They began telling our field people to just document the good stuff.

"We tried to help them. We'd say, 'Hey, you need a permit to build this incinerating facility in Valdez.' Then they'd say, 'Naw. We're going to claim this spill is an emergency and just push it through. We don't have to worry about those permits.' They were trying to find the shortcuts.

"The VECO supervisors really didn't like our science types

working for them. They wanted to review everything our people wrote down to make sure that nothing bad was recorded. If something looked bad on one of our reports, they'd say, 'You can't put that in. Give me that piece of paper.' They'd have one of their fellow VECO employees submit the information they wanted. We either had to put down what they wanted us to say or get canned. They fired fifteen people, including myself, in one day. Essentially, VECO made the decision to can the whole environmental monitoring program.

"I don't mean to downplay the massive logistical problem that Exxon and VECO faced, because it was staggering. Exxon couldn't have done it by themselves. VECO has a good capability to manage laborers and deal with hassles, but it could have been done in a spirit of cooperation with the other players. They had a choice—people in regulatory agencies, like DEC, were desperately seeking to work closely with them. I think industry made a conscious decision to do it their way, identifying agency people as the enemy. VECO was more concerned about liability and a show of getting something done than about really cleaning up those beaches."

One VECO beach worker reported that "I found oiled birds while I was cleaning up the beach, and my supervisor told me to hide them in oil bags—that Exxon did not need the publicity."

In another incident, journalists on a public relations tour were impressed with the appearance of a beach that had been "cleaned." The rocks looked clean until Marvin Fox, Jr., a young Native man working for VECO, pushed the nozzle of his pressurized hose a foot into the gravel. Oil gurgled up.

"After those reporters left, a VECO foreman shoved the kid," said Bill Barnes, Fox's uncle. "They grabbed him, twisted his arm, and said, 'What the hell do you think you're doing? We don't need this kind of crap around here. You're fired!'

"What they're doing makes me sick," Barnes continued. "They mess up our homeland and then treat us like a bunch of animals. I quit. They can keep their instant potato money."

Here again, consequences of the convoluted chain of authority were unfolding. Because the government maintained its stance as monitor only, the cleaning of hundreds of miles of sensitive, pristine shoreline had been delegated to a company that showed gross disregard for both the local people and the environment, as myriad horror stories brought back from the beaches confirmed. The chilling fact was that the national response system was rooted in failure: the government was to intervene only if a spiller failed. This policy had lulled the government into relying on an industry that staunchly proclaimed preparedness but was in fact utterly *un*prepared to respond to a spill of this size. Now the federal government was allowing the spiller's failure to play itself out, which meant allowing VECO to attack the shoreline no matter how inadequate its actions or how atrocious its attitudes. As with other aspects of the spill response, neither the state nor the Coast Guard stepped out of its passive, watchdog role to assert authority and direct Exxon's shoreline cleanup.

"As far as actual authority over the cleanup, I have none, unless I take over the spill," Coast Guard Vice Admiral Clyde E. Robbins reiterated. "My only hope is to get Exxon to do what I want to get done through jawboning and coercion."[7]

Even so, Vice Admiral Robbins, representing the Coast Guard, which in turn represented the federal government, had his hands full. He became the mediator between Exxon and the state of Alaska, which began disagreeing on almost everything, from which beaches needed cleaning to which cleanup methods would be used. "The admiral is like Daddy," observed a DEC spokesman in Valdez. "We're always running to Daddy saying, 'Tell Exxon not to do that anymore.' Exxon is always running to Daddy and saying, 'Tell DEC to leave us alone.'" Still, Commissioner Kelso argued that Exxon did not have to listen to anyone's advice or directions. In the future, he remarked, "We have to make sure that the spiller is not in charge of deciding how much work to do, how long to do it, or even how to do it."

A VECO supervisor, who asked not to be identified, agreed. "Exxon is trying to save its image," he said, and "VECO is reaching for a piece of the pie. What we really need is a professional oil spill cleanup company, like a fire department that's on twenty-four-hour call. We need an independent strike force on call to take care of disasters like this."

There was nothing new about this idea. Such crisis-cleanup teams are in place to respond to spills in other countries. "There is not one man from the oil companies on our response teams," said Ranier Leo, managing director of Leo Consult, a large pollution control company in West Germany. After the wreck of the *Exxon Valdez*, Leo flew to Alaska at his own expense to offer assistance. "We always thought the best technology came from the United States. But on television we saw pictures from Alaska and we were astonished. We saw people wiping rocks with absorbent pads. Each rock. Unbelievable."

Leo explained that "the *Amoco Cadiz* spill off the coast of France initiated us into getting oil spill equipment and developing response plans. We learned that you can't leave it to the oil companies to do their own cleanup. To save money they will always say, 'Things are fine.' To have an oil company in charge of cleaning up a spill is like calling the fox back in to take care of the mess he's made in the hen house. Here, the government pays highly trained crews to be on twenty-four-hour alert. They are prepared. That's their job. It's simple. And it works. When it's all over, the bill is sent to the oil company that caused the spill."

While debates regarding authority and procedures raged on, Exxon continued to spend money on shoreline cleanup with continually diminishing returns. One unexpected source of potential help arrived in the form of oil-eating bacteria.

Oceanographers at Alaska's Institute of Marine Science found an abundance of oil-eating microbes in Prince William Sound. The possibility arose that the microorganisms' consumption of oil could serve the cleanup effort, in a process termed bioremediation. However, in normal circumstances, these bacteria feed on complex hydrocarbons emitted in small doses by forests, and it was by no means clear that they would forego their natural food to consume North Slope crude. After the spill, the federal Environmental Protection Agency committed $5 million to assess the oil-eating ability of the indigenous bacteria. "It's natural. It's promising. It's based on good, sound science," said EPA administrator William Reilly of the bacterial cleaning process. "They are native Alaskan bugs. It's all local hire."[8]

EPA researchers found that oil-eating microbes run short of phosphorus and nitrogen, so, on the EPA's recommendation, Exxon ordered a dietary supplement for the microbes: 500 metric tons of fertilizer from France. Exxon's plan was to fertilize up to 700 miles of Alaskan beaches to encourage the bacteria to eat their way through the oil. However, some scientists questioned the effectiveness of the fertilizer. Remarked Dr. Jacqueline Michel, of the National Oceanographic and Atmospheric Administration, "It's funny. The EPA folks are trying real hard to show that they are improving the bioremediation process, but we're finding very little difference between where they've used fertilizer and where they haven't."

Reilly admitted that the EPA had to take some blame for being unprepared. "The country became complacent," he said. "Over the past several years, our priorities have been directed to some other problems. The response technology for these spills is primitive. We are all learning from this spill. I hope we are learning the right lessons."

One well-known ecological lesson was apparently being overlooked in this rush to stimulate microbes with fertilizer: change in one part of an ecosystem can have unpredictable, far-ranging effects elsewhere. Dr. John Farrington, a widely respected oil pollution expert, cautioned that "microorganisms have a community structure of their own, a sort of mini-ecosystem within an ecosystem. Many components of this microorganism community have essential functions to play in cycles that support the food web in Prince William Sound. If we overstimulate certain parts of this web, we may not only break down oil, which would be a good thing, but we may also stimulate some parts of the microbial population more than others—including some that are not breaking down oil, but doing something else within the complex ecosystem. So, while I favor people doing experiments, a great deal of care has to be exercised."

While Dr. Farrington warned of possible ecological consequences of using fertilizer, Lynette Clark of Fairbanks, Alaska, worried about its effect on people. Clark worked with a bioremediation team and had not been warned of any potential risks of handling the fertilizer. But she became alarmed when some of her coworkers began urinating blood. "Our team members were tested for blood in their urine," she said. "I'm concerned about kidney and liver damage down the road for some of these eighteen- and nineteen-year-old kids who were using this stuff."[9] It was confirmed that the toxic fertilizer could be absorbed through the skin and cause red blood cells to break apart, which released hemoglobin that was excreted in the urine. VECO advised workers that they did not have to work near freshly treated areas. No one knew how many small beach organisms the fertilizer would kill.

No one was certain, either, how effectively the fertilized bioremediation process would clean the shorelines. At best, the oil-eating microbes would break down the oil into a less harmful substance. However, on the beaches themselves, while the bacteria devoured some types of oil, they shunned most tar balls and the asphaltlike substance that had begun hardening on beach rocks. Dr. Michel explained that the microbes "eat the easy stuff first, leaving the asphalt and waxes, the black residue that's going to stay behind." Nevertheless, Exxon continued to view bioremediation as one of its most promising means of dislodging the oil and continued to spread great quantities of fertilizer.

The search for effective beach-cleaning techniques escalated throughout the summer. Independent chemists and inventors arrived in Alaska touting everything from oil-absorbing duck feathers to one-of-a-kind oil-scooping machines. "We've encouraged Exxon to try some of the alternatives that are available," Dennis Kelso said. "Fishermen in Homer, for example, have designed a rock-washing machine. It probably needs a little work to make it as effective as possible, but it's the kind of thing that ought to be tried. People in Kodiak are using geotextile fabric to seine up mousse and tar balls before they hit the shoreline. They'd like to have Exxon work with them to get that going. Those are the kinds of lower-tech, lower-intensity efforts that show some promise, and we ought to be using as many of those alternatives as possible, rather than just the large crews and large vessels."[10]

Low-tech options seemed a wise choice—and soon rather than later. Some feared that Exxon's high-pressure hoses and its army of workers invading the oiled shorelines were causing as much damage as the oil. In mid-July, Congressman Wayne Owens from Utah visited Alaska to see for himself whether beach cleanup might actually be counterproductive. At a May 6 congressional field hearing in Valdez, Owens had heard rumors that Exxon's heavy equipment was doing more harm than good. He decided to return to Alaska in July, slipping in unannounced—no advance warning, no press conferences. For a guide and boatman he chose Kelly Weaverling.

"We had a wonderful time out there together," Weaverling said. "He's a politician, so he's somewhat suspect, you know. A lot of them are junketeers. They don't really listen. They just want to appear on the scene, get a little mileage out of it. But Owens was genuinely concerned.

"So we went out and poked around. Surprised a few people," Weaverling recalled. "Here's Owens—clean shaven, wears glasses, short hair, dressed like a fisherman. A pretty average-looking guy. No one knew who he was. Some of those VECO bosses probably thought he was a rock scrubber goofin' off.

"We'd mosey up to a beach-cleaning crew and watch them blasting everything from barnacles to limpets with jets of water," Weaverling said. "Owens started seeing some of the things I'd already found on the beaches—graffiti scratched on rocks, orange peels, watermelon rinds, cigarette butts, oily gloves. On the beach at one little bay were thirteen smudge pits, where people had made fires above the high-tide line. We found burned pop cans and half-burned logs, discarded rain gear and sunglasses. And there were smooshed-down areas with toilet paper in the woods above the beach.

"I think Owens began to realize that there was no sensitivity involved in what VECO was doing out there. It's overkill to the max. Hundreds of people on a beach. High-power hydraulics, boats, and helicopters everywhere. That's going to bother wildlife."

At some camps, Weaverling and Owens found barges equipped with giant hot-water boilers and flexible boom normally used for pumping concrete. On the most high-tech barges, called Omni-booms, six oil-fired burners heated 100 gallons of 40-degree seawater to 160 degrees in one minute. The steaming water was then shot at oil-covered rocks from nozzles at a pressure of 80 pounds per square inch. Barring mechanical failure, the hot-water blasters worked around the clock. The blasting did dislodge oil, but, as critics pointed out, it also exterminated virtually all the living organisms it struck.

In a single day, Exxon's shoreline cleaning equipment, much

of which had been designed from scratch or modified on site, could process 200 million gallons of water, an amount equivalent to the daily needs of a city of one million people. At work on the shoreline were fourteen Omni-boom barges for spraying hot water, irrigation systems for flushing cold water over beaches, and fireboat nozzles mounted on barges for spraying inaccessible rock faces. With approximately 1,000 heaters putting out up to 7 million BTUs per hour, Exxon could wash the shorelines with nearly 17 million gallons of warm water per day. At peak activity, there were about 11,000 people working on the spill, with about 3,500 deployed on the beaches.[11]

By the first of August, Exxon's Otto Harrison proudly spoke of the accomplishments of this widescale effort—700 miles of shoreline treated and 16,000 tons of oily debris collected, with more coming in at a rate of 2,000 tons per week. However, critics were quick to point out that the term *treated* did not mean clean. Oil remained on the surface of Prince William Sound beaches, and subsurface oil had not been dealt with at all.

"It's going to take time. You can't do it in a hurry," Kelly Weaverling explained to Congressman Owens. "You can't move rock walls. And those are the places you want to use hot water, to lower the oil's viscosity, loosen it up, and skim it. But hot-water blasting doesn't work on most beaches. We need to remember that every beach is a little bit different. We can't clean these shorelines with zillions of people and billions of dollars. Instead of a lot of high technology, we need low-impact methods. More than anything, we need a lot of sensitivity."

When he returned to Washington, D.C., Congressman Owens, now clad in a suit and tie, peered down from an elevated podium and spoke to Bill Stevens, president of Exxon U.S.A. "I am one who believes that much of your high-tech operation is doing more damage than good," Owens said. "In Northwest Bay on Eleanor Island, where I visited ten days ago, you have 400 to 500 people in thirty-five to forty-five vessels. Unannounced, I talked to your foreman there, after having reviewed a lot of what's going on with all of those high-pressure, 160-degree water hoses, and after seeing all those boats plying that beautiful pristine—previously pristine—harbor. And I said to him, 'How much oil are you collecting here with this massive operation?'[12]

"His answer was seven barrels of oil a day," Owens said. "I can't imagine that the [impact] of 400 to 500 people . . . can be offset by the seven barrels of oil that's being recovered. It's the high-tech part of what you're doing up there that bothers me.

"Just north of there, your foreman showed me how hand implements really work much better than those big supersuckers. He was using a hand rake with a piece of screen on it to lift oil. He was lifting it up and putting it in a bucket, while this super machine with its twenty-five disks was getting nothing. I am convinced, quite frankly, that those operations, though well intended—and intended as a palliative to the Congress, which last spring said you've got to do whatever you can—are not working. It's not getting the job done. And it's doing more damage than good.

"I'd like to see somebody go into Snug Harbor, where I picked up an eagle feather in a pool of oil that had not yet been treated. I'd like to see a couple of people go in, in a shallow draft boat with three buckets and one of these jerry-built devices I was talking about, and very quietly clean up those horrible pools of oil. I'm afraid you're going to send a multimillion-dollar operation in. And I'm afraid it's going to do more damage than good."

Dr. Michel agreed with Congressman Owens's conclusion that much of the highly mechanized cleanup was causing more harm than good. "NOAA's study of the Omni-boom's hot-water washing showed that not only was there a 90-percent reduction in living organisms in places where cleanup crews washed, but below, in the subtidal area, there was also a 90-percent reduction, because of oil flowing down with the hot water," said Michel. "Concentrations of oil in the lower intertidal zone jumped up by two orders of magnitude after treatment. The fact is, we see death and destruction at all the treatment sites and we see much less in places that haven't been treated. We have killed a lot of organisms by blasting with hot water."

While debate on methods ensued, VECO cleanup teams spread out over dozens of beaches, trying to pry loose oil that had stuck like freshly laid asphalt to beach rocks. Time and the weather were having their own effects on the oil, adding another level of complexity to the problem. As the oil weathered, it became thick, tarry, and, when the weather cooled, tacky to the touch. Warmed by the sun, it would soften and become stickier.

Oil penetrating the beach surface remained fluid longer, and it drained down between rocks and permeated the fine sands. Oil in this form might leach into the marine environment for years. There appeared to be only one way to remove oil from beach substrata: to wash every cobble and nubbin of gravel, every grain of sand.

Though the objective was simple—clean the beaches—diverse aspects attracted specialized attention and yielded their own hotly argued controversies. While thousands of VECO workers and billions of bacteria worked on the spill, for example, chemists at Exxon Research and Engineering in New Jersey were trying to develop a chemical that would loosen the oil's grip on rocks. They came up with a kerosene-based substance called Corexit, and the chemical immediately became the focus of controversy, caught between Exxon's desire to apply it and the state's concern over pouring tons of a new, untested, and potentially toxic compound on Alaska's shorelines.

"Exxon proved without a doubt that Corexit has little to no toxicity," said Dr. Michel, adding that the state, which had to approve the use of this new chemical on Alaska's shorelines, "was so terrified to use Corexit that they required tremendous, I mean *outrageous*, amounts of toxicity testing and delay. They really didn't want Exxon to use Corexit, because, if it caused more damage, responsibility would have fallen on the state.

"DEC has been tremendously overzealous," Dr. Michel continued. "I think they've been counterproductive. They've been part of the problem and not part of the solution from the very beginning. DEC represents the state, which is suing Exxon. As far as I'm concerned, the state's damage assessment for litigation has totally screwed up the spill response. I do a lot of oil spill damage assessment, and I've never seen so many problems. Everybody is trying to figure out how much money they can get, rather than trying to solve the problem."

Commissioner Kelso responded, "Of course we wanted Corexit to work. Everybody wanted there to be magic. Exxon is trying to put up a litigation smokescreen. They read the *Amoco Cadiz* litigation, in which Amoco was able to escape much of its liability by claiming that the French government had refused to let them use dispersants. So Exxon wants to do the same thing, at every turn. In the case of Corexit, Exxon wanted to use an untested chemical that had never been used in this kind of setting. It doesn't make much sense to me to approve the use of a chemical unless it meets two criteria—it needs to be effective, and it needs to be safe. Given the emergency, we said, 'If you do what you propose, and give us toxicity data that looks safe, then we'll authorize trial applications as long as the monitoring goes on.' Of course, they didn't like that. Carte blanche is what they really wanted."

Another point of contention between DEC and Exxon was the incineration of tons of oily wastes. Exxon sought emergency permits to burn in excess of normal air quality standards while Kelso refused to compromise the standards, forcing Exxon to ship thousands of tons of oily debris to designated waste disposal sites outside of Alaska. Exxon complained that by insisting on the standards the state was hindering the cleanup. "I think it's unfortunate that, to a large extent, DEC elected to take a somewhat adversarial role," Otto Harrison commented later. "DEC manages on an adversarial basis. They made things difficult."

Kelso called Exxon's complaints over delays in incineration permits an "absolutely bogus argument."

However, a DEC official involved with the cleanup said, "DEC kind of led on Exxon. At the outset, many of our field people favored doing what's practical—let Exxon burn the waste. Others, who eventually won out, said, 'Let's sock it to 'em. Apply the air quality laws 100 percent. Let them deal with the problem.' No one had thought through how we should enforce our normal regulations in a crisis. So, with all the media attention focused on us, some of our people feared any waiver of standards would be seen as going soft. DEC was trying to preserve its image, but it actually slowed down the cleanup.

"After a while, a lot of us got fed up and didn't want to go back to the confusion in Valdez," the official continued. "DEC was thrust into an arena where we had no expertise. We didn't know how to clean beaches, so we kept waiting for Exxon to come up with the magic bullet. After helping to save the hatcheries, DEC lost its focus. It retreated into a legalistic shell and an adversarial role."

According to Alaska oil spill coordinator Dr. Robert Le-Resche, "Kelso could have cooperated more, if his decision had been that getting the oil cleaned up was more important than having hearings. There are a lot of strict state laws with wiggle room in them, and the commissioner can make a finding that it's in the state's interest to run a permit through and grant it today rather than a month later. But if he did that, his strongest constituency [conservationists] would have come down all over him. I tried to explain it to Exxon. I said, 'Look, if Kelso does everything you want, then he's going to be sued by these guys. He's got to walk down the middle.'"

Permits for incineration, bioremediation, and Corexit all remained points of contention as the state and Exxon fought each other for moral high ground in the press and for billions of dollars in court. The protagonists, entrenched with their lawyers and press agents, became increasingly isolated from each other. The result in many instances was that the battles took precedence over the problem. Too often the oil cleanup effort appeared to be driven more by legal and public relations strategies than by scientific considerations. And the common goal of restoring the coastal environment frequently seemed to get lost in the shuffle.

Vice President Dan Quayle's brief visit to Prince William Sound was typical of what Associated Press writer Paul Jenkins described as Exxon's "daily dog and pony show." Quayle helicoptered onto Smith Island's north shore, where he observed hundreds of Exxon workers flushing thick crude from the beach. Quayle walked the beach on a boardwalk (hastily constructed so he wouldn't slip in the oil), sprayed oil-coated rocks for a few minutes, and then left for a press conference, where he said, "I have a very good feel for what's going on."

Two days later, Paul Jenkins inspected the same beach and found it empty, but still covered with oil. The army of Exxon cleanup workers had vanished without informing either the state or the Coast Guard. "Smith Island's north beach remained blighted by oil," Jenkins reported. "All that was left of the cleanup effort were some booms and stacks of orange plastic garbage bags. An oily sheen floated on the water. That very day,

Exxon's public relations people in Valdez insisted that the cleanup workers were still working this beach."

In another incident, scores of workers were helicoptered to a remote beach on the Kenai Peninsula two hours before a USA Today television crew arrived to film beach cleaning. When asked if this was a made-for-TV cleanup episode, Exxon representative Dean Peeler said, "A planned media event? No way." But within an hour of the time the television crew left, three helicopter flights swooped off ten to twelve workers at a time, and another four left by skiff. Said one of the cleanup workers who had been shuttled to and from the beach, "Exxon was definitely putting on a show."[13]

Many involved in the spill response can recall when they first sensed that good press and damage-assessment dollars were becoming more important than actually cleaning the beaches. For Admiral Nelson, who had been dealing one-on-one with Frank Iarossi, whom he trusted, that moment came when he saw that every suggestion, every move, would have to be processed through a firm of faceless, liability-conscious attorneys thousands of miles away.

For Bob LeResche the spirit of cooperation deteriorated as soon as that first storm came howling down from the Chugach Mountains. He said, "After oil hit the beaches, everybody had a chance to kind of get the lay of the land as to how he personally was going to come out of this—that's when everything started to break down. And once this happened, there was no longer any morality in the conventional, old-time sense. The morality that began guiding everybody's actions was defined by liability laws and the bottom line. Shouldn't Exxon fully admit their environmental abuses? Well, no, because, if they did, it would cost billions and they might lose the company. Shouldn't we just admit that there weren't enough DEC guys around? No, because then the state wouldn't collect billions in damages. This mentality ruins everyone ultimately. It's too bad. But I think this is a fact of life in the late twentieth century."

LeResche made an effort to have all three parties sit down together and discuss the issues. "We need to talk about this like big boys and make some deals," he said. "It's a lot harder to hate a guy you're talking directly to. The closer people stand together, whether on a beach or in an office, the more responsive they are." However, the litigious roles became ever more entrenched as Exxon wiped and scrubbed and skimmed its way toward September. One Exxon official, a key cleanup strategist who asked not to be identified, acknowledged that for Exxon "the actual recovery of oil and the money spent became secondary to its public image aspects. The squeakiest wheels, the places where people had the most clout, were where beaches got cleaned, regardless of the amount of oil."

This official said that, by early June, Exxon felt the cleanup had "hit a point of diminishing returns. But quitting was not politically acceptable. Cleaning may have been causing more destruction than leaving the oil. But any time Exxon voiced that, DEC would say, 'Oh, Exxon is just trying to get out of their responsibility.' Sometimes the truth is not publicly acceptable."

This perception of the truth was also fraught with a disturbing irony. If, as Dr. Michel and others would attest, Exxon was continuing with cleanup methods that were counterproductive, then it was paying hundreds of millions of dollars to enhance its environmental image by being environmentally destructive—and all of this to please DEC and environmentalists. In any event, if Exxon believed that the shoreline cleanup was mostly for show, its interest in exploring a variety of innovative techniques may well have been dulled. Using these techniques might have resulted in significantly cleaner shorelines.

Said Dr. Michel, "As far as we were concerned, Exxon was not being very creative. They were interested in Corexit, bioremediation, and washing the beach. We had a list of ten or fifteen techniques that we wanted them to start using and have in their tool box. But they didn't really want to screw around with anything else."

That Exxon refused to try every cleaning possibility overlaid the irony with a sense of tragedy. The fact was that the magnitude and complexity of the spill doomed Exxon's handful of techniques to certain failure. In the course of the cleanup, methods became very site specific: what worked in one place wouldn't work elsewhere. With the oil moving, weathering, and changing consistency, cleanup efforts became time specific as well: what worked one day wouldn't on another. In retrospect, the entire cleanup can be viewed as a series of windows of opportunity that were open for a while but then closed. The first seventy-two hours had presented opportunities for skimming, burning, and dispersants. Later, there were chances to catch oil before it spread to new areas or sank into beach substratas. With every passing day, more windows closed, cutting off opportunities for safe and successful beach cleaning.

Among the lost opportunities were pools of oil that lingered on a number of beaches and just offshore through May and June. "When we did the surface washing, we knew we weren't getting the subsurface oil, so the remaining pools of oil were a big concern," said Dr. Michel. "By not getting the pooled oil in time, it was going to soak in deeper. Exxon had these supersuckers that were not being used, except occasionally to unload skimmers. So I told them, 'Where in hell are those supersuckers? I want you to go out there and start picking up that oil.'"

The following week, Dr. Michel returned to the areas of pooled oil. "I couldn't find any pooled oil anymore. It was all soaked in by that time. With the sun beating on it, the oil had soaked into the beach where we couldn't get at it."

By the September 15 deadline, Exxon's SCAT teams had surveyed more than 3,500 miles of coastline. The oiled areas had been broken into 1,100 segments, and all of these, after interagency and Coast Guard review had taken place, were deemed "treated." Exxon had spent well over $1 billion to treat 700 miles of beach, but there was no consensus on the results.

"Yes, there are still some shorelines that have some oil on them. You can find rocks that are tacky. But I find the progress very remarkable," said Exxon's Bill Stevens. "However much we've sought to mitigate the impact and deal responsibly with the cleanup, we know that in the eyes of some, our efforts have been lacking. But we've been here, we've done our best. We did not run and hide."[14]

However, neither Stevens nor anyone else at Exxon would commit to further cleanup work in the spring. They said they would wait to see what the beaches looked like and to hear what the Coast Guard had to say. Exxon's commitment to complete the shoreline cleanup finally rested on the words of Dr. John Farrington: "It all comes down to this. How clean is clean? And who decides what is clean?"

Chapter 14

How Clean Is Clean?

In his landmark study, *Oil Pollution: A Decade of Research and Monitoring*, Dr. John Farrington made it clear that oil pollution in the ocean involves much more than broken ships, oil-soaked birds, and blackened beaches, striking and dramatic though such images are. After visiting Prince William Sound following the wreck of the *Exxon Valdez*, Dr. Farrington focused on the profound complexity of the spill's consequences. "Nature is complex in and of itself and we have dumped a complex mixture of chemicals into this system," said Farrington. "Then we wonder what's going to come of all of this. One reaction is to throw up our hands and say it's too complicated, we'll never understand it. But, of course, we can't do that. So we have to try to understand what's going on to the best of our ability. And the problem that the scientific community, the government agencies, the public, and Exxon face is, How much money and effort do we put into this cleanup? The question of How clean is clean? ends up being a value judgment."

For Exxon, the question of How clean is clean? became not only a practical matter of picking up the oil, but also a public relations challenge: When would the public be satisfied that Exxon had done all it could do? With the oil's impact continuing to strike month after month on the shorelines of Alaska, Exxon mounted a PR campaign to convince the American people—and the U.S. Congress—that indeed it *was* doing everything possible.

At the outset, Exxon decided to provide day-to-day information about the spill through its people working in Alaska. "There was a lot of discussion about how to best make information available," said Exxon Corporation president Lee Raymond. "Our conclusion was that the people up there on the ground ought to be the people doing the talking, because that's where the information was. That has a certain risk, in the sense that they were saying things before we even knew it."[1]

From the start, the daily open-door press conferences in Valdez drew the public's frustration and anger away from Alyeska and focused them on Exxon. On the other hand, instead of seeing executives and ad agency wizards managing the spill from their glass towers in Houston and New York City, the public saw real people trying to do their best in remote sites in Alaska. Showing people like Frank Iarossi struggling with the problem helped humanize Exxon's effort.

"Exxon's move to send Frank Iarossi out in blue jeans and a flannel shirt was brilliant," said Ron Dalby, the managing editor of *Alaska* magazine. "When Iarossi said that he, instead of some PR person, would be providing information, he had the press eating out of his hand. Then, after about thirty-six hours, we began seeing that all the information about booms and skimmers wasn't making any difference: the oil was just sitting there. At one point, Iarossi said the tanker had been boomed: we flew out and saw that it hadn't been. Now, maybe he was being given incorrect information, but the press just got madder and madder. By Sunday everybody was out to get Iarossi."

While Frank Iarossi bore the brunt of anger in Alaska, Exxon Corporation's executives dealt with the spill on the national level. Violating a cardinal rule of crisis management, Exxon CEO Lawrence Rawl did not go to Alaska immediately after the spill. Even a brief, one-day tour of the affected areas would have shown the public that Exxon's top executive cared enough to see the damage for himself. More importantly, had Rawl and other top executives walked the oil-soaked beaches, picked up some dead birds and otters, and seen the fear and anguish in the eyes of Alaskans, they might have become more sensitive to the devastation that was unfolding. Not coming to Alaska at the outset served to keep the top executives emotionally isolated and disconnected from the oil spill. This reinforced an inclination to treat it as more of a public relations exercise than an environmental tragedy. Rawl explained that he wasn't in Alaska during the critical first three weeks because he didn't want to divert the attention of his people in Valdez and wanted to devote his attention to supporting the response from New York. However, shortly after the spill he found time to go to Washington, D.C., reportedly to lobby against double-hull tankers.

At the annual shareholders' meeting on May 18, Rawl faced a firestorm of criticism from both shareholders and the general public. Thousands of people across the country had already cut up their Exxon credit cards and mailed the pieces to Rawl. Crowds of protesters marched in the streets outside the meeting. Some stockholders wanted an environmentalist on the board, while others demanded the resignation of top management. Pension fund representatives holding large amounts of Exxon stock made it clear that they would be watching Exxon's cleanup performance.

In an attempt to soothe public and shareholder wrath, Rawl presented an Exxon video production whose message was that the shock and disbelief after the spill was giving way to a feeling that Prince William Sound could be cleaned up soon, not later. Further, the video production stated that 75 percent of the oil that had poured into Prince William Sound had been cleaned up, evaporated, or otherwise dissipated. Exxon scientists stated in the video that there were no water-toxicity problems as a result of the spill. The film ended with dramatic footage of unspoiled beaches and of whales swimming through clean waters. While some shareholders may have been reassured by the presentation, others were incensed that Exxon would try to cover up the devastation so blatantly. "I'm not an environmentalist," said one shareholder who saw Exxon's video. "I'm just an everyday kind of guy. But I think these guys should be charged with gross criminal negligence."

After the annual meeting, Rawl said, "I know we've got a lot of shareholders pretty upset with us. We've got to communicate better." Here again, Rawl was treating the oil spill as more of a public relations problem than an environmental challenge. As part of his effort to communicate better, Rawl wrote an open letter to the public that appeared in $2 million worth of newspaper ads across the country. In the ad, he apologized for the accident and said, "We believe that Exxon has moved swiftly and competently to minimize the effect this oil will have on the environment, fish and other wildlife."

But when *Fortune* magazine asked Lawrence Rawl what advice he would offer other CEOs for handling a similar crisis, Rawl did not speak of quicker or more efficient response methods. He said, "You'd better prethink which way you are going to jump from a public affairs standpoint before you have any kind of problem. You ought to always have a public affairs plan, even though it's kind of hard to force yourself to think of a chemical plant blowing up or spilling all that oil in Prince William Sound."[2]

Exxon received some public relations assistance from the Alaska tourist industry, for whom the answer to How clean is clean? was, Clean enough to keep visitors coming to Alaska. After the first grim images of oiled beaches and dead creatures were televised from Valdez, advance summer reservations dropped off. Tour boat operators worried that tourists would avoid the scenic cruises they offered. And when *Alaska* magazine devoted its June 1989 issue to "Paradise Lost—The Wreck of the *Exxon Valdez*," the Alaska Visitors Association became incensed. In the article, a fisherman was quoted as saying, "We found a snapper out there today that had come up off the bottom so fast after getting hit with oil that its eyes and bladder had popped out. Its gills were totally ringed in that black tar." Another spoke of the "black, oozing evidence etched on every rock, every dead and dying animal and bird."[3]

This issue of *Alaska* was the most popular in the magazine's history and won praise from other journalists. Nevertheless, the advertising committee of the Alaska Tourism Marketing Council, representing many of the magazine's major advertisers, voted unanimously to withdraw advertising. Looking back on their response, the magazine's publisher, Ron Dalby, recalled that members of the tourism council "wrote me scathing letters, often indulging in name calling and questioning my ethics. They suggested that Alaska was going to lose a lot of money because of the magazine's reporting of the oil spill."

Denial, an underlying cause of the accident itself, was manifesting itself again, as powerful economic interests pressured

Alaska magazine to virtually deny the spill ever happened. A string of advertisers, led by the Princess and Holland America cruise companies, canceled their display ads. Ostracized and threatened with further financial sanctions, Ron Dalby bravely addressed the marketing council. "I can appreciate the fact that you are concerned with the potential for the tourist industry to suffer losses as a result of the *Exxon Valdez* crashing into a rock last March," Dalby said. "What I can't appreciate is the prevalent feeling that *Alaska* magazine should have ignored the event or minimalized coverage of it, all in the name of tourism.

"Those of you miffed at our coverage, particularly those pulling their ads from *Alaska* magazine, might want to stop a moment and reconsider," Dalby told the tourism executives. "Did you walk the oiled beaches counting dead birds as my photographer did? Did you stand vigil with the bird and sea otter specialists? Were you in Cordova when a fisherman's wife collapsed in the middle of a city street, sobbing so hard she could no longer maintain her balance? My managing editor was . . . I directed my staff to prepare 'Paradise Lost.' There are some stories an editor simply cannot ignore or downplay. You do not dictate copy and content of *Alaska* magazine by virtue of your advertising."

Ron Dalby didn't back down to his advertisers, but the Alaska Visitors Association, which represents many of the same interests that had pressured *Alaska* magazine, became involved in an even more direct effort to counteract the bad publicity related to the spill. Exxon gave $4 million to the state tourism division for image enhancement, and, citing the urgent circumstances, the state bypassed its purchasing regulations and gave the money directly to the Alaska Visitors Association. The association took the money and its ideas to a public relations firm.

"Interestingly enough, it was the same firm that handles the Alyeska account," observed Valdez Mayor John Devens. Exxon essentially put $4 million into its own public relations and sent it out under the legitimacy of the state of Alaska."

The ad agency chose the late movie star Marilyn Monroe over wolves, bears, or whales as a symbol for Alaska's environmental purity. The ads, which appeared nationally in both magazine and television versions, featured Marilyn's face without her beauty mark, the small mole on her cheek. The text, comparing

Prince William Sound to Marilyn's mole, suggested that Alaska was just as beautiful without Prince William Sound as Marilyn Monroe would have been without her beauty mark. "Unless you look long and hard, you probably won't notice her beauty mark is missing." This peculiar conclusion segued seamlessly with Exxon's official story—that the situation just wasn't that bad.

Exxon's documentation of bird and otter fatalities gave it another opportunity to diminish the spill's significance. The number of oiled creatures reported depended not only on the actual number of dead birds and otters but also on the effort made to find them. By hiring the wildlife rescue boats, Exxon was in effect paying a lot of money for reports that would damage its public image. On April 15, barely three weeks after the wreck, the company put a stop to an effort it apparently deemed unacceptably self-defeating. On that date, Kelly Weaverling, who was directing the wildlife rescue fleet, was about to deploy newly contracted boats to an area just then being hit with oil. He received orders from Exxon not to send the boats out.

"I suddenly got word from Exxon to stop these new vessels," Weaverling said. "And further, we were to remove one vessel from each of the eight existing rescue units. They were reducing the fleet right before the spring migration, just as we were expecting 20 million birds to come through."

When Weaverling asked Exxon why they were cutting the wildlife fleet so drastically, he was told that this abrupt cutback had originated with Dr. Alan Maki, Exxon's chief environmental scientist. "I had been put in charge of the wildlife rescue fleet, and if there were going to be changes made, I at least wanted Maki to talk with me," Weaverling said. "So I called Maki. He wasn't in, and I left word for him to call me, but he never did."

Later, Weaverling learned that the wildlife fleet had been cut back because the number of dead birds being found was decreasing. "They created a self-fulfilling prophecy," Weaverling said. "Dead birds are still coming in. Spring migration is just beginning. However, each area now has just one boat looking for birds. They can say, 'Oh, yes, the bird count numbers are dwindling. Things are getting better.' Of course they look better. If you haven't got as many boats looking for birds, you aren't going to find as many."

By July, Weaverling had been fired, the number of wildlife rescue and retrieval boats had been cut down to four, and captains of the remaining boats had received word that their contracts would expire on August 3. "It was incredible. We were still picking dead seals out of the water," said Jim Shetler, a crewman on one of the four remaining boats. "Just yesterday, we found a dead deer near Perry Island. It had oil around its head and was just floating with the tide. We started seeing dead birds and animals left and right, and they cut our contract.

"After they got rid of Weaverling, there was no boss, no set schedule of where to go," Shetler said. "It became a joke. They didn't want us to find dead animals. They were just throwing money away. This whole thing was a payoff scheme, a way to buy off the communities and make everything look nice and clean."

Public relations efforts can alter reality just so far, and Exxon still had to deal with the observers' judgments of how clean they were actually getting the shoreline. In the Valdez press conferences immediately after the spill, Exxon sounded clear and unequivocal. On March 27, Frank Iarossi had said, "We are going to clean it up if it takes months, many months." Three days later, Exxon spokesman Don Cornett said that "We are going to pick up, one way or another, all the oil that's out there. . . . We are not going to walk off. The Coast Guard and the state are not going to allow us to walk off and leave any oil anywhere. . . . If we can find it, we will clean it up."

In April, Rawl had assured Exxon's shareholders at their annual meeting that Exxon would clean the shorelines and that "our objective is to complete the job by mid-September." However, later in May, "completing the job by September" had come to mean not cleaning, but "treating" the beaches.

Rawl had also assured Exxon shareholders and the public that Exxon was committed to returning the next spring to finish the cleanup: "In any event, we will return to the area in the spring of 1990 to reinspect the area to assure that the job has been properly done, and if not, to put it right." However, Exxon's embattled executives were feeling a great need for closure—to get through the summer and get this nightmare behind them. As management, they had to consider the interests of their stockholders. This meant balancing fiscal responsibility against the treatment of 700 miles of beaches, mending the company's tarnished image against cleanup costs that could reach $2 billion. And at some point in the spring, Exxon executives had come to realize that no amount of money could make the beaches as clean as they had been before March 24, 1989. They were looking for a way to cut off the hemorrhage of funds.

On July 19, Exxon's commitment to "finish the job" was thrown into doubt by a memo written by Exxon's cleanup chief, Otto Harrison. The terse memo informed Exxon managers that the company's "only commitment for the spring of 1990 is to survey the shorelines." It said that Exxon alone would select the dates for curtailing cleanup operations. "These are not negotiable points," wrote Harrison. "In discussion on these matters, you should stress the safety and operational factors. We are willing to discuss those factors. We are not willing to discuss the decisions."[4]

DEC commissioner Dennis Kelso responded that the most important thing to the state was Exxon's commitment to continue the work. He charged that the Harrison memo "makes it clear that Exxon doesn't care what anybody else cares or thinks. This breaches the promises the company made to Alaskans and the country that they would stay until the cleanup was done. This is outrageous and totally unacceptable."[5]

California Congressman George Miller told Exxon that "some fly-by-night operations wouldn't belly up to the bar and pay the freight to the extent you have to date. But if you believe that this is gonna be resolved by whether or not you [treat] 600 miles of beaches, or 800 miles of beaches, we've missed the point here. We're talking about [restoring] a total environment."[6]

Miller warned that Exxon apparently "intends to abandon oil cleanup activities based on calendar and investor considerations rather than on concern for the environment and the people of Alaska." To ascertain Exxon's cleanup intentions, Congressman Miller called a congressional hearing on July 28. "The bottom line is that we want you to know that we will not be satisfied until the cleanup is complete," Miller told Exxon U.S.A.'s president, Bill Stevens. "That's the kind of assurance that we heard from you when we were in Alaska earlier this year. And it's those assurances we've asked Admiral Robbins to build on. Then, along comes the 'Harrison memo,' which suggests that Exxon is now going to take a series of unilateral steps." The most alarming implication of the memo, Miller stated, was that Exxon was "only going to come back in the spring for the purpose of a survey."

As a reply to Miller, Bill Stevens restated Exxon's cleanup commitment, and it came out somewhat differently than it had in May, when he had said to Congressman Miller, "We are committed to cleaning the mess up. Whatever the volume is, we will get it done." Now, at the July 28 hearing, Stevens said, "The goal for this year's cleanup activities is fairly clear. And that's to try to treat all of the impacted shoreline. And we're now up to about 730 miles, with about 530-plus of that being in the Gulf of Alaska. . . . Now, what do we mean by 'treated'? Remove gross contamination and render the impacted shoreline environmentally stable. That is so that through the course of this winter there will not be mobile oil which will interfere with flora, fauna, birds, fish, and other wildlife on the shoreline."[7]

Stevens said, "Now, in retrospect, the wording in Mr. Harrison's memo was unfortunate, and he would be the first to say so, were he here. He doesn't take a lot of time to carefully word memos . . . but more importantly, what we're doing every day, in terms of the operation up there, would say that we will follow through."

However, that same week Exxon Corporation president Lee Raymond said, "Well, I don't know if we'll be back next spring." Raymond, who was considerably above Stevens in Exxon's hierarchy, said from his office high above New York City, "When you look at it from the shareholder's point of view, we're not willing to go anywhere and do anything anybody says. It is not in the interests of our shareholders for management to do that. There has to be an end to this. And no matter when we say there has to be an end, we're going to have an argument about it, because some people don't want it to end. They have a different agenda than we do in trying to clean up the beach."

Raymond suggested that some might feel the beaches were not clean enough because they had a vested interest in them being oiled. "In my view, there are still a lot of people who don't want to see the shoreline cleaned up," Raymond said. "There are some very, very narrow economic interests. You know, this has

been a boon to the state of Alaska. And there are a lot of environmentalists that are going to be disappointed if they can't go walk
on a bunch of beaches next spring and see a lot of oil."

While Exxon made public assurances that it would be back the
following spring to decide on further cleanup, Lee Raymond indicated that Exxon had already made some of those decisions.
Raymond made it clear that if the Coast Guard made unreason-
able requests for further cleanup, Exxon would not come back.
Raymond said, "I can tell you right now that even if there's something to be done next year . . . we're not going to have 10,000
people working on the thing."

Lee Raymond also suggested that the answer to How clean is
clean? was a matter of expectations. He pointed out that Alyeska's contingency plan stated that in a large spill a significant
quantity of oil would contaminate beaches. By approving that
plan the state had, in effect, accepted having oiled beaches. Raymond said, "That was an approved plan. We didn't make it up
and in the dead of night slip it under the door or throw it over
the transom. That was an approved plan that had been around
for years and had been recently updated. . . . Now, maybe all of
us in hindsight would say that we should never have a plan that
says a significant amount of oil will get on the beach. . . . Maybe
we all made a bad judgment." Raymond emphasized, however,
that the plan made it clear that "some oil is going to get on the
shore. Now if people don't understand that, they haven't read
the plan. I'm not responsible for that. If they approve it without
reading it, that's their problem."

DEC commissioner Dennis Kelso, who had approved the contingency plan—which stated that large spills would require a
long-term shoreline cleanup—said in the first week of August
that "we are not close to deciding How clean is clean? There is
still too much oil on shorelines where even the gross removal has
not been completed. . . . As a practical matter, it may well be that
the question is not How clean is clean? but rather At what point
do you have to make the practical decision that you can't get sufficient recovery of oil any longer?"[8]

Nevertheless, the state was able to make a clear, unequivocal
determination of How clean is clean? for Alaska fishermen,
whose primary concern was safeguarding the commercial value

of the fisheries. To protect fish products from oil contamination, and also to protect the perceived quality of Alaska seafood products, the state initiated a zero-tolerance policy: if any oil was sighted in a fishing district, that district would be closed.

"Zero tolerance is a marketing decision, not an environmental decision," charged Otto Harrison, Exxon's cleanup chief.[9] He considered this state policy a public relations ploy to protect the image of Alaska's fish products. Harrison pointed out that comprehensive testing at the canneries would have accomplished the objective of keeping tainted fish from the marketplace. Zero tolerance was closing tens of millions of dollars worth of fisheries in areas where only small amounts of floating oil, tar balls, or mousse were found. In each of these areas, claims would be made against Exxon for lost seasons. Harrison believed that very few of the fish would actually be contaminated.

At a meeting in Valdez, John Sund, a fisherman from Ketchikan, challenged Harrison. "The state's salmon industry was almost crippled a few years ago because of a few contaminated cans that led to a botulism scare. There's no way that the state or the fishermen are going to let that happen again because one or two salmon get on the market tainted by oil."

The state used the zero-tolerance policy as an environmental standard to protect the fishing industry, but it failed to establish equally clear and decisive standards for the overall environmental cleanup of Alaska's impacted coastline. Commissioner Kelso attributed this failure to the state's lack of authority: "Neither the state nor the federal government, under current law, has the legal authority to require Exxon to do any more work than the spiller wants to do in Alaska. We are all at the mercy of the spiller's sense of moral obligation to finish the job."

However, one attorney working for the state, who asked to remain anonymous, said, "The state clearly had more authority than it used. The state can't just march in and take over, but it definitely had more authority to go in and get what it wanted from Exxon. Why the state didn't use all of its authority is a sensitive area."

Michele Brown, an attorney working for DEC, concurred, citing DEC's ability to issue compliance orders and emergency orders to have a polluter cease polluting and clean up its mess. She said, "DEC had authority to issue specific orders, but for some reason opted not to. To make an order effective it would have to be very detailed, and Exxon would have the right to contest it. Exxon could have told the state, 'If you're dissatisfied, take over the cleanup.'"

Brown said she had advised DEC of its powers, but that others had made a policy decision not to use them. Douglas Mertz, an attorney in the state attorney general's office, said that for a large spill, "compliance orders just aren't very good tools." He added that a cooperative approach with Exxon was deemed more practical.

However, Patti Saunders, an environmental lawyer not affiliated with any of the oil spill litigants, charged that "the state was simply afraid to direct Exxon through a series of compliance orders. It's outrageous that we had to sit around and wait for Exxon to agree to do things. All the agencies twiddled their thumbs, saying, 'We don't have the authority to make them clean it up.' That's hogwash! They do have the authority. What they don't have explicitly they have implicitly, and the state should just take it and use it.

"The state of Alaska could have told Exxon, 'Clean all the oil up, try all the possible techniques, stay out there till it's done.' But the state was in over its head," said Saunders, who had spent six years of enforcing pollution laws for the state of Pennsylvania. "If Alaska had had a history of issuing compliance orders for oil polluters, it would have known how to handle this kind of situation. But when this big spill happened, the state simply didn't have the guts to stand up to Exxon and demand that the oil be cleaned up. Dennis Kelso has put himself in a position where he can play being Mr. Rough Tough. He says all this stuff in the press, but he doesn't do anything about it. By not asserting the state's authority, he doesn't have to take responsibility. The state was pulling its punches because of the legal ramifications. The state knew that if it began directing the cleanup, Exxon could come back with a counterclaim."

Here was a crucial value judgment on the state of Alaska. The state faced a tradeoff between doing everything in its power to restore the environment and protecting its position in damage claims and counterclaims with Exxon. If the state pushed the limits of its authority and directed Exxon with compliance orders, Exxon could claim interference and thereby reduce its liability for damages. When asked why the state wasn't using compliance orders on Exxon, Governor Cowper said he had been advised by his attorneys not to do so. To the extent the state backed off for fear of jeopardizing its damage claims against Exxon, it was sacrificing the environment for financial considerations.

Whether from inexperience, lack of confidence in its enforcement powers, or fear of compromising its claims against Exxon, it's clear that the state did not exercise its authority as forcefully as it could have. As a consequence of this policy decision, cleanup opportunities were lost. When the first cleanup plans were formulated in April and May, the state could have ordered Exxon to recover all the oil, both on and under the surface of beaches, instead of pursuing the policy of removing gross contamination from the surface. Further, the state could have demanded that Exxon try the numerous cleanup techniques to which NOAA's Dr. Jacqueline Michel had made reference. It could have insisted that Exxon collect the pooled oil that appeared through May and June. And it could have established shoreline cleanup standards as clear and unequivocal as the fishing industry's zero-tolerance policy. But instead of taking advantage of these opportunities, the state played it safe, protecting itself from liability suits and bolstering its ability to go after Exxon for damages.

To try to compel Exxon to complete the cleanup, the Sierra Club Legal Defense Fund and several other environmental organizations brought suit against Exxon. As Lori Adams of the Defense Fund said, "We are not seeking monetary damages. We don't want Exxon's money. We just want Exxon to complete the cleanup to the fullest extent possible."

A complete cleanup could entail washing every rock on every contaminated beach, which could take a hundred years or more. How long should Exxon continue to pay tremendous sums of money to render shorelines only slightly cleaner? Naturally, Exxon wanted to stop the spill-inflicted financial hemorrhaging as soon as possible. Others felt Exxon should continue to pay until the environment was completely restored. If Exxon went bankrupt in the process, that was just part of the cost of doing business. "My monkey wrench nature says seize Exxon's assets and liquidate the corporation," said Patti Saunders. "We should put Exxon's assets into a trust fund and spend it for as long as it takes to keep fixing things. We are talking about strict liability, and it should be very strict. I believe in the corporate form of capital punishment."

However, even the staunchest environmentalists, including Patti Saunders, agreed that further cleaning should not be required if it caused more harm than good. With a sense of resignation, Governor Cowper said he feared that "there will come a time when Exxon and the state of Alaska and the federal government, all three of us, are going to have to go to the public and say, 'Everything that can be done has been done. It's still a mess. But we can't clean it up anymore.'"[10]

Over the course of four months, the term *clean*—in the question How clean is clean?—had come to mean "treated," which itself came to mean "environmentally stable." The definition of the latter term was "no longer fatal to wildlife." The irony was that, while everyone continued to argue over How clean is clean? the concept of cleanliness as we usually understand it gradually disappeared. Zero tolerance defined *clean* for the fisheries; Marilyn Monroe without her beauty mark defined *clean* for the tourist industry. But by August, no one was talking about the beaches actually being clean again. If the governor's prophecy held, the word *clean* would come to signify "we can't clean it up anymore."

While Exxon tried to put the spill behind it and the state guarded its damage claims against Exxon, Congressman George Miller made it clear who he thought had the authority to decide How clean is clean? "Exxon can argue until it's blue in the face on one side of that issue, and Mr. Kelso can argue until he's blue in the face on the other side of that issue. But the determination of responsibility is with the Coast Guard at this point."[11]

Miller's staunch interest in the question would lead him to sponsor legislation giving states more clearly defined rights in determining How clean is clean? but the U.S. Coast Guard would remain the arbiter for the *Exxon Valdez* spill. "*Cleanup* is probably a misnomer," said Vice Admiral Clyde Robbins, who continued through the summer as the Coast Guard's on-scene coordinator. "Those beaches in Alaska are never going to be clean. This oil is tenacious stuff. We're never going to get it all off the rocks. And we're not going to be able to call these beaches pristine again in this lifetime. My aim at this point is to make the area as environmentally sound as it can be. . . . I don't want people saying I killed Alaska."[12]

Vice Admiral Robbins was willing to listen to anyone's opinion on how much more cleaning Exxon ought to do. However, he would rely heavily on the recommendations of NOAA, whose Dr. Jacqueline Michel said, "Exxon did a good job. Better, I think, than anybody else in the world could have done. At times [Exxon's people] felt that they weren't getting that much oil removed from the beaches, but they kept going. I'm sure that early on they made a decision that they had to go through this first year and do whatever it took to save their public image. Their only target was cleaning the surface of the beach. They never tried to go for the subsurface oil.

"Eventually this oil will break down and go away. It's not something like PCBs or DDT, which accumulate through the food chain. Prince William Sound is going to recover. The sound was pristine, and now it's going to have oil on it. Oil won't be everywhere. There are going to be some problems, but it's not the end of the world."

However, many Alaskans felt that a part of the world they loved had indeed come to an end. After surveying the "treated" beaches of Prince William Sound, Valdez Mayor John Devens said, "There are at least twenty tons of animal carcasses in storage for disposal, and more are dying. The beaches are not clean. We still have places where, if you step ashore, the beach will squirt oil on you. I want to keep the pressure on Exxon, can't let them off the hook until the beaches are clean."

On Kodiak Island, Dolly Reft, a Native Alaskan said, "It's empty around here. It's like a morgue. It's just not the same. We have continued to count dead birds, sea otters, deer, fox, and numerous other carcasses. Exxon is repeatedly trying to convince us that everything will be okay. We are not convinced. We have been here too long. We know better."

Don Moore, city manager of Cordova, said, "I appeal to the world to watch. Prince William Sound was one of the two most beautiful places on earth. I leave it to each of you individually to decide what the other one is. We all have a special Shangri-la in our hearts and minds. Think of yours when you contemplate what happened to ours."

John Devens, Dolly Reft, Don Moore, and thousands of other Alaskans caught in the wake of the *Exxon Valdez* had their own, entirely personal impressions of How clean is clean? They weren't oil pollution experts; they were fishermen, carpenters, schoolteachers, truck drivers, loggers, and family people. They didn't have to be conversant in lighter-molecular-weight hydrocarbon fractions to recognize the stench of oil on their beaches. They might not have studied the Clean Water Act or state compliance orders, but they did what they could to protect their communities, shorelines, and fishing grounds.

As the oil spread outward from Prince William Sound, managers of national parks and wildlife refuges and residents of more than twenty communities began to feel the impact of the advancing oil, the cleanup effort, and Exxon's public relations campaign. These phenomena ran out of control through the summer of 1989, and as they intermingled, they obscured the fundamental shoreline question: How clean, in the end, is clean?

Part **III**

The Wake

Chapter 15

Valdez

In the series of communities that would be impacted as the oil spread along the coast, Valdez was, of course, ground zero. And although prevailing currents carried the oil away from Valdez, the town was immediately inundated by people responding to the spill.

By nightfall on March 24, 1989, the town had begun to fill with an influx of divers, underwater welders, oil recovery specialists, biologists, bureaucrats, reporters, and television crews. Within a week, its population had swelled from 2,300 to more than 5,000. Hotel rooms that had gone for $45 a night sold out at $100. All the rental cars were taken. Phone lines were jammed. The sleepy Valdez airport, which normally handled about a dozen flights a day, averaged 300 to 400 a day, reaching a peak of 687 flights on March 30.

"This means millions for us," said Jan Buccini, a Valdez cab driver whose pay tripled after the spill. "This town is going to grow."[1] Gas stations, motels, cafes, bars, and liquor stores reported doubling or tripling their normal income. However, as soon as Exxon began hiring oil spill workers at $16.69 an hour, local businesses started losing employees and had a hard time replacing them. "It's really swamped down here. People are having to work long hours. There is a lot of stress," said Connie Harrison, who was desperate to hire more people for her 24-room hotel, bar, and restaurant. "I have ads in the newspapers for everything—dishwashers, buspeople, waitresses, housekeepers, bartenders, cooks, you name it."

By mid-April, a second wave of immigrants began arriving in Valdez, drawn by the prospect of getting some of the millions of dollars Exxon was spending on the cleanup. At times, it appeared as if the workers who had built the pipeline had suddenly returned to Valdez. Men with tattoos, battered cowboy hats, and a week's worth of stubble on their faces milled about on the sidewalks and around the hiring hall. Some drove pickup trucks to town; some hitchhiked in. Bars and camper parks overflowed. Street vendors hawked hunting knives, silver belt buckles, and glow-in-the-dark velvet paintings of Mexican bandits and naked women.

"Most of these hard-luck cases pouring into Valdez don't care about restoring the sound, they just want the bucks," said Kelly Weaverling, who was directing the wildlife rescue boats out of Valdez. "They're toasting Joe Hazelwood for bringing easy money. If they don't get jobs, they steal. They vandalize. They break and enter. The crime rate is out of control. People are squatting everywhere. Breaking bottles. Making fires. Defecating in the bushes. Throwing trash."

At the peak of the summer's frenzied spill response, the population of Valdez reached 12,000, more than five times its original size. Many of the transients feared they wouldn't be hired. "It's a waiting game," said Ken Kent of Fairbanks. "I'm too far into it now. I'm broke. I can't go home. I can't go nowhere."[2]

The townspeople feared outbreaks of disease among the tightly packed campers and squatters. They feared the infiltration of drug dealers, and they watched the rate of serious crimes rise 300 percent. City Manager Doug Griffen explained that the police couldn't chase off the people sleeping in vacant lots and on the edge of roads because they had no place to go. He added, "We're fearful that there are a lot of crazies coming in. One guy almost got the drop on one of our cops, drawing a gun. That doesn't usually happen around here."[3]

Alyeska and Exxon came to fear vandals and assassins even more than the press. Exxon stationed security guards wherever its employees worked or lived. "The rent-a-cops aggravated us no end," said Valdez Mayor John Devens. "It irritated me to have to tell some stranger in my community why I was going into a building, who I wanted to see, what I wanted to do. It's just rubbing salt in the wounds of a community when you no longer have free access to your stores and your buildings."

Exxon's security guards even restricted access to the community's Robe Lake Recreation Area. "A lot of parents and grandparents take the little kids out there to a little beach," Devens said. "It's not much of a beach. It's not really even much of a lake, but you can go out there and have a picnic. It's our one place where the water gets warm enough to swim. Well, all of a sudden we find that Exxon has guards out there. They were out there to guard a couple of Exxon's float planes, but they were telling everybody the whole lake was off limits. One lady went out there with two of her grandchildren, as she does every summer, and they chased her out."

"We needed security guards," said Alyeska spokesman Tom Brennan. "Every morning when I got out of bed, the first thing I'd do is inch my way over to the window and peep through the curtains to see if a sniper was waiting for me."

Devens, on the other hand, recalled that Exxon's biggest scare was self-inflicted. "I got a call saying that someone was trying to kill Exxon off. People were alarmed because someone had found two cans of gasoline under the steps of the Exxon building. We had the local police investigating to see who was trying to blow the place up. Come to find out, two Exxon employees didn't know what to do with their cans of gas, so they just stuck them by the building."

The flow of Exxon's cleanup money into Valdez sent the town's economy reeling. Apartment rents rose by as much as $500 a month, causing hardships for residents on a fixed income. In contrast, some kids on their first job made $35,000 scrubbing beaches over the summer, more than some of their parents made all year. And one young man in his early twenties leased his skiff, worth about $6,000, to Exxon along with his services as skipper. He had started the spring flat broke, but by the end of the summer had earned $700,000.

A quite different financial fate was experienced by KCHU, the Valdez public radio station. Always operating on a tight budget, the tiny station extended itself, providing extensive coverage of the oil spill. Soon it was broke, uncertain how to pay the phone bill and the next week's payroll. Exxon offered a grant of $32,283 to help cover the station's cost of reporting on the spill. This left the station with a tough decision: refuse Exxon's money and go out of business, or accept it and lose credibility. After considerable soul-searching, Exxon's money was not accepted. The station eked by on small contributions from sympathetic listeners.

For many longtime residents of Valdez, the loss of control over their community combined with the trauma of the spill itself proved overwhelming. "The stress down there in Valdez is incredible," said Tom Scott, director of the region's Emergency Medical Services Council. "People need to be aware that stress is going to be affecting them. Children in the Valdez area will be among the first to show the signs. Mental health professionals should plan on seeing stress-related problems for two to three years at least."

In April, Scott set up a twenty-four-hour crisis telephone line. The mental health professional staff began taking calls from people suffering from increased drinking, anxiety, depression, and domestic violence. A statement about mental health was placed in the local paper: "The oil spill in Prince William Sound is entirely different from other disasters," explained Dr. Richard M. Gist, a specialist in emergency services. "Rather than a single cataclysmic event, it is an ongoing progression of events. The 'low point' of a disaster is usually much easier to identify, and therefore 'turning the corner' is usually much easier. The oil spill is staying at a crisis level for an extended period." Dr. Gist then advised people feeling depressed to seek the help of a mental health professional.[4]

While people in other communities had to deal with the shock of seeing oil on their beaches, Valdez residents had to grapple with the transformation of their town. They also had to deal with the consequences of having hosted Alyeska for so many years. "Valdez has always been one of the most prodevelopment communities in Alaska," said Valdez councilman Lynn Chrystal. "We probably still will be. But we feel very let down and very cheated. It's almost like you found out your wife is cheating on you. At first, there's shock and disbelief, then you're angry, then you're sad, then finally you start to accept it."[5]

The sense of betrayal was heightened in Valdez because the community had always considered Alyeska a member of the family. Alyeska and its parent companies were the primary source of community stability, identification, and pride. Alyeska provided 90 percent of the city's annual budget, $33 million in 1988—four times what other towns of comparable size had to spend. Around city hall, Alyeska was affectionately known as "Uncle Al." However, as the spill focused attention on Alyeska, a darker side of the town's benefactor emerged.

"This is a story," said Douglas Baily, Alaska's attorney general, "about the ability of people with substantial economic power and influence to cause perceptions to be different from the way things really are—and to discourage others from making successful inquiries. Over the years, there have been very few inquiries into Alyeska Pipeline Service. There's been the state DEC [Department of Environmental Conservation], the *Anchorage Daily News*, and there's been Chuck Hamel."[6]

For the past ten years, Hamel, now fifty-nine, had been investigating Alyeska. He believed that Alyeska drove him out of business by leaving too much water in the oil he was brokering. Hamel lost $12 million and his reputation in 1980 and since then has been obsessed with proving that Alyeska spiked the oil with water when loading the tankers he brokered. "I didn't start out being obsessed," said Hamel, who has been described as having the determination of Rocky Balboa in the body of Mickey Rooney. "I started out being pissed off. I lost my business, I lost my reputation—everything. It became a matter of principle. How can you get screwed by people and let them get away with it?"

At first, Hamel couldn't figure out why Alyeska was picking on him—a small, independent shipper of oil. Then he realized that, by shipping the oil at nearly $5 a barrel less than the major companies, he was exposing their inflated shipping rates. "When I came in with that lower price with my little company, I thought I was a genius. And that was my first mistake," Hamel said. "British Petroleum, Exxon, and ARCO were going bananas trying to stop me. I knew I was nipping a little bit into their business, but at the time I didn't realize I was showing up their scheme to inflate shipping costs in order to save on taxes." Hamel estimated that the oil companies, by manipulating their shipping costs, may have diverted more than $1 billion in state and federal revenues into their pockets.

As Hamel's investigations led him into a maze of Alyeska's misconduct and regulatory violations, he encountered the coercive and violent undercurrents often found in a community dominated by one industry. "I wasn't trying to shut the terminal down, just upgrade its operations," Hamel said. "But I was threatened. I got beaten up. It was so spooky. I became paranoid and started traveling under assumed names." On the other hand, some Alyeska employees began confiding in Hamel. "People picked me to divulge what was really going on. I found out Alyeska was not only cheating but poisoning their people as well."

One person Hamel came in contact with was Erlene Blake, who had her own very personal reasons for being concerned about Alyeska's operations. Blake had worked for Alyeska for about six years. When she needed help in 1984 in filing a worker's compensation complaint, she hired attorney Douglas Baily, who was also handling Hamel's water-in-the-oil case. Blake told Baily that part of her job was to test the water content in oil and that her bosses regularly directed her to underestimate the amount of water. "If I got a sample that was very high in water content," she said, "I'd call my supervisor. He'd get another sample that was going to be the percentage they wanted. I jokingly used to say he was getting his samples from the miracle barrel."[7]

In addition to confirming Hamel's suspicions that Alyeska was leaving excessive amounts of water in his oil, Blake added that Alyeska also dumped oily wastes into Valdez Bay. "If there was ballast water with toxic levels of sulfides that they didn't want to take the effort to treat, they would push it through after everyone had left, so no one would smell it. If some chemical was exceeding its permitted level, it was run out in the night. We did a lot of things after dark."

In Alyeska's laboratory Blake had to work with highly toxic benzene in a small room that had neither a ventilation system nor a window. Blake recalled that she had to "boil the benzene off with nothing covering it. We tried to get a fan. We tried to get some changes, but it was like pulling teeth. We went on using a storeroom to boil off benzene for several years. It's a wonder the place didn't blow up." She began to develop health problems. "When I washed my hands, they cracked open and started bleeding," Blake said. "I started having headaches. My nose would bleed and my eyes were always bloodshot. On my weeks off, it began taking longer for me to feel better. I noticed massive mood changes and problems remembering things."

A blister on Blake's toe wouldn't heal. The sore festered and spread. Gangrene set in. She spent much of 1983 in a hospital and had most of her foot amputated. "Right after coming out of surgery, Alyeska wanted me to sign papers saying it wasn't their fault. They would come into my hospital room and say they didn't want me to do anything against Alyeska. Finally I signed papers, and I probably could never come back on them if I got sick with leukemia." Blake eventually received a worker's compensation settlement of $1,000 a toe. "Then, through Mr. Hamel's help, I got to specialists in toxic medicine," she recalled. "They said my symptoms of not being able to heal, memory loss, nosebleeds, headaches, and mood swings made up a classic case of chronic toxicity." She said that an Alyeska supervisor confided to her that Alyeska never expected to keep anyone in the lab for more than two years, so that when people got sick years later they wouldn't ascribe it to work in the lab.

In 1985, Blake agreed to testify in Hamel's water-in-the-oil case. However, Hamel could not afford the million dollars or more that it would take to fight Alyeska in court, so he laid his case before the Alaska Public Utilities Commission. Showing considerable courage, Blake acknowledged to the commission that she had falsified tests for Alyeska. "I polluted as much as anybody in the name of money, until my conscience got to me. They can buy people. They can buy whatever they need. But I have to speak for myself now. . . . Those violations were so senseless. Alyeska was doing it basically to save money, even though they would still be making a profit if they installed the needed equipment. Nobody was there to enforce regulations. Nobody was standing up to Alyeska. They have their own society, above and beyond the law, in which people are expendable."

The Public Utilities Commission ruled that Hamel's evidence was irrelevant to their proceedings because it pertained to previous violations, not current Alyeska practices. "They could have corroborated my findings," Hamel said. "They could have recognized a serious problem, but they chose not to delve into the matter further."

After speaking out, Blake's problems took on a new dimension. By the time she returned to Valdez, news of her testimony about Alyeska's unsavory practices had appeared in the newspapers. One night, a Molotov cocktail—a homemade bomb of gasoline in a jar—was thrown at her house, causing a fire and extensive damage. Another time, three men accosted her during a walk with her dogs and tied her up with wire. "They threatened me and beat me up," she said. "One of the voices sounded familiar. I feel they were Alyeska employees. In a way, I can understand why they were upset. Nobody wants to lose an $80,000-a-year job. But I was trying to help the workers. The police didn't want to get involved. Alyeska owns everybody in town."

After the beating, Blake had to have numerous stitches and couldn't walk for several weeks. Her attorney advised her to move away from Valdez. She said what bothered her most was "the mental terror. I never knew what to expect. On my door they painted the words 'get out.' And I was finally driven out."

Few people seemed to care about the plight of Erlene Blake or the evidence gathered by Chuck Hamel until the wreck of the *Exxon Valdez*. The case Hamel couldn't afford to make in court and couldn't win at the Public Utilities Commission, he presented to the public. A week after the spill, he rented a house in Valdez that became a library for documents, leaked memos, statements by Alyeska employees, and environmental reports. He installed four phone lines and two fax machines and began dispensing information to national newspapers and magazines and to state and federal investigators.

"If one can throw a congressional hearing the way you can a wedding," said *Newsweek*'s Pamela Abramson, "then Chuck Hamel's the one to do it." It was Hamel who encouraged California Congressman George Miller to hold hearings on May 7 in Valdez rather than in Anchorage and to focus them not only on the spill but on Alyeska's chronic violations of standards, laws, and the public trust. "This oil spill was no simple accident," concluded Miller, promising to pursue Alyeska's legacy of deceit. "This disaster is not just the story of a drunken sailor. It's the product of a systematic dismantling of environmental safeguards associated with the Trans-Alaska Pipeline system. The industry has reneged on its assurances to Congress and the people of Alaska."[10]

Among those in Valdez who felt profoundly betrayed by the oil industry was Mayor John Devens. "I don't know how many times in the past I've stood up and talked about our good corporate neighbors. But my attitudes have certainly been altered by what's happened," Devens said. "I have always been very prodevelopment, but we can never be put in this kind of situation again. For me, the first lesson is that a community shouldn't put its faith in big business or big government. This is not to say that Alyeska and Exxon are evil. But they are profit-making corporations. And their first loyalty is to their stockholders. A company's priorities are different from a community's."

When Devens began speaking critically about Alyeska and Exxon, he also became the focus of his community's mixed and anguished emotions. "At the terminal, signs were posted calling me a Benedict Arnold and demanding I be removed as mayor," Devens said. "Others cheered me when I pointed out that a beach that had been cleaned eleven times still had oil on it. Some tried to deny that there was a problem at all. They would have liked to ignore both the spilled oil and Alyeska's failings. Friends turned on friends."

To Devens and many Valdez residents, it soon became evident that Exxon was capable of using the kind of heavy-handed control exercised by Alyeska. Valdez and other coastal communities were becoming financially strapped and emotionally drained by the spill. But to get assistance, they had to plead with Exxon. "It's insulting to me to have to go to Exxon for everything this community needs," Devens said. "We're experiencing a lot of social problems related to the spill—fights, depression, divorces. We asked for a counselor, but Exxon turned us down and then gave the $20,000 we requested to Seward to enhance its summer celebration. A community shouldn't have to come begging to a company, and it bothers me that we are getting their handouts. It's as if we need a meal and they're saying, 'Here, kid, go see a movie, get some candy.' Exxon treats us like a child: 'No, son, we don't think you need that, but we'll give you this.'"

Devens became incensed when he noticed a great disparity in how Exxon was responding to the needs of the oiled communities. Towns that got more media attention and could afford attorneys received much better treatment than villages that were

out of the limelight and didn't have the resources to stand up to
the corporation. "Exxon went from town to town and got away
with whatever it could," Devens said. "If a community yelled and
screamed loud enough, it got some help from Exxon. But what
the company did in one place, it would refuse to do in another.
Exxon took advantage wherever it could. It was the worst kind
of manipulation."

In an attempt to make Exxon accountable for the social as well
as the environmental problems of the oil spill, the leaders of
coastal communities formed an association in April. The mayors
faced Exxon united, asking for fair treatment for villages that
couldn't afford lawyers and lobbyists to press for help. "We had
twenty-five separate villages and communities that were heavily
impacted by this spill," Devens said. "There was absolute solidar-
ity. We didn't want even the smallest of our villages to be taken
advantage of."

At first, Exxon refused to work with the association, prefer-
ring to deal with each community separately. When the mayors
held firm, Exxon was forced to consider their request for an
overall agreement to reimburse spill-related costs. Many of the
towns had spent much of their available funds paying for log
booms, anchors, tools, fuel, and other emergency supplies. They
also faced mounting costs for increased crime, mental health
problems, domestic violence, as well as extra demands for water
and waste disposal.

Instead of making direct reimbursements for these costs,
Exxon proposed that the communities become subcontractors to
Exxon. As subcontractors, city officials and their families were
supposed to promise not to do anything that was not in "Exxon's
best interest." Attorneys for the association said, "With this kind
of provision, Exxon is trying to buy the silence of the
municipalities."

Devens said, "Exxon is deliberately stonewalling us." The
mayor of the small Native village of Port Graham concluded that
"Exxon never intended to come to any agreement with us."[11]
The outraged mayors refused to accept Exxon's proposal, and
overall agreement was never reached between the oiled communities and Exxon. Each community was on its own to confront
the oil and deal with Exxon.

Chapter 16

Cordova

Cordova was also ground zero, but in a different way from Valdez. While Valdez was overwhelmed with people, the people of Cordova were so deeply connected with Prince William Sound that they felt personally wounded by its devastation. Many expressed the feeling that part of themselves was dying out there with the birds and the otters.

In the aftermath of the spill, Jim Brown stared pensively at his fishing boat, idle in the harbor. "There are few things in this world I enjoy more than sitting on my boat and seeing my nets smoke with fish, or cracking crab, or watching a mama bear with cubs ambling down the beach. We had a pristine environment," he said, choking back tears. "What we've got now—well, it's a loss of innocence."[1]

Brooke Adkinson came in from Hinchinbrook Island, where he and his wife had built a home at the edge of a meadow of wild strawberries and raised four kids. Since his wife passed away, Adkinson has lived there alone. At sixty-three, he chops his own firewood; to pick up his mail, he canoes across a cove and then hikes five miles over the crest of a hill. "I came to Alaska forty years ago with the feeling that here was a land still unspoiled. There's this vast solitude, like you're alone with your creator," he said. "I never wanted that pipeline. I fought it tooth and nail because I knew what would happen. They killed something vital in me when they spilled that oil.

"You see, there's a rapport, a kind of kinship you sometimes develop with a particular place. It becomes sacred to you. That connection has been severed for me. Oh, Hinchinbrook Island is still there. The ground is still there, but the part that gave me feelings of joy and beauty has been ripped out. I notice this joy in the wild creatures. They live in the moment, no worries about the future. Every animal and every bird I've ever watched showed this joy of living. You see it in the way bear cubs and baby otters play. You see it in the hawks and eagles in spring—they're gliding and looking. Their joy is to be one with the wind. Now a lot of those birds are dead—and they died a horrible death, their insides burning with oil. If anyone wants to know what this oil spill is all about, they should imagine themselves in the position of the otters that were blinded."

When Adkinson walked through the streets of Cordova after the spill, he said he felt that a darkness had descended over the town. "The snow was still bright on the mountains and the sun sparkled off the sea, but I could feel this darkness everywhere, see it in everyone's eyes. It was like something had literally torn the souls of these people. I remembered the Cordova fire of 1963. The town burned, and the people rebuilt," he recalled. "After the 1964 earthquake, boats were wrecked in the harbor. Once again, the people bounced back. But this time their spirit has been crushed. It's the first time I've seen this—so much anger, fear, distrust, and despair. I wonder if their joy for life will ever return."

Environmentalist and fisherwoman Riki Ott described seeing the people of Cordova go through several stages of emotion as the spill unfolded. "First there was all this positive energy to do something—'Let's go! Let's get that oil!' When we made repeated calls to try to help and ran up against Alyeska's stone wall, our feelings turned to anger and frustration. It got real negative. Then, when the oil took off, Cordova hit rock bottom. That's when people were mad at everything."

The tension was so great that CDFU, the fishermen's union, kept a "decompression" room where they sent people who were so stressed they felt they were about to explode. As wildlife rescue organizer Kelly Weaverling recalled, "When Exxon and Fish and Wildlife were driving me over the edge, a woman from CDFU whisked me across the street and put me in a room at the

Prince William Hotel. She said, 'Look, CDFU keeps this room for people who get too hot. We stick them in here and close the door for a while, until they cool down.'"

After seeing the bird rescue fleet shut down, Weaverling eventually collected himself and started a volunteer corps for Prince William Sound. Operating solely on private donations, the corps patrolled for injured wildlife and kept a watchful eye on the operations of Exxon and the various government agencies. For his persistence, *Newsweek* magazine made Weaverling its unsung hero of the year for Alaska. "It's a great honor," he responded, "but it's kind of an embarrassment—all the ragging I get from my friends. I told *Newsweek* I wasn't really interested, and they told me I didn't have a choice. It's just that so many people exceeded themselves out there."

The fishermen of the Mosquito Fleet who, full of anxiety and determination, went out to save the hatcheries were also widely regarded as the heroes of the early days of the spill. One visiting congressman compared their efforts to the English fishermen in the World War II Battle of Dunkirk, who went out in skiffs and dories to rescue stranded soldiers. Jack Lamb, Riki Ott, Rick Steiner, and many other Cordovans, who worked relentlessly to save the hatcheries, now kept the pressure on Alyeska and Exxon.

And then there was David Grimes, smack in the midst of it all. Grimes didn't belong to the fishermen's union or draw pay from any agency or company. He was just a guy with a beautiful singing voice and an old battered truck. In a roomful of people yelling and screaming over the lack of skimmers and booms, Grimes, his hair pulled back in a ponytail, would calmly say, "When there's nothing you can do, you're freed from limitations; you can go for it." He had a way of appearing when needed, an ability to soothe angry feelings. He was with Jack Lamb at the command post in Valdez during the chaotic first week of the spill, and he flew to Scotland with Rick Steiner to see how people dealt with oil spills in the North Sea.

"Grimes is flying without a net," Weaverling said. "He never knows what he's going to do or say next. His perception of reality is beyond the concrete, more into the ethereal and spiritual. He's just out there, everywhere and nowhere—elusive. He's an inspiration. Some of us help rescue injured birds and otters, and he has a way of helping us heal inside."

Feeling the need to help people come to terms with some of the more personal and spiritual aspects of the spill, Grimes put all his savings into an aging wooden fishing boat, the *Orca II*. He used it to take groups of people—from industry officials to workers worn down from months on the spill—out on Prince William Sound. He showed them both the devastation and the surviving beauty—dark-stained beaches as well as coves with sparkling water. He'd say, "You know, as we help heal the sound, it's going to help heal us as well."

The lives of many people in Cordova were torn apart, not just by the oil but by the cleanup effort itself. Fishermen of the Mosquito Fleet had gone out to save the hatcheries as volunteers, with little thought of compensation. When Jack Lamb asked Exxon for help, Frank Iarossi had said, "How many boats do you have? Twenty-six? Okay, I'll hire them all in one whack."

Iarossi's response helped the fishermen protect the hatcheries, but it also brought them onto the payroll of a company they despised. Exxon began contracting fishermen to chase, contain, and clean up the oil if they could, and many of those who had gone out initially as volunteers started getting paid quite well. Although the prevailing sentiment in Cordova was that Exxon's effort was too little too late, there was no doubt that the oil company's infusion of cash sustained cleanup efforts.

Exxon's money also raised the specter of a big oil company buying off its most vocal critics. The first contracts required fishermen to sign a statement saying that they would not talk to the press about what they saw in Prince William Sound. The fishermen found this statement outrageous and nearly all refused to sign it. When the attempt at censure was eliminated, many did sign up. But the money itself gave rise to conflicting feelings. The contracts meant lots of cash. A person who refrained from signing on might have to watch his friends get rich. One fisherman, not from Cordova, believed that his boat was worth $500 a day. He decided to ask for $1,000 a day and approached Exxon tentatively. Before even asking his price, he was offered a contract at $3,000 a day.

"That money could mean a lot to me," said Cordovan Dennis

McGuire, "but I just can't do it." McGuire is an imposing, mus-
cular man, with wild, silver-streaked hair and beard. His wife,
Pat, is an artist who has developed ink and dye techniques to
make prints of salmon, herring, squid, and other creatures of
the sea. "We just bought this house," McGuire said. "We need a
good year to get our feet on the ground. But if I take Exxon's
money, what do I have to give up morally? I'd have to live with
the consequences the rest of my life.

"The money Exxon is throwing out is destroying this town,"
McGuire continued. "Iarossi says, 'Whatever it takes to make you
whole.' He thinks money can buy you back to where you were
before it happened. I don't care how much money they pour into
it, that devastation is there. Have you ever had a relative die?
How can you raise the dead with a dollar bill?

"I'm hurt—inside. Exxon will just write off the costs. For them
to throw money at us is just disgusting. If I keep all these feelings
inside, I'll get sick. This is the kind of stuff that kills people. The
trust is shaken. Doesn't anyone give a damn anymore? But
maybe this is what it takes to swing America into thinking about
the world around us. Someone has got to protect this planet. We
live here! This is our planet. Baby, this is it!"

Still, for some who fished out of Cordova, protection of the
planet was not as immediate a concern as the Exxon money floating around town in large amounts. People who fish for a living
are competitive by nature; they make their living by beating one
another to the catch. Some went after Exxon contracts as if the
contracts were a new species of fish and wound up with $200,000
to $300,000 for the season. This created a new division of wealth
in the community, not to mention a new brand of jealousy. Some
felt this sudden change in the local economy would upset the
competitive balance within the fishing community. Those with a
bundle of Exxon money could suddenly buy faster boats, better
sonar, more nets. Those who avoided Exxon's money as a matter
of conscience hoped they could pay their bills and stay competitive with their old equipment.

Tom Copeland, the man who, with his five-gallon buckets, had
scooped up more oil than Alyeska's best skimmer, felt people
who fished and also worked for Exxon might have to take drastic
steps to clear their consciences. He said, "Sure, Exxon's trying to

pay off the fishermen. But it could backfire on them. The problem is that a fisherman has to live with himself. If you're whoring on these wads of oil dollars now, the only way to cleanse your conscience is to take an extreme position down the road. We're not going to go down in history as the guys who got bought.

"The oil companies have ruled Alaska for the last fifteen years, and they will continue to do so. But we're not powerless. We can shut down the pipeline in a nonviolent manner. We can put 500 boats in the Valdez Narrows and challenge the navy to get us out of there. They could bring in the entire Pacific Fleet, but we'd be in there in November when it's dark, the wind blowing 90 miles an hour, and we could resupply. Eventually our demands for protecting Prince William Sound will be met or we'll be radicalized enough to shut down the pipeline."

Christine Stanford was one of the people who felt that doing cleanup work was a way to help restore the sound while earning needed money. She had grown up in the mountains near Anchorage and was attending the University of Oregon in Eugene when the *Exxon Valdez* went aground. She came back both to earn tuition for school and to help restore the sound.

"I've gone kayaking out there, watched the kittiwakes and puffins. We'd camp on a beach and look for whales rising in the mist. It was so fresh and magical," Stanford said. "It really hurts to think of those places covered with oil. You wonder if they'll ever be the same again. I can't bear to go back and look. But I wanted to do something, whatever I could, to help clean up the sound."

Stanford went to work at the boat cleaning facility in Cordova, washing boats that had been in the oil. "When people first came to work here, they were excited. A lot of them were like me. They thought they could make a difference, help heal the sound," she said. "But sometimes, for days on end, there was nothing to do, no boats to be cleaned. We just walked around. The boss said, 'If anyone from Exxon comes around, look busy. Get out your clipboard. Point at things.' Our motivation started to slip away. The prevailing attitude became make your money for the day and stay out of sight. Don't think about anything other than what they tell you this hour. Efficiency wasn't rewarded; the supervisors didn't want it. If you had a better idea, you learned not to mention it. Getting something accomplished was seen as getting one step closer to closing down the operation. They liked to see you find ways to prolong tasks. The longer a job took, the more money their company made."

Stanford described the techinques in use at the facility. "Simple-green—sounds so nice, doesn't it? That's what they called the chemical we used to clean the boats. 'Pass the simple-green.' 'Pour on some simple-green.' Workers started getting intense headaches. When VECO saw how sick people were getting from simple-green, they switched to orange-plus. Now that sounds like a new citrus drink. Well, people got so sick from orange-plus that VECO had to switch back to simple-green.

"I noticed a loss of short-term memory in myself. I got dizzy and had severe headaches. At night my whole body would be flushed, beet red. As soon as I quit working around simple-green, the symptoms went away."

As the people of Cordova lived through the prolonged tension and torment of the spill, their despair and frustration deepened. To reaffirm their connection to the sound, they set aside a day to focus on positive feelings about the sound and its place in their lives. The event was called "Sound Love" and was held on April 23 in the high school gymnasium. Letters and crayon drawings received from children all over the world were taped to one wall. On another wall an enormous scroll painted by the children of Cordova was hung. Each child, from kindergarten through sixth grade, had been asked to "try to turn your anger and hurt into a picture of the way you'd like the sound to be." At the very bottom of the scroll, preschoolers had scattered their handprints, like so many shells in the sand. Over their outstretched fingers danced urchins and crabs and octopuses with dozens of arms. Up through the water swam red fish, blue fish, pink fish, brown-and-black fish, polka-dot fish, and one fish with a green-plaid tail. Whales broke through the surface of the sea. Eagles and gulls flew over the waves. There were fishing boats with families waving their arms. There were rainbows and smiling suns in the sky. And above it all was written: "Prince William Sound—Our Home."

For "Sound Love," children of all ages crowded into the gym with their parents. One elderly lady sat in a wheelchair. Groups of students sat together in the bleachers. Many wore small paper hearts reading "Sound Love" pinned to their jacket or shirt. Grade school children sang a song they'd composed for the sound. Then, one at a time, people rose to share their feelings.

One woman played her guitar and sang: "I'm proud to be a fisherman's daughter. And I'm proud he married my cannery-working mother. When their fishing is over, they tie up at the dock and go a dancin' all night. . . ."

Another woman gave an emotional reading of the Declaration of Independence. As she spoke the words of the nation's founding fathers trying to liberate themselves from British oppression, everyone felt their own need to throw off the oppression that had descended over their lives.

"This is not just an issue of biology or economy or corporate policy," one man said. "This is a moral issue. We must find the sensitivity and determination to make sure this never happens again. Not just here—this must never happen to other communities and other beautiful places."

Department of Environmental Conservation commissioner Dennis Kelso, much loved because of his support of the fishermen, described going out to Knight Island after the oil had passed through. "The island was hit very hard all along the curve of the beach. I stood there on a spring morning when one would expect the sounds and smells of spring. But it was quiet and there was only the smell of the oil. I felt very sad. But as I was standing there wondering how long it would take the sound to recover, I heard breathing—the deep, explosive breathing of a large pod of killer whales. Their flukes slapped the water. They were huge ones, swimming together in synchrony. They passed close and headed out to open water, leaving the oil behind. We must go like the whales, leaving this sadness behind us."

The oil did move on. It spread southwest toward the Kenai Peninsula, and no one knew how far it would go. Prevailing sea currents and winds made the *Exxon Valdez* oil spill a continuing calamity. Every time it reached a new region or community, the oil spill effectively became a new and separate disaster. While the people of Valdez and Cordova felt the first impact, others would also have to deal with the grief and frustration, the struggle between conscience and greed, and the dilemma of not knowing what to do.

Chapter 17

The Kenai Fjords

When the spill happened, we followed it for a few days in the news," said David Ames, assistant director for the National Park Service in Alaska. "Like everyone else in the nation, we thought of the spill as something that happened in one place. That's how I pictured an oil spill, kind of a glob of oil around the tanker. It was terrible, but we were all very thankful that it was not happening along a national park shoreline. At least *we* didn't have to deal with it."

Then, on March 29, five days into the spill, the interagency regional response team, which was advising the Coast Guard, told Ames that there was a slight chance that some of the oil would drift out of Prince William Sound. As the currents flow, the first landfall outside the sound is Kenai Fjords, one of the most spectacular areas in the national park system.

Kenai Fjords is a roadless park southwest of Seward and reachable by boat from there in two hours when the sea is calm. When storms strike the outer Kenai Coast, 40-foot waves crash against exposed seawalls. The deep-cut fjords angle back into the coastal peaks and the Harding Ice Field, a remnant of the Pleistocene ice fields that once covered much of Alaska. This frozen sea still extends over some 1,145 square miles and is the origin of more than forty separate glaciers that carve the steep rock as they grind and tumble their way to the sea.

The steep and polished granite cliffs of the Fjords have been only recently released from hundreds of feet of ice. Here one can witness the birth of a new landscape—blades of grass sprout from thin crevices, and yellow flowers bloom from bare rock. While the landscape has a raw and barren grandeur, the sea spills over with life. It is a sanctuary for whales, seals, sea lions, and otters. Seabirds swirl around their sea cliff rookeries, and bald eagles glide along the coast. Occasionally, a peregrine falcon cuts through the sky in pursuit of another bird.

"With all that oil headed for the Fjords, we didn't know what to do," said Ames. "I had never faced an oil spill before." He had, however, faced volcanic eruptions and hot lava flows when stationed in Hawaii's Volcanoes National Park. "I didn't know what an oil spill would do, but in Hawaii I'd gotten used to dealing with an unpredictable force that was coming at you. You learned to respond quickly.

"A lot of people were trying to make us believe that since oil is organic, it would just evaporate and dissipate and we'd never see it," Ames said. "I'm not a chemist, but it seemed like it wasn't going to be so simple. I just knew this blob of stuff was coming and we had to respond to it."

With more oil than it could handle in Prince William Sound, Exxon wasn't interested in rushing people over to the Kenai Fjords. The regional response team said that there was only a remote chance of the oil leaving the sound. However, Anne Castellina, superintendent of Kenai Fjords, called Ames. She said, "The National Oceanographic and Atmospheric Association's worst-case scenario is that no more than fifty barrels would escape the sound. And the Coast Guard told me, 'You won't get any oil. You don't have a problem.' But local fishermen are telling me to watch out."

Castellina learned that Dr. Tom Royer at the Institute of Marine Science in Fairbanks was confirming the fishermen's fears. The prevailing currents would carry much of the oil straight onto the outer coast of the park. Seward, the town closest to the Fjords, asked Castellina for help in coordinating a response. After flying over the spill, city officials told her, "It's huge and it's coming our way."

"The city was trying to take action, but we couldn't really figure out what to do," said Jack Sinclair, a resident of Seward. "So we approached the National Park Service and asked for assistance. We said, 'You're a federal agency. Can you help get a response together?'"

Ames agreed with Castellina that they had to try to keep the oil from hitting Seward and Kenai Fjords. "But I just didn't know what we were going to do without some help," Ames said. Then they got lucky. Ames had used an Incident Command Team before. One of these emergency strike teams, made up of individuals from different federal agencies who are trained to cope with sudden disasters, was available. "This oil spill was looking a lot like a fire to me," Ames said. "It was chaotic and destructive, and it was moving fast. With only six people on the Kenai Fjords staff, we didn't have the people or experience to deal with this kind of emergency. So I called for an Incident Command Team and was told, 'The Alaska team went to Valdez. But it wasn't being utilized. We were sending the team members home, but we can send them on to you.'"

Ames said he wanted the team right away for the park and to help the residents of Seward, who knew the oil was coming and feared that neither the Coast Guard nor Exxon planned to offer protection. But he ran into an unexpected wall of resistance. "The Department of Interior's environmental coordinator, Paul Gates, told me, 'You shouldn't send an Incident Command Team down there. You can't do that. You know the Coast Guard is running things for the federal government. You can't do anything unless the Coast Guard tells you to, or the National Park Service won't get reimbursed.'"

When Ames checked with the Coast Guard, he heard again its original, highly optimistic projection that if the oil ever did come out of Prince William Sound, it would just drift out into the gulf and vanish. It wouldn't hit the Kenai Fjords. It would move offshore and disappear. Ames realized that to try to protect the national park he would have to go against the plan the Department of Interior was insisting he follow. He said, "Other agencies, such as the state Fish and Wildlife Service, seemed to be heeding the warning to do what they were told or they wouldn't get paid for it. . . . But our responsibility is a national park. No matter what others were doing, we had to try our damnedest to protect the park."

Nevertheless, Ames felt cautious about bucking both the

Coast Guard and the Department of Interior. He sought advice from Boyd Evison, Park Service director for Alaska, who was in Washington, D.C., at the time. Evison told Ames to get the Incident Command Team to Seward as fast as he could. To Evison the priorities were clear: "Our mandate is the act which created the National Park Service and the laws establishing parks. Our job is to protect parks. We have to gather information on the park's coastline in order to protect key resources and to assess the impacts of this spill."

In Washington, D.C., Evison was sensing that the restraint on the Park Service was emanating from behind the scenes. He could see that Paul Gates was getting directions from Vern Wiggins, a political appointee well known for his prodevelopment views. In the late 1970s, Wiggins had been executive director of a pro-industry lobbying group that fought the creation of new parks and refuges in Alaska. That battle was lost in 1980, when the Alaska National Interest Lands Conservation Act more than doubled the national park and refuge systems in the state. However, during the Reagan administration, Wiggins was appointed federal cochairman of the Alaska Land Use Council, in which capacity he tried to achieve administratively what he had failed to do politically. In the waning days of the Reagan administration, Wiggins was appointed Interior's deputy undersecretary for Alaska, wielding considerable authority over the parks and refuges whose creation he had fought. Jack Hession, the Sierra Club's Alaska representative, observed, "Wiggins failed to block the Alaska Lands Act, but since then he's made a career of undercutting the parks and refuges created by this act. And as soon as the oil spill happened, Wiggins went to work subverting the proper response of Fish and Wildlife and the National Park Service."

After the wreck of the *Exxon Valdez*, the Bush administration designated Wiggins as Interior's oil spill coordinator. "I was at the first briefing that was given to the Secretary of Interior, and it was run by Vern Wiggins," Evison said. "Vern belittled the threat of oil hitting anything outside the sound. He said if it did, it would be broken up into tiny little tar balls, inert and harmless. He wasn't pleased when I told him that the oil was already within a couple of miles of the Kenai Fjords—and that it wasn't in the form of little tar balls."

Rather than backing down in the face of Wiggins and Interior's bizarre directive to wait and see, Evison told Ames to use the Incident Command Team as effectively as possible. The command team was in Seward the next day and immediately went to work with Superintendent Castellina, drawing on the abilities of her staff and local people. The command team helped set up emergency phone lines, located boats, assessed supplies, and developed lines of communication within the community. To get people working together, the team helped the community form its own Multiagency Advisory Committee, or MAC group, to set priorities for oil spill work. Castellina was chosen to chair the meetings, and her first task was to draw all the key parties into a concerted effort. However, Exxon had no one in Seward and wouldn't send anyone over for the first meetings.

"The day before our first MAC meeting on April 3, the Coast Guard boat left Seward for Ketchikan for a dry-dock inspection," Castellina said. "They told me they had scheduled this checkup for a year and couldn't change it. That boat was the only Coast Guard presence in Seward. They didn't send us anyone else. Meanwhile we scouted the spill from the air and saw it coming closer. It was creeping closer and closer every day."

Castellina asked Alaska Senator Ted Stevens for help in getting the Coast Guard back to Seward. "He called the Coast Guard and complimented them on what a great job they were doing in Seward," she said. "He knew they weren't doing anything. He used this ploy to coax them into getting someone over here."

Boyd Evison was surprised that the Coast Guard, like Interior, was trying to underplay the spill. "We sat face to face with them in a briefing with a senator and a bunch of generals and they denied oil approaching the national parks," Evison reported. "But the oil was there. Our people had seen it. The Coast Guard was upset at us because after they denied how far the oil had advanced, our on-scene people got up and said, 'But it's there and there and there.' Threats were made against our people. 'We're going to the highest levels of Interior and get you,' they told us." Interior could apply pressure through budget restrictions, censure, or transfer of Park Service staff.

Meanwhile, at park headquarters in Seward, Castellina was trying to get containment boom out to the most sensitive shorelines and streams. City officials said that if she could help provide the organizational expertise, they'd get the money to buy the boom. "The oil was coming down on us, and we were working with people in the community to figure out the highest priorities for streams both inside and outside the park," Castellina said. "Our responsibility was larger than the park. We couldn't just look at the boundaries of our own turf. We had to look at the ecology of the entire area. And we had to get boom out there right away."

However, in Washington, D.C., the National Park Service got orders from the Department of Interior not to deploy boom. Officially, Interior was saying that there was no threat, no need for action by the Park Service or Fish and Wildlife. But the oil was coming; the shorelines of parks and refuges were threatened. Castellina said, "I couldn't understand why they didn't want us to do anything." There was no clear answer. Perhaps Interior officials were simply too far from the spill to perceive the danger it posed to parks and refuges. Perhaps they were worried about how much it would cost to ward off the oil. Or perhaps, as some suggested, Interior wanted to play down the magnitude of the spill, hoping it would somehow fade away and not cast a shadow over the department's plans to develop oil in other offshore areas and in the Arctic National Wildlife Refuge.

For Boyd Evison, Interior's motivations may have been obscured, but the orders were unequivocal. He said, "We were told not to put any boom out there to protect Kenai Fjords. The order came through Paul Gates, but it must have originated with Vern Wiggins. In any event, I told our people to go ahead and do what they felt had to be done."

Castellina agonized over what to do. She knew Evison was relying on her judgment. And she knew that if she acted against the wishes of Gates and Wiggins, it could mean not only her job but Evison's career. "By the letter of the law, I had no authority to deploy boom," Castellina said. "The Coast Guard had that authority. I begged for their help, but they didn't see the threat. They weren't here. If anyone was going to deploy boom, it was going to have to be us. It was a difficult decision for me. I had always been a good little bureaucrat, doing what I was told. Now the Coast Guard had called and chewed my butt, and I felt threats from Interior. If we deployed that boom, we'd be going out on a limb and taking a lot of good people out there with us.

But how could we sit here and do nothing? The Park Service had hired me to do a job: protect the resource. And that's what I was going to do."

By April 3, the leading tendrils of oil were within 3 miles of the Chiswell Islands and headed for the national park several miles away. Over the next few days, oil hit the Chiswells, killed thousands of murres, and edged closer to the park. The Incident Command Team sent boats and aircraft along the coast to evaluate the danger to wildlife and intertidal zones. As the boom ordered by Seward began to arrive, Castellina had it deployed to the most critical habitat areas. By April 10, the leading edge of the slick had already struck the headlands of the park and was working its way into the fjords.

On April 17, the Incident Command Team turned over its deployed boom and other emergency operations to Exxon, which needed to work on several fronts at once—maintaining the boom, collecting debris from the beaches, retrieving dead birds, rescuing live birds and otters, and trying to clean the beaches with hot and cold water washing and bioremediation.

The MAC group, chaired by Anne Castellina, established the retrieval of dead birds and otters as the highest priority for Exxon. "We had to get the oiled wildlife out of the food chain," said Castellina, who started a reconnaissance of the Kenai Fjords shoreline on the day Exxon arrived to begin cleaning up. As her boat entered Thunder Bay, she was overjoyed—there was no sign of oil on the beach. A hundred feet from shore, those onboard saw only clean rocks. Then they saw an eagle on the beach. Its wings were partially extended, and it was shaking. Even before going ashore and reaching the bird, they saw the problem. The surface of the rocks was clean, but between every stone and cobble, oil was thick as molasses. In deep puddles of oil they found lumps that had been birds, and they realized the eagle had been feeding on the black carcasses.

"I poked around with a stick, and every crevice was filled with dead birds," said Castellina. "I'd been living this thing day and night for a long time, but this is when it really hit me. It hit so hard I couldn't talk. Then I began asking myself, 'What have we done? What has humanity done? What could I have done differently?'"

Meanwhile, Evison observed that the Fish and Wildlife Service was moving very cautiously. "You have to understand they were following instructions. I know their director felt that we were overreacting. But it was clear that Fish and Wildlife people in the field would have liked to be doing a whole lot more than their bureau was doing. Heck, they came to us to volunteer to help on their own time. They wanted to be out there with us, keeping track of the oil, trying to divert it. But for a very long time the only Fish and Wildlife participant in Seward was one person who just happened to be a member of the Incident Command Team."

Castellina came in contact with some of the Fish and Wildlife Service people who were trying to help regardless of the orders coming from Washington, D.C. Castellina said, "They were being told that there was no problem, but they knew there *was* a problem. They were totally frustrated and apologetic. One of them told me, 'We should have been right there with you.'"

Meanwhile, another clash developed between Evison and Interior's spill response hierarchy over making information available to the public. "I received word that we should not be talking directly with the press," Evison said. "Everything should be cleared through the regional response team. For example, one of the television networks asked for use of some of our film footage for a news program. I was in Washington at the time, and we were told, 'You can't do that. You shouldn't give it to them.' And I said, 'Unless there's a legal reason for our not giving something out, we are going to make it available.'"

As the summer wore on, Evison was angered at finding that other federal agencies were allowed to receive reimbursement from Exxon, while the Park Service was excluded. "Early on, Vern instructed us to accept no funds from Exxon," Evison said. "But later I found out that other agencies had been collecting directly from Exxon."

In addition to not being allowed to be reimbursed by Exxon, the Park Service was chastised by Interior for the money it had already spent. "The Park Service did their thing, spent lots of money," Paul Gates said. "No one had reins on them. We just said, 'If you are running, make sure you know where you are running and how you are going to pay for it.' All the dollars spent didn't stop much oil."

However, as Evison had pointed out during the first days of the spill, the Park Service didn't expect to stop all the oil—but it needed to get the best possible assessment of the oil conditions, to try to divert oil from the most sensitive areas, and to try to keep the cleanup from doing more damage than the oil itself. In these efforts, the Park Service succeeded despite interference from the Department of Interior.

When Evison was asked if he felt he had risked his career trying to protect the park, he answered, "There was a time there, quite a while in fact, when it was rumored that I was going to be yanked out of here. But I didn't feel like I was risking my career. No, not really, because there is a lot of strength in just doing what's right."

Anne Castellina spoke more pointedly about the pressure brought to bear on Evison. "Those people in Interior who had been trying to stop us knew we had gone over budget, so they said, 'If you spent money you don't have in your budget, we can take you to court to make you pay for it personally. And if you can't pay, you'll go to jail.' We heard that if they couldn't get Boyd Evison any other way, they'd get him this way. When I heard that, I figured that if I'm going down in flames, I'm at least going to keep doing what's right."

With Castellina directing the MAC group and working with the Incident Command Team, more than 15,000 feet of boom had been deployed to ten priority sites—ten important salmon-spawning streams, nine of which were completely protected from the oil. But there was no way to cordon off the entire Kenai Fjord coastline, and 40 miles of it were hit with oil. In places, the oil worked down at least 12 inches into beach sediments.

By summer's end, the National Park Service's initiative in bringing in the Incident Command Team was widely recognized as the best response mounted by any community or agency. The Park Service had made the best inventory of shoreline resources before the oil arrived and the best assessment of damage after the oil struck. However, the Department of Interior assigned the task of preparing its official spill damage assessment report to the Fish and Wildlife Service. Noting the irony, Jack Hession said, "It looks as if the National Park Service has been excluded from writing this final spill report because it was so aggressive, thorough, and uncompromising in responding to the spill and gathering information."

Looking back over the five intense months of fighting the spill in Kenai Fjords, David Ames, who had initiated the Park Service's response, said, "There's just nothing that compares to what we've been through. It's possible that all the oil will disappear in a few decades as the ecosystem cleanses itself. But you have to be pretty optimistic to think it will ever be clean in our lifetime. There's never been this level of manmade damage to a national park, ever."

On September 6, Exxon wrapped up its cleanup work in the Kenai Fjords. After taking over from the Incident Command Team, it had mounted a massive cleaning effort in the area. Exxon's waste disposal plant near Seward had shredded and bagged more than a thousand tons of oily debris retrieved from beaches. But, as Boyd Evison observed, the beaches were far from clean. "Many people saw the oil on the shore and thought, 'What a mess, but clean it up and everything will be all right.' No way. Even if we found a miraculous way to suck it all off the rocks tomorrow, it would still be in the ecosystem. And it's going to affect it for generations."

Paul Gates said, "I don't think you can point any fingers. I think the system worked. There were some rough edges along the way, some shoving and pushing. But in the grand scheme of things it worked. The spill was so overwhelming, we weren't capable of controlling it. It didn't matter what we did."

However, Anne Castellina said, "In hindsight, I would have screamed and yelled a lot more about the oil getting out of the sound. It would have made a difference if they had listened to us sooner. They should have headed that oil off at the pass, never let it get this far.

"Whenever I've gone out to Aialik Bay in the Fjords, I've always been comforted by knowing it will be there for my children and grandchildren. When we violate a place like the Kenai Fjords, we destroy part of our country and part of our future. It's for our children that these beautiful areas must be saved."

Chapter 18

The Refuge Islands

While Anne Castellina and the Park Service struggled to save the Kenai Fjords, others tried to protect the widely scattered islands of the Alaska Maritime Wildlife Refuge, which extend from the southeast tip of Alaska, through the Gulf of Alaska, and out to the Aleutians and the Bering Sea. Some of the most fascinating and wildlife-rich parts of the refuge are the remote Chiswell, Pye, and Barren islands. Windswept and surrounded with thundering surf, they are home to great colonies of seabirds, otters, seals, and sea lions. And these islands lay directly in the path of the oil surging out of Prince William Sound.

"For the first few days we didn't react to the spill very much at all," said Mike Hedrick, deputy refuge manager. "Then we started getting the idea that this spill was not acting like the experts thought it would. The oil was moving faster and further than they had predicted. It was going to be far more destructive than anyone realized."

By April 6, the Chiswell Islands had been hit, and Hedrick flew out along the isolated, storm-wracked coast to see how bad it was. "Migrating gray whales were coming out from underneath the slick and getting ahead of the oil," he said. "Without even searching for whales, I counted seven pods with forty-two individual whales in an hour. We could see them spouting further out as we flew along the coast.

"The Chiswells were hit first and they were hit the hardest. They're on the outer coast and face into the gulf. There's a lot of wave action on those sea cliffs and the narrow beaches. I could see that the remoteness that makes these islands valuable for wildlife was also going to make protecting them impossible and cleaning them up very difficult."

As the leading edge of the spill moved southwest with the currents, oil swirled through the Pye Islands off the outer Kenai Coast and around the Barren Islands at the mouth of Cook Inlet. Oil washed ashore repeatedly as the tides rose and fell. Storm waves sent oil 40 to 50 feet above the mean high-tide line. Although the beaches were in a national wildlife refuge and were as heavily oiled as any place in the sound, no one rushed out with booms and skimmers or beach workers to clean them up.

"Exxon ignored these islands for a long time because they are difficult to reach," Hedrick said. "The Barren Islands were sort of 'out of sight, out of mind'—Exxon felt it could put off cleaning them. It took us a long time to impress on the company how seriously the spill could hurt wildlife in these areas."

In early July, Exxon turned hot-water sprayers onto the rock cliffs and boulder-strewn coves of the Pye Islands. After being prodded by Vice Admiral Clyde E. Robbins, Exxon sent crews to clean the Barrens in late July. However, the company preset a date for the crews' withdrawal: August 14. Exxon said that by that date the beaches would be treated and deteriorating weather would make further cleaning inadvisable. After Exxon's crews left, John Martin, the refuge manager who was now helping coordinate the Fish and Wildlife Service's overall spill response, flew out to inspect the islands. "I had heard all the horror stories about Exxon's cleanup, but when I got out to the Pye Islands it looked like they were doing a pretty good job," he said. "I'd say they probably got the rocks 75 percent clean. Of course since then they've been reoiled."

The Barrens were exposed to reoiling from patches of oil circulating with the currents and because of the nature of some of the beaches. Gravel slopes up from the water and then drops off to form small lagoons, where high tides stack up driftwood. Summer storms threw oil over the top of these beaches and into the lagoons. When Exxon workers arrived they gathered up oily stumps, snags, and strings of kelp tangled in the pools. But oil was still buried in the gravel, where it would periodically leach out and reoil entire beaches.

Exxon, anxious to move on to other beaches, said it wasn't going to dig into the gravel because it didn't contain a significant amount of oil. John Martin disagreed. "When I walked along the top of the beach, it had a slippery feeling. It was like walking on ball bearings because the gravel was soaked in oil. When you started walking, displacing that top layer of gravel, the oil would just ooze up."

Martin wanted Exxon to remove the oil imbedded in the sand and gravel, but, since the spill had not been federalized, he lacked the authority to make such a demand. Nevertheless, when Exxon asked Martin to give his unofficial approval for the company to demobilize and leave the Barren Islands, he refused. "This is a real bone of contention for us," he said. "The oil is still there, so I can't agree when Exxon asks for my blessing to demobilize. If I sign off, Exxon can say, 'Demobilization has been approved. The area is environmentally stable. We can leave.' But I didn't agree. Nobody but Exxon would have called those beaches clean."

Exxon was, of course, counting on winter storms and oil-eating bacteria to work for them over the winter. While effective in some places, they were unlikely to make much of a difference on many parts of the island. Because the oil-saturated berm was at the high point of the beach, it was out of reach of the oil-eating microbes that live in seawater. Exxon had fertilized the oily berm, but the granules remained undissolved on the gravel piled 30 to 40 feet above the waterline. Also, as the cold weather arrived, the microbes would lose their appetites and eat less oil. Martin thought the storms would probably break the oil out of the gravel, but only if storm waves coincided with the very highest tides. Otherwise, the waves wouldn't reach the oil. It had been a combination of storms and high spring tides that had thrown the oil over the top of the beach, and Martin feared that not until the following spring—when the birds would be back—would the tides and storms reach the berm and break the oil loose.

Martin had wanted Exxon to thoroughly clean these beaches during the summer. When Exxon failed to do this, he at least wanted to gain control over when the oil would break out of the gravel and reenter the water. "The only thing we could think of doing was a real bad trade-off, but it became our bottom line because nothing else could be done," he said. "We told Exxon to take a large bulldozer in there in late fall and push that oiled berm down to the bottom of the beach where the winter waves could clean it. Exxon said they didn't want to go out there in winter. So we told them, 'We'll give you a permit to ship your damn cat out there in summer and leave it. Then pick a nice day in the fall to fly out in a helicopter. Push the oily gravel down to the bottom of the beach where waves can get at it. Then park your machinery until you can come back and get it in spring.'"

When Exxon refused to try this last-ditch effort, Martin concluded that, for all its assurances, Exxon didn't really care about actually cleaning the beaches. "I always thought, if you cleaned something, it was clean," he said. "Exxon came in here and wiped down the rocks in a superficial way. They cleaned up the oil pools. They burned the logs. They collected all the oil-soaked kelp and debris on the beach. But they left all the oil in the gravel. I mean, it's not clean. And I don't think any beaches will ever be really clean as a result of this spill. I think we'll always be finding some of the oil. I don't like it, but there's nothing I can do about it."

When Exxon pulled out in mid-August, Martin was left to ponder the disaster that had befallen the refuge. The oil hit the refuge islands before some migrant birds arrived. However, the murres were already in the Chiswell, Pye, and Barren islands in early April, and 80 to 90 percent of them perished. While this loss may not seem significant in terms of the millions of murres throughout Alaska, it virtually wiped out these island colonies.

Martin was furious with Exxon for causing the accident but felt that the blame had to be shared. "I think that as users of oil we all contributed to it," he said. "The state probably contributed, because before this oil spill DEC was going downhill—the oil companies and the miners had their thumbs on DEC. I know that the Fish and Wildlife Service contributed. Last year we did a comprehensive plan on the refuge that looked at all the major environmental problems, and we didn't even list the possibility of an oil spill. Didn't even list it!"

The Fish and Wildlife Service's tendency to deny the possibility of a large spill developed into a desire to downplay its reality once the spill occurred. Martin recalled his trip to Washington, D.C., to prepare the testimony on the spill that the director of the Fish and Wildlife Service would give to Congress. "If I talked about so many 'deaths of birds,' they took those words out. It became 'oil impacting' this or that. I got to see the internal controls that the appointed officials have over the 'professionals.' When I wrote what was happening, it was watered down by taking out harsh words. Instead of how many deaths we really had, they'd say, 'approximately this many.' I think Fish and Wildlife officials in D.C. thought, particularly during the first weeks of the spill, that they could mute the effect this spill might have on the oil companies, because ANWR [oil exploration in the Arctic National Wildlife Refuge] was still alive."

Here was denial reappearing in the wake of the crisis. According to Martin, the pre-spill complacency that had contributed to the devastation caused by the *Exxon Valdez* was reemerging, fostered by officials at the highest levels of the Fish and Wildlife Service. By watering down Martin's field reports, appointed officials in the nation's capital were smoothing things over, reassuring Congress and the president that the spill really wasn't all that bad and encouraging people not to worry about it too much. Political appointees within the Department of Interior told Martin's director not to allow field people to talk to congressional committees—they preferred to do that themselves. Martin felt that they "wanted people to view the spill the way this administration wanted it to be viewed."

Dr. Calvin Lensink, who had worked for the Fish and Wildlife Service for thirty-three years, also critiqued the agency's oil spill response. "The Service didn't have a good biological contingency plan," Lensink said. "It had other commitments and didn't know where the money was coming from for this. It was reluctant to get in there and hire people to work on the spill. Fish and Wildlife decision-makers were even reluctant to divert people from other projects. To have somebody doing anything with birds, you were going to have to charter boats, and where was the money going to come from? Nobody knew. Basically, [people at] the refuge weren't turned loose until the middle of June to start doing anything on damage assessment. . . . Damage assessment should have started on March 25."

Deputy refuge manager Mike Hedrick hoped the government would learn from this spill and make some responsible changes. "There *will* be other spills," Hedrick said. "In fact, the islands of the refuge were hit with more than thirty oil spills in 1989 alone. While none was nearly as large as the *Exxon Valdez* spill, the cumulative, year-to-year effects of these smaller spills could be just as devastating. Will the Fish and Wildlife Service be prepared to protect wildlife from future oil pollution, or are we going to perpetuate our mistakes spill after spill, until the accumulated impact becomes irreversible?

"The Fish and Wildlife Service is the trustee of the nation's wildlife for all the people of the United States, but it's part of the political process. We've gone through a period of ten to twelve years in which this nation has been in the mode of developing natural resources. Our charge was to develop rather than to moderate development to accommodate wildlife."

To Hedrick, the response of Fish and Wildlife to this oil spill was indicative of a larger problem. "Early in this spill, the wildlife managers in this agency realized there was going to be a major impact on wildlife in Alaska," Hedrick said. "But we weren't out front the way some people wanted us to be, because from a political standpoint it probably wasn't healthy to be out there.

"I'm sure that some people back in Washington, D.C., viewed this spill and wondered when it was going to go away. Congress was considering opening the Arctic National Wildlife Refuge for oil development, and this administration and our Secretary of Interior are in favor of opening it up. To proponents of oil development, this oil spill and its impact on wildlife was bad luck, an inconvenience. I don't think the public appreciates how oil-related politics touches so much of this."

After Exxon packed up and went home in September, Mike Hedrick surveyed the damage. He thought the islands would recover, but not soon, "not in the way we measure time." John Martin said, "I'm madder than hell about this cleanup. I wish I had been able to tell Exxon that they had to clean up the gravel beaches and they had to do it before fall. But all I could do was make recommendations."

Exxon was hoping that winter storms would scour oil from the sea cliffs and beaches. Hedrick, Martin, and other Fish and Wildlife Service officials feared that oil would remain buried in the gravel and fine sands, slowly leaching out and endangering wildlife for years to come.

Chapter 19

Kachemak Bay

On March 30, six days after the grounding of the *Exxon Valdez*, a small notice on an inside page of the *Homer News* said, "The Prince William Sound oil slick may be headed this way." At the time, the main body of oil was flowing through the sound: herring fishing seasons were being canceled, the Cordova Mosquito Fleet was working around the clock to protect the hatcheries, and the National Oceanographic and Atmospheric Association (NOAA) was still predicting that only small amounts of oil would escape into the Gulf of Alaska.

In Homer, most people viewed the spill as a catastrophe that happened 250 miles away. However, a week after the grounding, a thick sea of crude oil escaped the sound and hovered off the outer coast of the Kenai Peninsula. Its western edge had reached Aialik Bay, where Anne Castellina was fighting to save Kenai Fjords National Park. It began to look as if offshore currents and the prevailing northerly winds might carry most of the oil toward Kodiak and the Katmai Coast. Then the forecast changed to winds out of the Bering Sea, winds that could conceivably push the oil into Cook Inlet, toward Kachemak Bay and toward Homer.

"Homer Braces; Oil Enters Cook Inlet" read the *Homer News* headline on April 13. Throughout that weekend, frustration focused on Exxon. The company hadn't made it to Homer yet. "Exxon's absence reflects a larger problem," wrote Tom Kizzia, the newspaper's managing editor. "The Homer area's plight, however serious, is not ranked by officials elsewhere with the crisis in Valdez, Seward, and even Kodiak."

Two days later, the first sheets of oily sheen and patches of mousse rounded the corner of the Kenai Peninsula and entered Kachemak Bay, one of the most productive and scenic coastal areas in the world. Here, glaciered peaks rise from green waters containing an abundance of crab, shrimp, herring, and salmon. The bay has been called the Big Sur of Alaska, both for its landscape and the many artists who are drawn to its shores. Some beaches are so smooth and sandy that at low tide people gallop their horses along the edge of the surf. Seldovia and the small Native villages of Port Graham and English Bay are tucked into coves along thickly wooded slopes leading back to glaciers and high mountain ridges.

Homer, with a population of 3,500, is the largest town on Kachemak Bay, and it's literally the end of the road: get on a highway anywhere in the United States and you can't drive any farther than Homer. Over the years, it has become a sanctuary for people who want to be part of a small community set in one of the most inspiring landscapes on earth. Residents of Homer and its environs are extremely protective of their bay. When the state sold oil leases in the outer bay in the early 1970s, local residents protested that Kachemak was one of those special places where oil development simply wasn't worth the risk. They stood up to the oil industry and made such a persuasive case that the state took the unprecedented action of buying back the oil leases it had sold. Now the people of Kachemak Bay had oil from the *Exxon Valdez* heading their way.

"Nobody knew how frightened we were," said Marge Tillion, an energetic young woman who combines motherhood with work as a medical aide, volunteer firefighter, and commercial fisherwoman. "Fishing is my life. If you fish and have done it for a long time, you're not in it for the money. It has adverse conditions and unstable income. You fish because you love that way of life."

Anxiety rose around the bay as people began to realize that the oil was coming and that the fate of their coast lay with the wind and tides. Tillion began compiling a list of fishermen and their boats willing to combat the oil, and within forty-eight hours she had more than a hundred signed up.

Following the approach that had worked in Seward, Homer formed its own Multiagency Advisory Committee (MAC) to organize the local response. Borough mayor[1] Don Gillman appointed Loren Flagg, a fisheries biologist and fishing guide, to be the group's first chairman. "We set our priorities at that first MAC meeting: 30,000 feet of boom was needed immediately to protect the major salmon streams and critical habitats," Flagg said. "But we couldn't get any boom from Exxon. We needed an Exxon rep to work with. When we finally got one, he was a retired public relations man who'd never worked in Alaska and knew nothing about an oil spill. This was just unforgivable. It showed us their callousness, their lack of care and understanding. As a result, very little got done for two weeks. We kept hammering away, but Exxon didn't get us any boom. And this prompted area residents to take matters into their own hands."

By the third week in April, fishermen and loggers banded together to build their own boom from logs. They worked in volunteer shifts throughout the night, limbing and notching spruce trees on the beach near the harbor. Nobody had ever built a log boom before, but nobody in Homer was willing to sit around and watch oil reach their hatchery, coves, and streams. Across the bay in Seldovia, people began making a boom to string across the mouth of Seldovia Bay, which sheltered their town. They used whatever they could find: logs, fishnet webbing, Typar (a permeable construction fabric), and crab pots. Junior high and high school students were let out of school to help fill sandbags for anchors.

Meanwhile, Gillman secured funds from Exxon and the state for the Homer MAC group to defend Kachemak Bay. Now Loren Flagg and the MAC team didn't have to depend on Exxon to order commercial boom. "That's when we knew for sure that Exxon had been giving us the runaround," Flagg said. "Because when we got the money in our control, we ordered boom and got 5,000 feet within two days. This was a prime example of our frustration with Exxon's lies. They had told us there was no boom available. But they just hadn't tried to get it. They deceived us."

The people of Kachemak Bay were so incensed with Exxon that they tried to get Alaska Congressman Don Young and Senator Ted Stevens to eliminate Exxon from the cleanup. As Flagg recalled, "It was an attempted coup by the citizens of Homer to overthrow Exxon, just get them out of here and have the state or federal government take over the spill."

When the attempt to replace Exxon didn't work in Homer, John Mickelson, a fisherman from Seldovia, tried to make a citizen's arrest of the Exxon representative during a MAC meeting. As Mickelson recalled, "It's a federal misdemeanor to convey or impart false information with reckless regard for human life. The chaotic response to this oil spill was definitely endangering lives, and the Exxon representatives were intentionally giving misleading facts. When you boil it all down, it's against the law to lie if it means you are endangering somebody. And if you see a crime being committed, and you know it's a crime and don't intervene, then you're guilty too. I saw what was happening, so on a moral basis I had to go ahead and arrest that Exxon man. He said, 'Okay, you do what you have to do.' I think he'd been instructed on how to respond, so I didn't have to wrestle him down. However, I couldn't get an officer of the law to take him to jail, so he went free."

By April 24, gale-force winds had broken open containment boom on the outer Kenai Coast. Oil rushed onto the beaches, coating the estuaries of salmon-spawning streams. As storm waves pounded the coast, Exxon's skimmers were far from Kachemak Bay, bottled up in sheltered coves. When the storm cleared, sheen and chunks of emulsified oil were seen near Seldovia, and sheets of oil were approaching the Native villages of Port Graham and English Bay. A combination of commercial and handmade log booms were stretched between the coves and streams and the advancing oil. However, the oil took its toll on the vast stretches of unprotected coast wherever winds and currents broke through the patchwork defense.

By mid-May, globs of oil were washing up on the seaward side of Homer Spit, a sliver of land extending more than a mile into Kachemak Bay. Within hours, volunteers and Exxon workers were combing the beach for tar balls. Exxon announced that about 500 feet of beach had been hit, but officials at the Homer Center for Disaster Assistance reported oil on more than 2 miles of beach.

Some of the oil unexpectedly moved past Kachemak Bay and

on up Cook Inlet, where fishermen in Kenai were readying their drift nets to catch salmon. "When the Coast Guard said oil was going to curl up into Cook Inlet, we didn't think it was going to reach our fishing district," said David Horne, vice president of the United Cook Inlet Drifters Association. "When the first tar balls started showing up, we thought the currents would turn the oil around and wash it back out Cook Inlet. We wanted to fish. We kept waiting for the season to open. But the oil stayed, and Fish and Game kept closing the season, week after week."

Only scattered patches of oil reached the rich fishing grounds near Kenai, but with the state's zero-tolerance policy it was enough to close the entire summer season. There were 585 fishermen who weren't allowed to fish. Many of them had been unable to fish in 1987 when the tanker *Glacier Bay* spilled 125,000 gallons of oil in Cook Inlet and in 1988 when an oil slick from an unknown source appeared in their fishing district. "I feel so frustrated with the oil companies, because we've faced these problems before," Horne said. "I expected them to have learned something. We kept hearing that the oil companies had all this new equipment and their response would be better next time. But it wasn't. There was absolutely no difference. I realize now that the technology just isn't available to handle a spill of any magnitude. The way things are going, we might never get to fish again."

Meanwhile, Kachemak Bay area residents were becoming increasingly incensed with Exxon's lack of resolve to clean up the hard-hit beaches of the outer coast. Gore Point became the focus of their frustration. As Gore Point was oiled and reoiled by sheets of oil, the Homer MAC group and local residents pleaded again and again for Exxon to clean it up. However, by the end of May, the area was still heavily oiled, and Vice Admiral Clyde E. Robbins and DEC commissioner Dennis Kelso came to Homer to demand an explanation from Exxon for delays in cleaning Gore Point and other beaches in the Kachemak area.

"I'm tired of hearing about Gore Point. I want it clean—whatever it takes," said Robbins, who also said he sensed that Exxon was more interested in stilling local criticism than in collecting oil. "I get the feeling Exxon's idea is, 'Let's throw 140 men at the beaches and that'll keep 'em quiet for a while.' Well, it isn't keeping them quiet. I want to see a plan, and 140 men won't hack it. The last time I came down here, there were a thousand excuses why it wasn't done."[2]

Cleaning Gore Beach was difficult because the waves had buried oil in the sand and gravel. To actually remove the oil, Exxon would have had to resort to a type B cleanup in which heavy equipment is used to dig down into the beach substrata. Exxon resisted this costly cleanup method. "I cannot give you a better answer on whether we will dig up Gore Beach or not because I don't have it," responded Exxon representative Dean Peeler at the May 31 Homer MAC meeting. "I can't give you what I don't have. And I don't know where we're going by continuing to ask the same questions over and over."

When Peeler presented a new plan for sending workers out to Gore Point and other area beaches, a Homer man said, "We would all like to be optimistic about your new plan. However, this is about the fifth reorganization we've seen. We all know the level that needs to be done. One beach at a time. A hundred men."

"I'd like to say on behalf of the Coast Guard," interjected Robbins, "that we have a signed paper from Exxon saying that they cannot clean up Gore Point. But it's the Coast Guard's opinion at this point that there will be a type B cleanup on that. If a type B cleanup isn't done, 80 percent of the oil will be left on the beaches."

"Based on what I saw today, they have a long way to go," Kelso broke in. "When I was here several weeks ago, someone said, 'Gore Point needs to be picked up.' The oil could have been picked up. It was in the water. It was on the shore, but it wasn't yet in the kind of condition where we had a massive pebble-by-pebble cleanup problem. If Exxon had acted then, we wouldn't be talking about digging up the beach now."

"Mr. Kelso," said a Homer resident, "this has been a problem for all the people here in Homer. We get something like cleaning Gore Beach approved, then we walk up to Exxon's door and it's locked. There are other people from Seldovia and Port Graham who have innovative beach-cleaning techniques. We all run into the same problem. How are we supposed to be able to do something if we keep walking up against the door and it's locked?"

By this time, Mike Hedrick had replaced Loren Flagg as chairman of the MAC group. When he was manager of the Kenai National Wildlife Refuge, he had dealt with oil companies exploring for oil in the harshest of winter conditions. He said, "I'm surprised at Exxon's attitude. I'm used to oil companies doing whatever they set out to do, overcoming every obstacle. But on this spill I've seen an entirely different attitude. Exxon went through the motions of cleaning up because they had to for their company's credibility. But they tried very few innovative things. They should have harnessed the talents of individual Alaskans, who were truly motivated to clean up their own back yard. Exxon didn't care as much as the local people and it showed.

"You know, I've watched Exxon in the Homer zone start out with shovels, giving a twenty-person crew shovels to pick up oil from the beach," Hedrick recalled. "Then Exxon took their shovels away and gave them garden trowels for picking up oil, because they were picking up too much sand when they used the shovels. The sand was giving them oily waste they simply weren't committed to handle. There are a number of beaches on the Kenai Coast where crews were scaled back on tools because they were picking up too much waste."

Exxon had wanted to burn much of the oily waste from the beaches, but restrictions by DEC forced the company to haul the waste away in boats. Since Exxon didn't have enough waste-disposal boats, it began cutting back on the amount of waste being picked up. At Windy Bay, on the south side of the Kenai Peninsula, beach cleaners had been using shovels effectively until Exxon took the shovels away. "Now we can only use our hands," said Ephim Anahonak of Port Graham. "We can't use any kind of tools now. Oil's hard to pick up just in gloves. It goes through your fingers. We can't even pick up any gravel. Every time we have a successful plan, they stop us from using it."[3]

After inspecting the Homer cleanup zone, Robbins said, "Exxon hasn't been doing any strenuous cleanups here. The local people are very concerned, and rightfully so. The problem is that Exxon has not acquired enough storage capacity for the oily debris recovered by workers."[4]

At one point, beach workers waited five days for containment vessels to show up that could store the oil they were recovering.

Frustrated, they dug a temporary holding pit, lined it with plastic, and threw in the oily debris. These workers were fired, apparently for their initiative. Others were reportedly terminated simply for working too hard.

"I saw a few people who were hard workers, and they didn't stay around very long," said Bill Kaehr, who grew up in Homer and cleaned beaches on the outer Kenai Coast. "People who work really hard disappear. A foreman will wander over and say, 'Pack up.' In two hours, they're gone.

"A little bit of rain, and everybody just stayed on the boat, getting paid to play cards or read books," Kaehr recalled. "In a two-week period we were only on the beach for twenty hours. But even then only two or three people were working, and fifteen to twenty were lounging around. Once I was sitting on a log and the boss came up, patted me on the back, and said, 'Good work there.' It was so lax, it was ludicrous. I wish we could have done more, but the bosses didn't really care. One time a foreman even told us, 'We're not here to get everything off the beach. We just want to spray it with water. Make it look like it's been touched. Check another one off the list. Go on to the next one.'"

Disillusionment with the cleanup added to the frustration people were feeling. In Homer, mental health worker Chris Laing described the vortex of emotions that were pulling many down. "People around here are closely connected to the land and ocean, so the death of birds and animals and seeing so much oil in the water has a deep impact on their lives. They get exhausted from the long hours of work and feel hopeless because there's no end in sight. There's a sense of loss of control and impotence because no one is truly in charge. They feel betrayed—not just by Exxon, but by the state and federal governments, which are supposed to be looking out for them. Money is precious to people around here, and they get angry seeing Exxon waste so much of it. Their sense of self-worth has been reduced because people in authority don't appreciate their knowledge and love of this area. This is their home, and it's been violated—so *they* feel violated. We're seeing a lot of intense anger, a lot of uncontrollable crying."

Because Marge Tillion had had emergency medical training, she helped counsel those who were overstressed. In confidential "debriefing" sessions, she helped people share their emotions and begin working through the stages of grieving. "They all talk about how they are doing, how they feel, and what they are angry at," Tillion said. "By the time a session is through, many people are crying. There's fist pounding. People are consoling each other. This helps people know that someone is looking out for them, that they are cared for. Unfortunately, in disasters the worst stress is often felt years later."

Tillion spoke quietly about one young man who must, she said, remain anonymous. "He had been hired by Exxon, along with four others, at the end of the first or second week after the spill. The job was to shoot otters and seals, including pups, that were oiled and alive so that they would sink. He's having trouble living with himself for what he did. He's been near suicide. The money was good. I guess it was cheaper for Exxon to sink the animals than to pay the cost of cleanup and rehabilitation."

Some Homer people found that volunteering—doing something constructive—was a way to work through their frustration. Billy Day, a young Homer man, became a driving force in the area's unusual volunteer response to the spill. He recalled how it all began on March 24. "I woke up in the morning, turned on the radio, heard the news, and immediately broke into tears. It seemed so close to me because I'd grown up exploring Prince William Sound. My father and both of my grandfathers fished the sound. My dad used to take me out there in the summer. So I feel very, very close to this country. I had to help. I didn't want to admit it, but I knew that as just one individual there was probably very little I could do."

Day noticed that, once Exxon came to town, most people stopped making their own decisions. "We sat back and decided we'd let them take care of it for us, tell us what to do," he said. "But we soon found out they didn't have any answers." So, when Alaska's division of Parks and Outdoor Recreation offered Day the job of patrolling for dead birds and animals near Gore Point, he took it, eager for a chance to help. At the time, Exxon was still arguing over what kind of cleanup it would attempt at Gore Point. Day and a few companions decided to try to do what Exxon was unwilling to undertake.

"There was nobody out there, just a lot of bird and animal carcasses," Day recalled. "I walked across the isthmus and through that long meadow to the outer beach. I could smell the oil from a mile away, and as far as I could see along the beach there was a thick layer of oil, maybe 4 feet deep, waves of it splashing ashore. I waded out nearly to my knees in oil. I watched a hundred or more murres landing, and all of them floundered and washed ashore. It was obvious to me that until we got this stuff picked up, we were going to have more and more dead birds. For me to just stand there and pick them up as they came washing in didn't seem like the right way to tackle the situation."

While camped above a short beach with a 10-foot-wide swath of oil, Day noticed a window of opportunity that no one was using—the oil had not yet sunk into the substrata and was easy to reach. "In five days a friend and I cleaned it up, using shovels and buckets, scooping it right off the surface," Day said. "I stacked up about two hundred bags of oily debris. There was probably 4 miles of beach that could have been cleaned this way, but three weeks passed with no sign of Exxon."

While they worked, Day and his companion watched a family of land otters that had to cross the swath of oil to reach the sea. At first there were six otters. A week later there were four. Finally, only two were left. After Day had been there for a month, an Exxon beach-assessment team flew in at high tide in a helicopter. They walked a few hundred feet of the beach and categorized it as lightly oiled. They said they weren't going to recommend any cleanup. "That's a mistake," Day told them. "Why don't you guys wait until the tide goes out and I'll show you around.

"They were reasonable guys, real personable," Day recalled. "They stayed, and as the tide went out I showed them the area. Their assessment of the beach went from lightly oiled to heavily oiled and needing attention right away. So I thought, 'Oh, good, they'll get a hundred workers out here and clean this beach up.' But after those guys left, two more weeks passed without anyone coming out. We continued to have dead animals wash in."

Billy Day and other state park workers were supposed to be patrolling for dead creatures, period. But Day and a couple of companions continued to shovel up as much oil as they could, inching their way along the seemingly endless expanse of beach. They stacked bags of oiled debris on the beach, and gradually, one bag at a time, the stacks got higher. When an Exxon-chartered barge named the *Rama Lee* came by, Day asked its skipper to take away the bags. The barge captain radioed his Exxon supervisor for approval but was told no, he was supposed to be standing by elsewhere. However, it was obvious to the captain that the collected debris had to come off the beach. He defied orders and, under cover of darkness, came ashore to hand-load the debris. It weighed in at 35,000 pounds.

"It stirred up our spirits when the captain of the *Rama Lee* defied orders and pulled in to help," said Day. "It was kind of a turning point. As boats passed by, more and more guys started coming in to help shovel oil. They weren't supposed to be recovering oil. But we realized that if we didn't take care of this beach, nobody was going to. I mean, it's not our mess, but it's our shoreline. We were going to have to deal with it, whether or not we had support from those in charge. It was miserable work—hot and fumy. But it was gratifying. And that was the birth of the volunteer project."

By July 1, Day was no longer working for Parks and Outdoor Recreation, but had become a full-time volunteer organizer of an all-volunteer effort to demonstrate how well a beach could be cleaned. To cover the volunteers' expenses, people in Homer raised money by holding bake sales, passing the hat in bars, and making pleas over the radio. Eventually, Exxon sent out a crew of beach cleaners to work alongside the volunteers. The crew came with shovels and buckets and started cleaning tidal pools. "They cleaned them up real well. I give them a lot of credit. They did a really great job," Day said. "Then they hit the beaches where there were larger cobbles. Exxon ordered them to stop using shovels to reduce the amount of material being picked up. I watched these people crawl around on their hands and knees and wipe rocks with absorbent towels, which came apart and stuck to the rocks. Everyone's morale was just devastated.

"There had to be an alternative. Surely Exxon could figure out how to wash oil from rocks. It's not that complicated. I kept thinking they'd show up with a big machine to wash the rocks, but it never came," Day said. "My last week out there I got very angry. I didn't even want the oil company people there anymore. I felt like they were belittling the place with a token effort. I became very adamant that we should do it ourselves. It's a tremendous undertaking for small groups of people, but it's the only way any progress is going to be made."

In mid-August, Day flew to Anchorage and spent his savings, about $5,000, to build a washing machine for rocks—a small cart with filters and high-pressure nozzles mounted on mountain bike wheels. He flew it back to the oiled beach. And it worked. Its capacity was limited, but it actually cleaned the rocks and drained off the oil. Day hoped it would serve as a prototype, but he wasn't surprised when Exxon said it wasn't interested.

After Exxon's crews went home in mid-September, the volunteers kept working on a beach near Gore Point they called Mars Cove. The volunteers, who came from Hawaii, Florida, England, Switzerland, and other distant places, as well as from Kachemak Bay, put in long hours of hard labor on the beach in the numbing cold. "If I was getting paid for this," said one worker, "I'd have quit by now."

Their goal was to work through the winter to determine whether beaches could be cleaned during the coldest months. Their most successful cleaning technique was brilliant in its simplicity. When the tide went out, they worked a single patch of beach, perhaps no more than a hundred square feet. First, they dug down to the deepest penetration of oil, usually about 18 inches. Then they lined this pit with a heavy waterproof tarp and shoveled the oiled rocks and sand into their handmade pond. Stirring and scrubbing with hands, shovels, and high-pressure hoses, they lifted oil from the rocks and siphoned it off with an adapted vacuum cleaner. When no more oil floated to the surface, they pulled out the tarp and went on to the next section of beach. "We're taking the beach apart and cleaning it rock by rock," said one of the volunteers. "It's not as big a job as you might think."

By the end of October, the volunteers had cleaned a quarter mile of beach. This was only a tiny portion of the hundreds of miles of beach where oil remained in the substrata. But this handful of people working without pay had done something that one of the world's largest corporations had been unable or unwilling to do. Their ingenuity and refusal to quit demonstrated that a badly oiled beach could be cleaned. Their perseverance would set an important precedent for other areas.

Chapter 20

The Katmai Coast

When the *Exxon Valdez* went aground, I didn't believe we were going to get any oil down here," said Ray Bane, superintendent of Katmai and Aniakchak national parks, which are more than 400 miles southwest of Bligh Reef. These parks are still wild regions. The Katmai Coast has towering sea walls, steep bouldered banks, cobbled beaches, and fine-grained sandy shores. Where this dramatic landscape meets the sea, it forms an unusually rich ecological zone. The cliffs, beaches, tidal flats, and estuaries are gathering places for eagles, seabirds, seals, sea lions, foxes, wolves, enormous coastal brown bears, and other wildlife.

When oil appeared in the Kenai Fjords at the beginning of April, Ray Bane came to Seward to familiarize himself with the Park Service's spill response. Bane said, "Okay, I might learn something that will help in a future crisis." The next day Bane was in a briefing in Seward when he glanced at a map on the wall. "That's when I realized that the currents were going to bring the oil out along the periphery of the Kenai Peninsula and into Shelikof Strait off the Katmai Coast. The moment I saw that map, I realized we were going to get a slug of oil on our beaches."

In their thirty years in Alaska, Bane and his wife, Barbara, had lived by the ocean in Sitka, in southeast Alaska, and in several rural villages on the Bering Sea and Arctic Ocean. He had been to sea in skiffs, kayaks, and Eskimo skin boats. Now he knew that the Alaska coastal current was drawing massive sheets of oil to the coasts of Katmai and Aniakchak, two of the most inaccessible places in the national park system. There are no roads to these parks. They are reached by air or by crossing the ever turbulent Shelikof Strait. Headquarters for both parks is at the town of King Salmon on the Alaska Peninsula. From there it is an hour's flight to the Katmai Coast over peaks often obscured by clouds and fog. Bane decided to confront the spill from Kodiak, where he would be only a short helicopter flight from the Katmai Coast.

"I went to Kodiak with hat in hand," Bane said. "I was looking for assistance, and the Kodiak people were overwhelmingly helpful. They took me in. We were all going to fight this thing together."

From its command post in Kodiak's Westmark Hotel, the National Park Service began developing its strategy for Katmai and Aniakchak. To string a barrier before the coast, which was spread-eagle in front of the advancing oil, would require hundreds of miles of boom. To withstand the high seas, the boom would have to be stouter than any made, virtually a floating Wall of China. Bane knew there was no way to boom the entire coast—Katmai and Aniakchak would get hit by the oil.

Since the parks were going to be oiled, the Park Service needed to be able to anticipate the size of the impact to help direct cleanup efforts. Bane sensed that the impact would be different from that in Prince William Sound, where the oil coated the rocky shores. Along the Katmai and Aniakchak coasts the oil was more likely to seep into the rocks, sand, and mud. The Park Service's first task was to determine the condition of the beaches before the oil hit. What birds and animals would the oil affect? Which shellfish and invertebrates? Which varieties of seaweed, beach grass, algae?

"The Park Service is woefully lacking in basic background information for these areas," Bane explained. "We simply do not know what's there. Now, these parks belong to every American. It's our job to protect them. But with all that oil coming, it was like running through a house taking inventory while the house was burning down."

On April 12, a helicopter pilot reported seeing oil at Cape Douglas, the easternmost point of Katmai National Park. The Coast Guard immediately made a reconnaissance flight, but sighted no oil.

Three days later, Bane flew over the same coastline in his Supercub. "At one point, I caught a glimpse of a glob of something
in the water," he said. "It was the size of a couch, just one glob.
But as I circled, I started seeing more and more oil. It was part
of a wide slick of broken mousse and sheen just 2 miles from
Cape Douglas. Before the oil hit, we needed to find out how
many colonies of birds and otters were out there. We needed a
picture of potential fish and wildlife losses at both Katmai and
Aniakchak. This was going to cost an enormous amount of
money, and we didn't know where the money would come from.
My regional director, Boyd Evison, was under a tremendous
amount of pressure. I know I was. How could we do our job at
Katmai and still pay the bills?"

Bane's annual budget was already stretched too thin for normal park duties. He didn't even have a boat to patrol the 400
miles of Katmai and Aniakchak coasts. However, in this time of
crisis, Evison pushed the limits of his authority to make some
funds available. In mid-April, three costly 90-foot vessels were
leased to do an extensive survey of the coasts. After making the
twenty-hour trip from Homer to the Katmai Coast, researchers
on the survey boats began their studies of intertidal resources,
water quality, bird and marine mammal populations, and cultural sites. They also began picking up oiled birds and debris.
Back in Anchorage, Evison was incredulous when he heard others insist that oil had not reached Katmai: "The Coast Guard and
NOAA denied in a briefing to Senator Stevens that there was oil
on the Katmai Coast. But we were already collecting it."

Unable to rely on Coast Guard and NOAA information, the
Park Service sent a boat to survey the Aniakchak Coast. But
rough seas often prevented the researchers from being able to
do onshore work. And before they completed their survey, gale
warnings were issued for Shelikof Strait. Winds rose to 35 knots
and the seas to 16 feet.

When the wind slackened somewhat on April 25, thirty-five
fishing vessels contracted by Exxon left Kodiak. The fishermen
were to look for oil approaching Kodiak and Katmai and "catch
it if possible." The next day, oil was sighted in Kashvik, the south-
ernmost bay in Katmai National Park. Splotches of oil were
found every 4 to 5 feet, between low-tide and high-tide lines

along 2½ miles of beach. The 435-foot Russian skimmer, *Vayda-ghubsky*, was sent by Exxon to Shelikof Strait to try to skim up some of the large pools of oil eddying offshore. "I flew over the Russian ship when it was trying to pick up oil," Bane said. "It looked like a waterbug dwarfed by the oil around it."

Meanwhile, a low-pressure front moved in from the Aleutian Islands. During the last week of April the storm struck the Katmai Coast. "We sent our boats out into some of the stormiest waters on the face of the earth," Bane said. "And the weather shut us down. High winds created waves that could engulf a two-story house. Visibility went to zero in fog and driving rain. And when the storm let up, it was like the dam had broken. Patches of oil had been coming ashore since mid-April, slowly collecting on the beaches and beginning to kill seabirds and otters. But the main body of oil had been gathering offshore. The storm slammed it onto our coast."

On May 1, Bane boarded a helicopter to inspect the Katmai Coast, starting at the southern end and working his way north. Flying over Shelikof Strait, he saw patches of oil floating offshore. Bane said, "It was like losing a friend, like watching a friend die. We saw bear sows with their cubs walking in the oil. The beaches were greasy brown. When the angle of the sun was right, the beaches glistened as if the whole coast had been freshly lacquered. In places there was so much oil in the surf that it changed the hydraulics of the waves. Instead of splashing onto the sand, the waves had this leaden quality. They fell with a thud.

"Hallo Bay is where it really struck home," Bane recalled of his trip up the coast. "We could see the sun hitting this sandy beach. White sand runs for 6 miles. It was one of the most beautiful beaches anywhere—glaciers in the background, escarpments of mountains. But now we could see the entire beach shimmering with oil. Mats of oil stretched as far as we could see, lying in rows where they'd washed up with the tides, one row higher than the next, row after row. And mixed into the matted oil were these little bumps. When we got close, we realized that they were birds.

"I tried to turn off the emotions. My job was to document. I filmed dead birds matted into the oily debris. About a thousand dead birds, mostly murres, were strewn on Hallo Beach. They had been killed in the water, washed in, and lay in the sand along the high-tide line. They were diving birds, and must have died of suffocation as oil filled their nostrils and mouths."

Bane was also concerned for the Katmai brown bears. They are the world's largest land carnivores, and Katmai National Park is their most protected reserve. Oil reached Katmai beaches just as the bears were emerging from hibernation, coming down to the beaches to eat seaweed and dig for clams. Bane observed bears eating oiled birds. He saw fox, wolverine, and wolf tracks leading in and out of the oil.

At Cape Douglas, Bane found foot-deep pools of thick, syruplike oil. On nearby Shaw Island, which had had a large colony of sea otters, he found no trace of the otters. At Douglas River, near the eastern boundary of Katmai, Bane watched an eagle that had been feeding on oiled birds. "It was covered with so much oil that it couldn't fly," he said. "This great bird was helpless, flopping into the river and out onto the rocks. We knew it was going to die."

Ray Bane's survey after the storm revealed that 75 to 90 percent of the Katmai Coast had been hit with oil in one form or another. Bane felt torn by the inescapable trade-offs involved with cleaning the shoreline. He wanted the oil removed, but he didn't want the remaining wildlife to endure further stress from the commotion of boats, planes, and hundreds of people. In setting cleanup priorities, his first step was to prohibit any large, shore-based operations, which would cause more disturbance, until it was certain that no more oil would wash ashore. However, no one knew when that would be. As the weather warmed up, the onshore oil softened: some of it seeped deeper into the rocks and gravel; some was picked up by high tides and tossed again on the waves. The few skimmers available were deployed to keep more oil from coming ashore. Onshore, the most urgent task was removing the oiled, dead wildlife to prevent scavenging by bears, wolves, foxes, and eagles. On May 8, a cleanup crew reported that 30 percent of the dead birds had already been scavenged.

As Exxon's cleanup crews traveled in and out of Kodiak, Bane received reports that the helicopter crews were harassing bears and that low-flying planes were scaring birds from their nests. He tried to work out these problems with the Exxon supervisors. "Most of the people I dealt with at Exxon were good people," he said. "I have no complaints about those individuals. The field people cooperated with us."

However, Bane found the results of Exxon's overall cleanup depressing. He inspected one hard-hit beach where Exxon crews had already removed 300 tons of oil mousse from less than half a mile of shoreline. "From the air it looked clean, like a post-card of Hawaii—white sand, sun sparkling on the water," he recalled. "I landed my Supercub and began walking on the beach. There were some tar balls in the high-tide zone, but otherwise the beach looked clean. Then, as I walked down the shore, I felt as if I were walking on a waterbed. When I stopped, oil started to seep up around my feet. It was buried 6 inches under the sand. I dug down and found veins of oil up to 4 inches wide. I'd seen guys work hard on this beach for the better part of a month. Three hundred tons is a lot of material to remove, but it didn't change anything."

Bane felt pressure from Exxon to sign off on these beaches. Although he had no explicit authority to certify that beaches had been cleaned, he had credibility, and Exxon wanted his stamp of approval before moving on to other areas. Bane said, "My rangers were being asked to say these beaches were clean when they weren't. And I'd tell them, 'No. Don't do it. We're not signing off on a mess like this.'"

Bane also felt pressure from the Department of Interior to refrain from talking too much about what he was witnessing. "It's not like someone called and said, 'Shut your mouth.' That's not the way business is done. But people were getting uncomfortable and wanted me to tone down my comments to the media. However, I feel we have a responsibility to let the public know what's going on. We were not going to exaggerate or over-dramatize anything, but we were not going to hide anything."

Bane said he had never before looked forward to summer being over. "I tried not to feel too much, so I'd still be able to function," he said. "Our people were working twenty-hour days, wearing themselves to the point where they had nothing left. People don't come to work for the Park Service to make money. Some ideal or concern brings us here. And when so much of what you consider precious is being destroyed, it takes its toll. It was hard seeing my rangers break down in tears. Part of it was exhaustion, but it was mostly emotional stress."

Toward the end of summer, the Park Service arranged for counseling for all of its oil spill workers, whether laboring on the Katmai Coast or in the Kenai Fjords. "Dealing with all of that death was more than some of them could handle," Boyd Evison said. "They were working fourteen-hour days and they cared intensely. It just overwhelmed them. I'd return from the oiled beaches stunned myself. The impact of all that destruction is indescribable. It just eats away at you."

By the end of summer, 95,151 bags of oily debris had been hauled from the Katmai Coast, 154 bags from Aniakchak. A total of 7,869 dead birds had been recovered from the Katmai Coast. Two hundred miles further southwest, on Aniakchak's beaches, 469 birds had been found. Thirty-three dead otters had washed up on Katmai beaches, one at Aniakchak. No one knew how many bears had perished after eating contaminated carrion. "To me, every animal in this park is special. I don't see the wildlife as populations," Bane said. "A park like Katmai is a sanctuary for individual animals. People say, 'Bane, one bear out of a thousand is killed. What's the big deal?' Well, if just one bear died from this oil spill it would be a tragedy. One bird's death is a tragedy. We have had 8,000 tragedies."

After accompanying Bane on a survey of the treated beaches in September, Evison said, "Nobody alive today will see the time when all that oil is gone. Our biggest fight right now is to get the wherewithal to figure out what's going to happen over the long term. But we know that the unspoiled value of the Katmai Coast is lost."

Ray Bane, who agonized over the desecration of the Katmai Coast he loved, said, "Exxon caused this mess, but it had plenty of assistance. I think all of us who have benefited from that oil have a responsibility to bear. Alaskans take too much for granted. It's a big land—good fishing, lots of animals, wild rivers. We take it all so damn much for granted. The oil spill is only a symptom of all of us closing our minds to the fact that there is always a price to pay when you develop oil, or cut down some trees, or build a road.

"All this devastation that should not have happened. I think we all fell asleep at the wheel, myself included. As a citizen, I have a responsibility to put pressure on state and federal officials so something like this will never happen again."

Chapter 21

Kodiak

Four hundred miles southwest of Bligh Reef, the green hills of Kodiak Island rise above the deep, cold waters of the Aleutian trench. The men and women who fish out of the town of Kodiak are among the toughest in the world. They have a saying: "Kodiak may not be the end of the earth, but you sure as hell can see it from here." Beyond the safety of the harbors lies a wilderness of ocean, fog, cyclonic winds, 80-foot waves, treeless islands, and a wealth of marine and bird life.

In 1988, Kodiak, the oldest town in Alaska, was the nation's highest producing fishing port. The bulk of the catch was king crab and salmon—reds, silvers, pinks, and kings. The community's 5,000 residents are mainly fishing men and women, cannery workers, and others related to the fishing industry. The *Exxon Valdez* oil spill seemed, at first, far removed from their lives.

"My initial reaction was that it was a big tragedy for the people in Prince William Sound," said Kodiak borough mayor Jerome Selby. "I felt badly for them and wondered if there was something we should do to help them. It never crossed my mind that it was going to become a problem for Kodiak Island. A week later it dawned on us that it was going to be our problem as well.

"Seeing the oil come closer and closer was a painful process for everyone," Selby said. "We had to face the reality that we couldn't boom off the entire island. It was very difficult for us to sit there and calmly say, 'Okay, scratch that bay. If oil comes, it gets oiled,' and then go on to the next bay. It's difficult to accept the fact that, no matter what we did, a part of Kodiak Island, which all of us love so much, was going to get destroyed."

While Valdez and Cordova were ground zero, Kodiak was at the far end of the spill and had a hard time getting the attention of Exxon and government agencies. As one state official said, "Kodiak was everybody's stepchild. When we were all working around the clock in the sound and not making any progress, nobody wanted to hear about Kodiak's problems."

But the oil was headed toward Kodiak and someone had to deal with it. "Rather than sit here and wait for the oil to get to us, the spirit of Kodiak is, 'Let's go attack that sucker,'" said Bill Barham, who had lived out in the Alaskan bush for two years and is known as Wild Bill. "This island has a history of overcoming some serious obstacles, like our weather. There are days when the sea looks like it's smoking—a hundred-mile-an-hour wind blows the water right off the surface. Here in Kodiak, we're used to adversity. We couldn't do anything about that Exxon tanker captain, but we could get after the oil."

Kodiak residents ordered containment boom from the Lower 48. Some built a log boom for the Afognak hatchery and for some of the key fishing bays. Others set up shop in an empty barn to make oil-absorbent boom from a synthetic material. Town meetings were held every morning. "We were calling Exxon almost daily, asking them to send somebody and let us know their plans for the defense of Kodiak Island," Selby said. "Exxon kept saying, 'Well, you guys don't have an oil problem. If you get hit with oil, then we'll be down to take care of it.' Our frustration just mounted. You could see the anger and anxiety at public meetings. People had to do *something*."

From the time the *Exxon Valdez* went aground, Exxon had three weeks to come to Kodiak to mobilize a response before the oil arrived. "But they waited until the oil actually hit Kodiak Island," Selby said. "Exxon didn't seem to understand our urgency to get the oil out of the water before it hit the beaches."

After Exxon arrived in Kodiak three weeks after the spill, many local residents felt control was being taken away from the community. "When we had the first oil spill meeting here, there was a tremendous amount of energy," said Brian Johnson, a Kodiak fisherman. "People were coming out of the woodwork, and we felt there was a lot we could do. Then Exxon walked in and took over the town. We completely lost control.

"It was hard to sit here and see all this oil on the beach and know that no one was going to go out and pick it up," Johnson said. "You saw the stuff getting baked on. With a spill like this you've got to use every available resource, and we weren't using them. There's a lot we could have done to help, but we were told, 'You can't do this. You can't do that.'"

In contrast to the prevailing frustration was the pamphlet Exxon sent to its credit card holders. *The Valdez Cleanup: A Progress Report from Exxon* stated that "by mid-May essentially all of the oil on the water had been removed or had dissipated. Progress has been good . . . From the earliest days of the spill, we have been working with local fishing groups to protect the fish hatcheries which are so important to the area's economy."

"We don't have time for this mumbo-jumbo," Johnson said of the pamphlet. "We saw lots of otters swimming in sheen, lots of new dead birds. We saw miles and miles and miles of area impacted and not one cleanup crew. We took our small rubber boat, and we could look down through the water and see oil on the bottom. The stuff was plastered all over the place."

Johnson and several friends went out with old nets and picked up 1,000 pounds of oily gunk. "It doesn't take a genius to come up with ideas," said one of Johnson's companions. "Any fisherman can do it." A group of draggers—fishermen who trawl with long nets—also loaded up gear and went after oil. With no previous experience and no promise of payment, the draggers collected emulsified oil for several days, as much as 20,000 gallons a day, from the water.

But as Exxon began writing lucrative cleanup contracts, fishermen were caught between making lots of money with Exxon or staying independent and broke. People were torn between their conscience and greed; between paying their bills and suffering financial ruin. For some the spill became their biggest payday; for others it remained their worst nightmare. Friends sometimes turned on each other. Rick Schoenberger, a fisherman who had been fishing out of Kodiak since he was eight, said, "This spill has ripped our town in half. Friends tell me, 'Keep your mouth shut so you can get a charter.' Well, I've had three different offers for oil charters and I've turned them all down. I won't do an oil charter if it means I've got to watch what I say. I won't keep my mouth shut. I'm going to be a watchdog."

Schoenberger and his crew spotted an oil streak on the surface of the sea. They followed it in their boat and discovered that it was 3½ miles long and had sunk beneath the water's surface in two places. "Unless we go out and look at the oil ourselves, we don't know what's going on," Schoenberger said. "Otherwise, we only hear what Exxon wants us to hear."

At fisherman Ed Monkiwiecz's house, a half-mile above the harbor, fishing men and women spent many hours sipping coffee and agonizing over the spill. In a dark corner, a cardboard box with an army jacket flung over the top held a frightened gull Monkiwiecz had rescued from the oil. The fishermen felt boxed in themselves. They were seiners who wanted to be out catching salmon, but their fishing season had been lost to the oil spill. Many had no alternative ways to earn money. "Initially, we were led to believe that Exxon was going to make us whole, that they were going to do well by us. They didn't, and we have no reason to believe they will," Monkiwiecz said. "They have a moral obligation to the people they hurt the most. We have no options." Particularly frustrating to Monkiwiecz and the other seiners was not knowing why Exxon contracted some fishermen and not others.

"The devastation to our island and our lives is mind-boggling. Yet trying to lay the blame for this whole thing on Exxon is very difficult for me to do," Monkiwiecz said. "The state should have had better safeguards in place. And ultimately, I think we're all at fault, every single one of us. We've got to have our cars. We use the fossil fuels. Maybe if we put more value on our environment, this wouldn't have happened. I didn't have much sympathy for all these nature groups before the spill, but now I'm beginning to appreciate what these groups stand for. The animals have no voice. This oil spill proved they need some representatives."

Monkiwiecz set out on his own solitary cleanup. "I've got Typar material to protect my boat from being contaminated," he said. "I got rags to catch oil and some 5-gallon buckets. I'm going to go out there and do what I can."

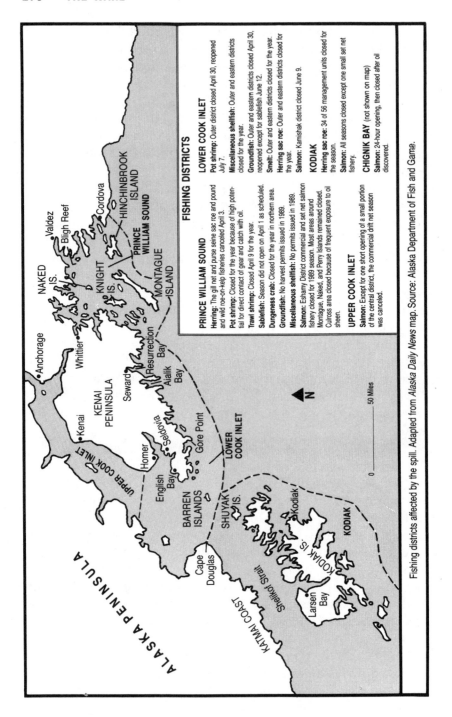

FISHING DISTRICTS

PRINCE WILLIAM SOUND

Herring: The gill net and purse seine sac roe and pound and wild roe-on-kelp fisheries canceled April 3.

Pot shrimp: Closed for the year because of high potential for direct contact of gear and catch with oil.

Trawl shrimp: Closed April 9 for the year.

Sablefish: Season did not open on April 1 as scheduled.

Dungeness crab: Closed for the year in northern area.

Groundfish: No harvest permits issued in 1989.

Miscellaneous shellfish: No permits issued in 1989.

Salmon: Eshamy District commercial and set net salmon fishery closed for 1989 season. Most areas around Montague, Naked, and Perry Islands remained closed. Culross area closed because of frequent exposure to oil sheen.

UPPER COOK INLET

Salmon: Except for one short opening of a small portion of the central district, the commercial drift net season was canceled.

LOWER COOK INLET

Pot shrimp: Outer district closed April 30, reopened July 7.

Miscellaneous shellfish: Outer and eastern districts closed for the year.

Groundfish: Outer and eastern districts closed April 30, reopened except for sablefish June 12.

Smelt: Outer and eastern districts closed for the year.

Herring sac roe: Outer and eastern districts closed for the year.

Salmon: Kamishak district closed June 9.

KODIAK

Herring sac roe: 34 of 56 management units closed for the season.

Salmon: All seasons closed except one small set net fishery.

CHIGNIK BAY (not shown on map)

Salmon: 24-hour opening, then closed after oil discovered.

Fishing districts affected by the spill. Adapted from *Alaska Daily News* map. Source: Alaska Department of Fish and Game.

Monkiwiecz's deckhand, Saskia Kilcher, expressed the frustration of not knowing what was going to happen next. "We live from day to day not knowing if we're going to be allowed to fish or not," she said. "Fishing is the only thing I'm qualified for, and fishing is a challenge. It's a certain feeling of freedom. When you've caught a lot of fish you feel just great. And I think we're capable of cleaning up the oil if they'd let us. We know our weather. We know our tides, our ocean, and our boats. When something has to be done, we do it. But now we can't *do* anything. Our lives are out of our hands. That's the worst thing. Exxon won't give us answers; they just let us wait around."

Those who did work for Exxon received lucrative contracts, but many experienced delays in getting paid. "A lot of people are going without because of Exxon and its main cleanup contractor, VECO," said Ray Monigold, who had installed computer systems Exxon used to track all its oil spill operations in the Kodiak region. "I've had to lay off five employees because of delinquent compensation from VECO. None of the village skiffs hired by VECO has been paid. Finally my conscience came through."

In an act of high-tech civil disobedience, Monigold shut down Exxon's and VECO's regional computer systems on June 14. Then he notified Exxon: "I will reinstate the functions when a system, any system, is implemented that is able to quickly pay the people of this state." He said that he was holding the companies as "computer hostages" because of their refusal to pay vendors and village workers. Monigold was particularly upset that some villagers had been paid and others hadn't. "It's a divide and conquer tactic—you create resentment among the village people toward each other. It's one of the oldest ploys. Genghis Khan used it, and VECO is using it now."[1]

Jolted by the computer shutdown, Exxon and VECO streamlined their payment system enough to convince Monigold to turn their computers back on. However, new problems arose shortly after the computers were running again. Four hundred angry cannery workers met with Exxon's Kodiak manager, John Peavey, to demand payment for lost wages because no fish were coming into the canneries. Normally, a cannery worker could earn up to $8,000 in one summer. On July 12, Exxon distributed an initial round of $1,000 checks to more than 1,000 workers who had been hired by canneries before June 1. The company called this an interim settlement; future payments to cannery workers were to depend upon whether commercial fishing seasons were opened in and around Kodiak. As the cannery workers picked up their checks, many feared this would be their only payment from Exxon. They all knew that the outlook for fishing was not good.

Deckhands and crew members of Kodiak's fishing fleet were also worried. They were forced to rely on their skippers to handle their claims and feared that they would not be compensated for lost wages. Said one deckhand, "Exxon is going to pay the claims of boat owners and skippers, and it's up to them to divide the compensation money. So the deckhands are really dependent on their skipper. We could really get screwed. There's very little protection for crew members unless they have a contract."

The Shelikof Lodge, a split-level hotel with a chrome-and-formica restaurant and bar, is five minutes' drive from Kodiak's boat harbor. This is one of the places where many Kodiak residents gather to vent frustrations and relax. A baseball game might have been flickering on the television screen, but through the summer, conversations focused on the oil spill. Becky Westbrook, a popular bartender at the Shelikof, said, "I hear stories from across the bar about Exxon trying to cover this up; trying to keep the full force of what has happened under wraps; hiding the carcasses of dead animals; firing people on cleanup crews who bring cameras with them; hiring special teams to go out and turn over rocks so that beaches look clean when the Coast Guard flies over. Friends of mine have been turned down for employment by VECO and Exxon because their priorities and their hearts are with the land and the people—and they just aren't willing to keep quiet. This kind of stuff brings on that feeling of helplessness. It makes me so angry. Sometimes you don't know what to do with this incredible anger."

Every time the people of Kodiak thought they had experienced the full magnitude of damage from the oil spill, it seemed to get worse. First there were dead birds and otters. Cherished beaches and coves were blackened. Fishing seasons were closed. People lived in uncertainty. And then came an unending chain of reverberations within the community—fear, jealousy, selfishness, disillusionment. "There's really no end to how it affects people in this community," Becky Westbrook said. "Some people have made marvelous money off the spill, and other people are going under completely. This creates a lot of anger and tension. It's tough seeing others make so much money when you're broke and have a family to feed or house payments to make. My fiancé finally went down to VECO and stomped his foot and said, 'I'm not from New York, and I'm not from Wisconsin, I'm from Alaska and I'm starving to death. Put me to work.'

"When VECO first got here a lot of people were quitting their jobs to go work for it, which left a lot of the small businesses in town up in the air. It has affected the entire economy of Kodiak. A false economy has been created, and once they pull out, the repercussions could be absolutely incredible. It's all part of the seduction with Exxon. They come in and offer all this great money, and it turns this thing into a get-rich-quick scheme.

"Each day people become angrier and angrier because Exxon keeps saying, 'Oh, it really wasn't all that bad. We've got things under control now.' Our anger runs so deep. Exxon is a multinational corporation, so there isn't any one person you can shake your finger at. I wish those executives in their glass towers who make hundreds of thousands of dollars a year could see the people here who are real scared about their futures. There's a salmon fisherman who comes into the bar on a regular basis. His wife just had a baby. He's been salmon fishing for years and has always made a real good living. This year he's been out of work. For so many people, there's just complete uncertainty and helplessness, wondering what's going to happen.

"There are extremely important lessons people need to learn from this. We need to wake up and realize that oil spills do happen, that we live in a world of high technology and there's a price to pay for that. We have to be responsible."

Chapter 22

The Native Villages

T he Native story of the oil devastation is different from the white man's story. It's different because our lives are different," said Walter Meganack, Sr., chief of the Port Graham people. "What we value is different. How we see the water and the land and the plants and the animals is different. What white men do for sport and recreation and money we do for life: for the life of our bodies, for the life of our spirits."[1]

The Native village closest to the spill was Tatitlek, just 6 miles from Bligh Reef. On the morning of March 24, 1989, the ninety-five Aleut villagers rose as usual. As the day started, the still mist filtered through the forest, and low clouds hung over the water. Then someone turned on a television newscast. An announcer thousands of miles away was talking about a huge oil spill in Alaska. The tanker was still leaking oil. And as the people of Tatitlek listened in stunned disbelief, they learned that the spill was just around the corner from their village, on the other side of Bligh Island.

Tatitlek's grocery store is the ocean. The villagers' immediate concern was whether they could still gather food from the sea.

When the *Exxon Valdez* went aground, the herring were about to spawn in Prince William Sound. After a long winter, their arrival signals the beginning of a new year. The herring come in on a high tide to lay their eggs on leafy kelp and other seaweed close to shore. At low tide, people run out to gather the herring roe. The crunchy clusters of eggs are a delicacy whether eaten straight from the sea or dipped in seal oil. What isn't eaten fresh is salted and frozen for later in the year. "The enormity of the spill didn't hit our village until the herring started to spawn off Tatitlek's beaches," one villager said. "The fish looked clean, but the people were afraid to catch them."[2]

Unfortunately, the villagers had no way of knowing how seriously the sea life was affected. Prevailing currents carried the oil away from Tatitlek, but birds, fish, and seals might come into contact with it as they moved through the sound. And contamination reports that reached the village were often inconclusive or conflicting. The people knew that clams and mussels were sensitive to very small amounts of pollution, but the Alaska Department of Fish and Game maintained that shellfish found on the beaches were dying as a result of an unusually cold winter. And Exxon was announcing that the oil would not sink to where bottom fish lived, but fishermen were pulling up anchors dripping with oil. Department of Environmental Conservation commissioner Dennis Kelso cautioned that no one really knew if it would be safe for villagers to eat their traditional foods—the birds, fish, shellfish, seals, and other creatures they take from the sea. This uncertainty became a source of great anxiety in Tatitlek and other Native villages.

"Mussels, clams, starfish—things are dying off and floating up on the beaches," said Gary Kompkoff, the village council president. "The tides come in and go out, come in and go out. The scientists do their research one day, and everything looks fine. But what about the tide coming in? There's frustration, uncertainty, and fear—a fear of what the future's going to bring. We go from fear to anger to frustration with this thing. It's going to be with us for a long time."[3]

On the third day of the spill, the people of Tatitlek were terrified when the sky darkened from a huge cloud of black smoke billowing up from Bligh Island. "Nobody told the villagers what the hell was going on," said Michael Smith, a resource planner hired by the association of Native regional corporations to help villages within the sound cope with the spill. "Nobody told people in Tatitlek that some of the oil was being burned off. All of a sudden the smoke comes. It comes and comes, and the people don't know what's happening. Is the whole thing on fire? Is the fire going to come blazing down on them? They've got no idea what's happening. Talk about fear! They tried to get their pregnant women out of there. Some of those people were scared to death."

The children of Tatitlek began showing signs of stress. A teacher reported that two of her students were having nightmares about people coming to hurt them. Some showed anxiety when their parents went off to scrub beaches or collect dead birds. "My children used to play by themselves all the time in the woods or down on the beach," said one Tatitlek mother. "Now they hear about things dying and their father has gone to clean beaches, so they cling to me. Wherever I walk, they're right beside me, hanging on."[4]

Many of the young people felt a deep sense of loss for the creatures that had been so much a part of their lives. "Just think, it's like they're taking all the fish and animals away from us," Jason Totemoff wrote in an essay. "I mean, it's so sad to see your life ahead of you drift away."

To replace the traditional foods gathered from the sea, Exxon sent in a boatload of groceries. "Gosh, they sent cases and cases of chicken," Jason said. "We're not used to chicken. I told the teacher, 'If they bring any more chicken, I'm going to charter a plane and bring it up to Exxon and tell them to keep it.'"[5]

Sixty-five-year-old Edward Gregorieff has lived his entire life on Prince William Sound; he raised seven children in Tatitlek. Looking out his window toward the sea, he said, "*Sad* is too mild a word to say for what we are losing." To Gregorieff, the oil spill was not an isolated incident, but part of a long series of changes pulling his people away from their way of life.

He remembered that when he was a young boy, neighboring villagers paddled up to Tatitlek in their *bidarkas*, traditional skin kayaks. In the days of his childhood everyone lived from the land and sea. He said now, "We Native people are balancing between the white man's way of life and our own. Natives would be better off staying with their own way of life. But how long can that way of life continue in Tatitlek?"[6]

The village of Chenega Bay lies 30 miles to the southwest of Bligh Reef. Chenega Bay had experienced an unexpected catastrophe before. Twenty-five years earlier to the day, the Good Friday earthquake set off a tidal wave that swept away the old village of Chenega. When the tsunami crashed ashore, children were literally swept from the arms of their parents. Swirling water crushed village homes—one house was swept away as a woman stood in the doorway calling to her children. The survivors had to leave Prince William Sound, and for twenty years they drifted between various jobs and welfare, always yearning to return. In 1980, village leaders finally found a way to rebuild Chenega, renaming it Chenega Bay. Homes went up. Families returned. People reestablished their bond with the sea. Then the oil spill hit.

The villagers' first reaction to the spill was to call for their priest. The region's minister flew in to offer consolation and support. He was soon followed by helicopters and float planes full of Exxon and state officials and reporters from as far away as London and Australia. With currents sweeping the oil toward Chenega Bay, boats of the Mosquito Fleet soon swarmed offshore, as fishermen tried to save the nearby San Juan hatchery. By April 10, the oil had reached Chenega Bay, and the quiet village had swollen from 80 people to more than 250.

"We've been inundated by anyone and everyone," said Darrell Totemoff of Chenega Bay. "We're all too busy to be depressed right now. Everyone is in shock and confused by all the activity in the village. Seems like Good Friday brought us another disaster."[7]

With so many people combing the beaches for oil, villagers feared that artifacts from ancient village sites and burial caves would be disturbed. These ties to their ancestors have a personal and often sacred value to Native villagers. The artifacts also have such tremendous commercial value that old village middens and graves are often vandalized. As protective measures, Exxon hired archaeologists to survey beaches in advance of the cleanup crews and instructed workers not to venture above the high-tide line or into caves. Nevertheless, problems arose.

"The less that's known about these places the better," said Michael Smith, who spent much of the summer trying to help protect cultural sites within the sound. "The spill blew the cover on an awful lot of these places. One tragedy involved a burial cave on one of the islands. It was found by beach workers who went into the cave and built a warming fire. As light from their fire lit the cave, a skeleton became visible in the shadows. They called a state trooper, who collected the remains and sent them in for forensic analysis."

The people of Chenega Bay were incensed that the bones of one of their ancestors, a young man, had been shipped off in a bag to be weighed and measured. The remains in this burial cave were so sacred that even the region's cultural heritage program, which had surveyed the sound for ten years, did not know the location of the cave; the secret had been kept by a handful of elders. The bones, which were eventually reburied by the village people, predated Captain Cook's voyages and the arrival of Russians in Alaska.

As the oil continued to wash ashore around Chenega Bay, wildlife died and people were physically affected. "There have been fumes in the air, and my face has felt as if it were burning," said Paul Kompkoff, Sr., sixty-six, who raised six children with his wife, Minnie. Normally, they would have been busy gathering subsistence foods and working at commercial fishing during the summer, but this year most of the family cleaned beaches. "We found three deer lying together on Knight Island," Kompkoff said. "People walked right up to them, thinking they were asleep, but they were dead. They had oily kelp in their mouths. On Seal Island, six seals were lying on the beach between the work crews. They were too sick to move."

Kompkoff recalled how in past years he watched whales, porpoises, and sea lions playing in Chenega Bay. This year, only the sea gulls were there as usual. "In some ways the village is doing fairly well," he said. "Free food is being brought in by Exxon, and most people are being paid for financial losses. But what's going to happen in two or three months? Exxon officials don't understand why the oil spill is so bad for the Native way of life."[8]

Chugach Alaska, an organization representing Natives of the region, has filed a lawsuit to recover damages for Chenega Bay and other Native villages. "What good will that do?" Kompkoff asked. "This spill has taken our lifestyle away and our livelihood. I keep thinking of moving, but where would I move to? The best anyone can do is start cleaning. The oil will be here for many, many years."

English Bay and Port Graham are two Native villages approximately 150 miles southwest of Bligh Reef. When sheets of oil came ashore in early May, the Native villagers faced things they thought would never happen. Salmon had always been their main source of food, but in 1989 the smokehouses and drying racks were empty. The pink salmon returned to the area, swimming and leaping thorough the clear pools and falls of the river near the villages. However, no one bothered to catch them after a villager caught one whose guts were oily and whose eggs were shriveled and blackened.

Offshore, a reef appears at low tide. Crabs scurry along the crevices, and clams, chitons, and mussels cling to the dark rocks. This year, for the first time anyone could remember, no villagers went out to the reef to gather food. Irene Ukatish went out to check the chitons, or *birdarkies*, as her people call this relative of the abalone. When healthy, *birdarkies* grip the rock so tenaciously they have to be pried loose with a strong knife, but now they were falling from the rocks with the slightest touch. "I don't trust food from the sea anymore," she said. "We're not getting any kind of seafood."[9]

Biologists began studies of English Bay and Port Graham seafood in April, but three and a half months later the results were still inconclusive. Some shellfish showed contamination; some didn't. Procedures to detect oil in seafood were difficult to develop. Dr. Thomas Nighswander, with the Indian Health Service, reported that samples of seal meat—another staple of the Native diet—were locked in freezers while attorneys debated legal issues connected with the *Exxon Valdez*.

Several times, Exxon representatives told villagers to go ahead and gather their traditional food and store it until test results were in. "But the beaches are stained and splattered with oil," Roberta Ukatish said. "Who wants to pick mussels, *birdarkies*, or snails where you can see that oil?"

At the end of August, Roberta's father, Vincent Kvasnikoff, said, "Every day we see that sheen out there. Tar balls are still washing up on the beaches. I asked Exxon's people, 'What about a year from now, when the oil has sunk to the bottom? What about the halibut, the cod, and other bottom fish?' They couldn't answer."

Large Exxon and VECO paychecks from beach cleanup work provided some villagers with enough money to ship in commercial brands of food. However, not everyone made money, and, in any event, buying food from a store isn't the same as getting it from the sea yourself. "The money is great to have, but it doesn't replace the sense of community people normally have from catching and preparing their own food," Wally Kvasnikoff said. "Every one of these houses put up at least 200 fish last year. We've been doing that for ages. Without that, we walk around like zombies. Exxon's money can't replace that part of our lives."

Port Graham Chief Meganack tried to describe why this subsistence way of life—the gathering of food from the land and sea—means so much to his people. "When the days get longer, we get ready. Boots and boats and nets and gear are prepared for the fishing time," he said. "The winter beaches are not lonely anymore, because our children and grownups visit the beaches in the springtime and gather the abundance of the sea: the shellfish, the snails, the chitons. When the first salmon is caught, our whole village is excited. It's an annual ritual of mouth-watering delight. When our bellies are filled with the fresh new life, then we put up the food for the winter. We dry and smoke and can hundreds of fish to feed each family.

"It was in the early springtime," Meganack said. "No fish yet. No snails yet. But the signs were with us. The green was starting. Some birds were flying and singing. The excitement of the season had just begun. And then we heard the news. Oil in the water—lots of oil, killing lots of water. It's too shocking to understand. Never have we thought it possible for the water to die. But it is true. We walk our beaches. And the snails and the barnacles and the chitons are falling off the rocks. Dead. Dead water.

"We caught our first fish—the annual first fish, the traditional delight of all—but it got sent to the state to be tested for oil. No first fish this year. We walk our beaches, but instead of gathering life, we gather death. Dead birds. Dead otters. Dead seaweed.

"Before we have a chance to hold each other and share our sorrow and loss, we suffer yet another devastation. We are invaded by the oil company offering jobs, high pay, lots of money. We are in shock. We need to clean the oil, get it out of our water, bring death back to life. We are intoxicated with desperation. We don't have a choice but to take what is offered. So we take the jobs, we take the orders, we take the disruption."

Chief Meganack saw his people losing their trust in each other and fighting. After being bossed around on the cleanup crews, some villagers showed signs of agitation. "Our people get sick," he said. "Elders and children in the village. Everybody is touchy. People are angry. And afraid, afraid and confused. Our elders feel helpless. They cannot work on cleanup. They cannot do all the activities of gathering food and preparing for winter. And most of all, they cannot teach the young ones the Native way. How will the children learn the values and the ways if the water is dead?

"The oil companies lied about preventing a spill. Now they lie about the cleanup. Our people know what happens on the beaches. Spend all day cleaning one big rock, and the tide comes in and covers it with oil again. Spend a week wiping and spraying the surface, but pick up a rock and there's 4 inches of oil underneath.

"We fight a rich and powerful giant, the oil industry, while at the same time we take orders and a paycheck from it. We are torn in half."

Charles Christensen, a large man of Aleut descent, is mayor of Larsen Bay on the north side of Kodiak Island. In a soft, gentle voice, he recalled the coming of the oil. "All of us were being told that the oil wouldn't get down this far," he said, "but fishermen know the waters. They know the winds and the tides. Once the oil started working its way to Shelikof Strait, everybody realized it was coming. We were sitting here watching for it. We knew it was going to hit."

When oil reached Larsen Bay, the villagers started cleaning the beaches without contracts from the oil companies. "You walk on your beaches and look at that mess," Christensen said. "All the birds and wildlife. When my wife was told how many died, she cried. Those living things have rights, too. They want to live their lives out. It's really sad.

"Everybody's mad, but what can you do? I guess we gotta make the best of it, get out there and clean it up. Our people have been cleaning beaches all summer—rain or shine, winds, storms. Smelling that oil every day and working in it makes some people sick. You just wonder what's going to happen next. What about our salmon? People are really afraid to even touch salmon.

There's oil all over. It's sunk down in those beaches. I don't know if we'll be able to touch the clams now for maybe years. How are we going to know when they're safe to eat again?"

As oil reached the other Native villages on Kodiak Island, people in each community faced the same agonizing uncertainty. At Ouzinki, near the northeastern tip of Kodiak Island, Mayor Zack Cichenoff said, "People are dying to have some fire-smoked salmon, but they don't have any at all. They're afraid. The oil has had a tremendous impact on us. People have been afraid to even kill any deer. They know that when deer want to get salt they go on the beach to eat kelp. Now the kelp is full of tar."

Cichenoff said that they tried to find out how poisonous their subsistence foods had become. "Time after time, we've asked NOAA and DEC and Fish and Game, 'Is it all right to eat this, or isn't it all right to eat this?' They won't tell us. They say, 'If it looks good and smells good . . .'"

According to Dr. Jacqueline Michel of NOAA, a definitive answer can't be given. "The Native people don't trust their food anymore," said Dr. Michel. "They don't trust the ocean. So we've set up this program to try to build confidence in their subsistence fisheries. We've analyzed about sixty-five samples, and none of the fish and only a few of the shellfish came up contaminated. But it's enough to be worried about. Since the spill occurred, most of the Natives in the villages aren't eating seafood. Some of them don't even want to go in the water. They're afraid there are carcinogens. They're terrified."

Alberta Aga of Larsen Bay recalled the scent of cottonwood leaves after a rain—"like a beautiful perfume, better than any you can buy in the stores." And she described how the scent of the land changed after the spill. "Hope Point stunk really bad," she said. "Some of the people had to use masks. It made me sick. I was working down there for a month and a half. When I got off, I was kind of light-headed for quite a while and felt nauseated. Now it's kind of worn off. I think I'm back to normal.

"This oil is so disgusting. I'd hate to think of something like this ever happening again. But, you know, it does give people work," Aga said. "Everybody's been able to make a few bucks. So that's the one good thing about it."

But Dolly Reft, an outspoken Native leader of Kodiak, questioned the value of money when a way of life is at stake. "The money isn't going to do it. These people can't live and exist off money," she said. She and her husband could have gone to work for Exxon or VECO, but they didn't. Instead, they spent their time and most of their savings trying to help the village people cope with the spill.

"The village people need their environment. Without it they can't exist, can't be who they are," Reft said. "When you pick up these dead carcasses day after day after day, you go through a mourning process. It's not only death in your environment, but in a sense it's a death of yourself, because you're part of that environment."

Kodiak's mental health workers reported a 700 percent increase in emotional problems in the months after the spill. "Right now the people are at their very weakest, when they essentially need to be at their strongest," Reft said. "If people don't have authority over their environment or themselves, their spirit and their will to live get weaker and they are more vulnerable to things they can normally handle. We are experiencing a high rate of alcoholism and suicide. This summer we've had eight suicides in six weeks."

Reft said that the Native villagers working for VECO or Exxon were not able to speak about their frustrations because they felt intimidated or had been told they would lose their jobs if they talked. "When you can't talk about something as vital as this, you have no place to vent your anger and frustration," she explained. "And when that accumulates inside you, it's very destructive. We have a lot of turmoil, a lot of mistrust and negative energy. People are bottling this up inside."

Exxon offered to fly fish into the villages. While this was a well-intended effort to help ease the need for subsistence foods, calories, protein, and even the taste of salmon were only part of what people needed. "The outside world still needs to be educated on what subsistence is," Reft said. "When you send fish into a village, what you've done is taken the people's spirit away because they don't have that joy of going out and providing for their families and getting the food. It'd be like me taking your job away with you having five children to feed. You'd have to go to a welfare system, and that would destroy your self-confidence.

"To think that their environment is being destroyed or put off balance is a very scary thing. In the villages, we know that if we aren't responsible to the land it will affect us next year. The land is a part of you. And it's like therapy to be able to go out and hunt and fish or dig clams and collect kelp. It's a way of recognizing who you are. When this is taken away from you, what do you do? This way of living has been handed down to you and you've done it all your life. How do you put a value on the destruction from this spill? There is no 'cost' that can be attached to a bird or a whale. It simply has to be reproduced. This is a different value system, a different reality.

"You cannot take people from a village and put them into modern society where others are competing for the dollar. It's a totally different way of thinking, a totally different way of living," Reft explained. "Subsistence is our last tie with who we are. In our subsistence way of living we are not competing, because it's not necessary. We go on hunts together. We go fishing together. We work together to help provide for our friends and relatives. This value system in itself is a sense of security. And this comes from living in nature, having the security and serenity of depending on the environment and of being responsible to it."

Each village in the wake of the *Exxon Valdez* experienced the spill in its own way. Each Native person, from small child to elder, had his or her own encounters with the oil, the turmoil, and the uncertainty. Chief Meganack of Port Graham searched for a sense of hopefulness in people's loss and fear. "What will happen to our lives in the next five years?" he asked. "What will happen when the cleanup stops and the money stops? We have lived through much devastation. Our villages were almost destroyed by chicken pox and tuberculosis. We fight the battles of alcohol and drugs and abuse. And we survive.

"But what we see now is death. Death—not of each other, but of the source of life, the water," Meganack said. "I am an elder. I am a chief. I will not lose hope. We have never before lived through this kind of death. But we have lived through lots of other kinds of death. We will learn from the past, we will learn from each other, and we will live. Where there is life there is hope."

Reflections

I watch spring return to Prince William Sound. Along the shoreline, snow begins to melt where the sun strikes it during the middle of the day. In places, eagles soar on the wind. Flocks of gulls fly low along the green, white-capped waves. Soon the great migrations of birds and whales will begin; salmon will search for their spawning streams.

Prince William Sound is certainly not dead. But the sound and the Alaska coast southwest to Kodiak and Katmai are not as wild and abundant as they were. Winter storms lashed sea cliffs, but more than 140 miles of exposed shoreline remain oiled. In more sheltered coves oil still clings to rocks, and patches of bright iridescent sheen still leach into the sea. Along hundreds of miles of shoreline, oil is buried in the sand.

Exxon officials insist that the oil spilled from their tanker did not create an ecological crisis. Indeed, on the spectrum of toxicity, oil is far from our most destructive pollutant. And the planet's air and water systems do have recuperative powers. The sea will continue ceaselessly to clean the shores. The impulse of animal species is toward regeneration, so barring further oil spills or other adversity, the bird, otter, and other animal populations of the sound are likely to return to their prespill abundance. Biologists estimate that some species may recover in twenty to seventy years—a way of saying that no one really knows how long—but all agree that no species has been wiped out forever.

An ecological disaster? asks Exxon. Now, a year later, where's the evidence?

Studies of everything from bald eagles to microorganisms will continue for years, and their results will spur controversies in and out of court for decades. Years from now, the resulting litigation could yield a precise accounting of the spill's consequences, though not if Alyeska's and Exxon's attorneys had had their way. The two companies had filed motions in Anchorage Superior Court that would have barred disclosure of information entered as evidence. Nevertheless, despite what National Wildlife Federation president Jay Hair calls this "blatant and outrageous attempt to hide the facts from the American people,"[1] unsuppressed evidence already confirms that the *Exxon Valdez* spill was the most devastating and costly oil spill ever.

One thousand sixteen dead otters were retrieved, making this spill the most deadly in history for marine mammals.[2] And no one knows how many otters and other sea creatures actually died. An undetermined number of seals and whales died in the vicinity of the spill, but their deaths may never be conclusively linked to the oil.

The U.S. Fish and Wildlife Service officially counted 36,460 dead marine birds, mostly murres—again, far more deaths than in any other spill. Moreover, scientists believe that this number represents only between 10 and 30 percent of the total mortality—that 100,000 to 350,000 birds might have died from the spill. By comparison, the next highest bird mortalities were the estimated 30,000 dead seabirds from the *Torrey Canyon* spill off the coast of England and the 20,000 killed by the *Amoco Cadiz* spill off the coast of France. The *Exxon Valdez* also affected more species of birds. Deaths were reported for eighty-eight species, with the highest mortality among murres, murrelets, kittiwakes, shearwaters, puffins, cormorants, and loons. There were also dead petrels, sandpipers, auklets, fulmars, swans, peregrine falcons, and 2,927 birds so badly oiled that they couldn't be identified.

The *Exxon Valdez* spill also set a record for dead eagles. One hundred fifty-one adult eagles were found dead, and, again, no one knows how many actually died. In the most heavily oiled areas, 83 percent of the bald eagle nests failed to produce young.

In measures of animal life alone, then, the spill was indisputably a major life-destroying event. But these numbers don't reflect the suffering of the dying creatures. The deaths represent only the most obvious symptoms of the extensive stress to the biomass. The oil also affected clams, mussels, urchins, fish, and a multitude of organisms in the intertidal areas. Furthermore, an ecological disaster is not defined just in terms of fatalities. Sublethal effects of the oil spill diminished the reproductive potential of species and rendered habitat virtually sterile. There was a tremendous loss of tiny invertebrates, an essential link in the food chain. The oil altered the complex interrelationships among a vast array of organisms. It upset the balance among species and set off chain reactions whose ultimate effects may not be detectable for many years. Finally, the death and ecological reshuffling caused by this spill were not isolated, localized events: many species, particularly migrating birds and whales, face other sources of pollution, other encroachments on their habitat, other threats to their existence. The multifaceted petroleum industry creates a network of problems: development of new fields disrupts wildlife habitat and wilderness; transport of crude oil and refined fuels precipitates pollution at sea and along inland waterways; oil consumption helps drive the greenhouse–global warming process. The *Exxon Valdez* oil spill is part of this ongoing ecological crisis of enormous proportions.

The social impacts of the spill are even more difficult to quantify than the ecological effects. How, for instance, do you measure the heightened sense of vulnerability of people living within hundreds of miles of the tanker operations? Their world has been forever changed by the passage of oil—and by the extreme sensitivity of their homeland to the massive cleanup operations. Native Alaskans depend upon resources of the sea; hunting and fishing make up their way of life and are essential to their cultural identity and survival. They now know that at any time another enormous swath of oil could sweep through their lives. And they know that once this force is loose, it will run its destructive course. It can be very hard to live a normal life when you fear that at any moment your world can be overwhelmed by oil.

Another nonquantifiable, almost inexpressible, loss is that of wilderness value, the sense that a region's landscape and ecology is as it was created, utterly undisturbed by human beings. This coast of Alaska was wild in ways in which it will never be wild again. It remains beautiful, but it will never again be pristine. No one will be able to return to a favorite cove or fjord, in memory or in person, without sensing the oil buried in the sand. This loss alone, in its effect on the human species' psychological experience of the natural world, marks the wreck of the *Exxon Valdez* as a tragedy of global significance.

With destructiveness and loss incontrovertibly established as the context, another thorny question arises: What is the extent of Exxon's responsibility in the perpetration of the spill? Judging Exxon's performance is no easy matter, partly because so many people in so many different arenas were involved. Yes, the captain of the vessel had a well-known drinking problem. Yes, crew fatigue and policy violations could have played a part. Yes, the Coast Guard was negligent in its vessel-tracking responsibilities. Yes, the state's laissez-faire attitude toward tanker operations fostered neglect. Still, the inescapable fact remains that the chain of command traces up to the company's policy- and decision-makers. In both practical and moral terms, Exxon is responsible for the grounding of its tanker.

As for Exxon's performance in response to the events, though unprepared for a spill of this magnitude, the company responded faster than any government agency and marshaled enormous resources to fight the oil. Lightering 40 million gallons of oil from the stricken tanker was a major accomplishment. Moreover, Exxon mounted its response amidst the confusion of state and federal officials trying to determine their roles, their responsibilities, and the extent of their authority.

In the future, companies causing large spills may not match Exxon's effort. A case in point is the mid-December 1989 explosion aboard the Iranian tanker *Khark 5*, which spilled some 30 million gallons of crude into the Atlantic Ocean. Following the explosion, a 200-mile-long slick drifted toward the coast of Morocco for *thirteen days* before any response was mounted. While the ship's owners haggled over salvage rights, they made no attempt to contain the spilled oil or lighter the remaining 53 million gallons, which a French observer called "a floating bomb."[3]

Also to Exxon's credit, the company promptly established a

claims process, which no law required. In one year, Exxon spent close to $2 billion as a result of the *Exxon Valdez* wreck, making this the most costly oil spill in history by more than a billion dollars. Exxon, with profits of $5.3 billion in 1988, is one of the few companies in the world capable of actually paying the costs of the spill, which could reach $4 billion by the time all the lawyers and claims are factored in.

However, for all its efforts, Exxon, according to government surveys, recovered only 3 to 13 percent of the spilled oil.[4] Regardless of all the efforts to divert, contain, disperse, and recover it, the massive slick inexorably ran its course.

The fact that Exxon did mount an extensive response makes the wreck of the *Exxon Valdez* a highly instructive case study. Experts and lay observers worldwide learned that no amount of money could get the spilled oil back in the ship and that the farther the oil spread from Bligh Reef the less benefit Exxon got for each dollar spent. The billions of dollars Exxon threw willy-nilly at the spill brought to mind a well-known scenario: all the king's horses and all the king's men—and, above all, all the king's money—couldn't put Humpty together again.

Frank Iarossi's appraisal of Exxon's response is telling: "I won't say that there weren't details that couldn't have been done better, but I've seen EPA and Coast Guard reports that basically give us a B+ or better on most of the response work. It's just that it was totally inadequate relative to the magnitude of the spill. I'd say the lesson to society is that a spill like this can happen: no matter how low the probability, the potential is still there for it to happen. Another lesson is in the inadequacy of current technology. What we have is just not good enough, no matter how finely tuned an organizational structure you have."

Exxon played out a lesson in futility that the whole world needed to learn: *no amount of money spent or personnel deployed can control a large oil spill.* "The industry has neither the equipment nor the response personnel in place and ready to deal with catastrophic tanker spills." When I first read these lines, I thought they must be from a conservation organization. But they come from an American Petroleum Institute report issued three months after the *Exxon Valdez* went aground. This report acknowledged that for a spill of 220,000 barrels or more, "the industry is not prepared anywhere along the coastal U.S. to deal with a spill of this size. . . . Even given adequate equipment and personnel, there are any number of variables beyond the control of a response team that can thwart a response to a spill at sea. Among these are: darkness, sea conditions, weather, physical properties of oil, location, logistics and safety considerations."[5]

The American Petroleum Institute went on to say, much as opponents of the Trans-Alaska Pipeline had said twenty years before, "Nothing can be promised to government or the public except a best effort to respond at sea. Further research into recovery technology can certainly help in this regard, but it is not considered likely that we can move to the point of guaranteeing containment and recovery at sea."[6]

During the cleanup, Alaska's Department of Environmental Conservation (DEC) expressed shock at how little oil was being recovered, but this result came as no surprise to those who had studied other large oil spills. The National Research Council's analysis of spills over the past ten years shows that "In many cases, mechanical cleanup capabilities may be only on the order of 1,000 barrels per day. . . . Spills much over 1,000 barrels per day have little possibility of being controlled by mechanical means."[7]

Exxon and other oil companies *must have known* prior to the wreck of the *Exxon Valdez* that mechanical recovery of spilled oil is extremely difficult to achieve. Of his initial reaction to news of the spill, Frank Iarossi said, "I knew then this was an uncontrollable volume."[8] And Alyeska must have known that its own contingency plans were based on wildly unrealistic projections. As it turned out, oil skimmed from the water during the first seventy-two hours was approximately 1 percent of the oil Alyeska had projected for recovery in this amount of time.

"The plain fundamental truth is that once oil hits the water it spreads rapidly and booms and skimmers have tremendous limitations," said Dr. Ian White, managing director of the International Tanker Owners Pollution Federation. (Over the past twenty years, this industry federation has analyzed more than 200 major oil spills; representatives of both Exxon and British Petroleum sit on its board.) "Unfortunately, mechanical recovery is in direct opposition to the natural tendency of oil to spread, fragment, and disperse. The reality, which people don't want to accept, is that there is a very limited chance of recovery. It is rare that as much as 10 percent of the original volume of spilled oil is removed from the sea surface as a result of cleanup operations. We remain unable to deal with spilled oil on the open sea and thereby prevent it from fouling beaches and damaging wildlife and coastal resources. The truth is that the problem is much more difficult than politicians, the media, and even parts of the industry itself are willing to acknowledge.

"The public, particularly in America, has been misled for many years," Dr. White continued. "A myth has been perpetuated that a large oil spill is solvable. A 10 percent recovery of spilled oil is tremendous and dispersants are no panacea. There is no magic solution or cure. Contingency plans must address this fact fair and square."[9]

The inescapable conclusion is that the basic premise supporting North Slope oil development was false: no safety net existed to guarantee effective spill response. Stated simply, environmentally safe oil development and transport were and are impossible: they always entail a degree of risk. The oil companies misled the U.S. Congress with assurances of their oil spill response capability when they sought approval of the Trans-Alaska Pipeline right-of-way permit. If either the state of Alaska or the Department of Interior had been more attentive and better informed, the industry's false assurances might have been revealed. Instead, the government agencies responsible for environmental protection swallowed whole the situation as the industry painted it. I remember attending a private gathering in Anchorage at the time when a federal judge's injunction barred the pipeline permit until potential environmental problems had been studied and alternatives explored. Someone asked then Secretary of Interior Rogers B. Morton if, as reported in a national news magazine, he was really going to consider the option of building an overland pipeline across Canada. Morton laughed and responded, "Naw, don't worry, guys. We're going to put that pipeline down through Alaska. But to get that injunction lifted I've got to make that judge think we really are studying alternatives."

It was clear from Secretary Morton's comment that the Department of Interior was willing to deceive a U.S. judge in order to shepherd the oil industry's pipeline plans. This collusion with industry and willingness to distort the truth appeared again when Interior announced safety criteria for the pipeline. The criteria were heralded as stringent environmental safeguards, but, as the secretary's special assistant John Horton acknowledged, "Those standards are designed so the companies will be able to meet them."[10]

It was deception, then, by both industry and government that helped clear the way for the Trans-Alaska Pipeline and tanker system. This same deception placed at risk both Alaskans living along the tanker route and Canadians in British Columbia, the latter having nothing at all to gain from North Slope oil. But even putting aside this mammoth deception, the safeguards Alyeska promised, inadequate as they were, never materialized. As the Alaska Oil Spill Commission concluded, "Public pronouncements by Alyeska and its owners that the company employed the best available technology and committed adequate resources to safety purposes turned out to be false."[11]

Offshore oil leases continue to be sold in Alaska and elsewhere, and with their sale other people become vulnerable to the myth of oil spill safety. "After all these years of hearing the oil industry tell us with confidence bordering on arrogance that it could clean up oil spills in even the most extreme marine environments, we're finally seeing more than 10 million gallons of truth spread across Prince William Sound," said George Jacko, state representative from the Bristol Bay region where offshore oil leases in the midst of the world's largest salmon fishery were sold in 1988. "The plainest—and the blackest—truth of all is that the oil companies have lied to Alaskans for years about their ability to clean up oil spills."[12]

An even darker side to this deception is the fact that both state and federal officials covered up for the industry. One official in the Department of Interior told me, "Our agency was constantly worried that we'd step on some oil industry toes." An incident during construction of the pipeline illustrates the state's complicity. Alyeska's construction camps were in full swing without the sewage treatment permits required by law. Gil Zemansky, who was single-handedly inspecting all the camps for DEC, reported that raw sewage was gushing into the nearest ponds and streams.

After he filed notices of violation, Alyeska persuaded the state to back off. As Robert Mead reports in *Journeys Down the Line*, "Alyeska turned its powers of persuasion from the gnat that had been stinging it to the commissioner and the governor himself, and Mr. Zemansky found himself transferred from Fairbanks to Juneau and, soon thereafter, fired. . . . Shortly thereafter, although little had been done to meet Gil Zemansky's objections, the DEC issued permits that allowed Alyeska to operate its sewage plants, and the law, if not the reality, was accommodated."[13] A similar situation arose after the *Exxon Valdez* oil spill: Alyeska objected to Dan Lawn's aggressive policing of its operations, and Lawn, DEC's most outspoken critic of Alyeska, was soon transferred to a new position.

As a result of the *Exxon Valdez* spill, Alyeska and Exxon are likely to pay substantial damage claims, but the companies will pass on most of these costs to consumers and continue making roughly $400,000 an hour profit from North Slope oil.[14] Still, there *is* a penalty that the oil companies fear—being barred from exploring for oil in the Arctic National Wildlife Refuge and on the continental shelf offshore from many coastal states. In the effort to protect this option, oil companies have sought to bolster the industry's reputation, sullied by the *Exxon Valdez* wreck, with an onslaught of expensive and potent public relations.

Prior to the spill, the industry advertised widely in Alaska, their magazine and television ads reinforcing the sense of well-being arising from the flow of oil revenue to Alaska's citizens. Immediately after the spill, the oil companies pulled all their ads in Alaska. This was a textbook public relations move—even positive messages would have reminded people who they were mad at. However, six months after the spill, Alyeska was putting out new ads, expensively designed to reassure Alaskans and the world that all was well. About this time, too, ARCO began running television commercials that interspersed bucolic images of Alaska and Alaskans with pictures of the oil industry, all tied together with a catchy theme song suggesting that "Alaska, the dream belongs to you." "Classical conditioning," said one public opinion pollster.[15] The myth of environmentally safe oil development was intact and in place.

The myth of safety in oil might have originated with the oil industry, but people in other sectors also had a stake in perpetuating it. The Department of Interior's Minerals Management Service (MMS), the lead agency for outer continental shelf oil leasing, had both motive and opportunity for furthering the myth in playing its dual and often conflicting roles of preparing environmental impact statements on lease sites and selling the oil leases themselves. Since a key part of this agency's mission is to evaluate oil spill responses and impacts, one would have expected MMS experts to have gone immediately to the *Exxon Valdez* spill, a real-life situation infinitely more instructive than the computer simulations they relied on. However, during the first critical days of the spill, no MMS experts visited Prince William Sound.

One Minerals Management official, who asked not to be identified, tried to explain: "Our risk-analysis people wanted to go out on the spill—to help and to learn—but word came down from Washington that 'it's in state waters so it's not our concern; stay away.' When one guy used his vacation time and paid his own way out to the sound, it became kind of a joke in the office—initially he was the only one who went out.

"Basically, Minerals Management was more worried about its political posture than the spilled oil," this official continued. "We're supposed to be the cutting edge of oil-in-the-environment awareness, but we had to be nice to the oil companies because we didn't want to offend them. We funded a few studies, but it wasn't until about three weeks after the accident that it occurred to someone in our agency that we'd be asked, 'What did you learn from the spill? How did this change your attitude about future oil leases?' This revelation prompted some cover-your-ass maneuvers. We tried to send out analysts but somehow couldn't make arrangements to charter a plane or a boat. Our specialists weren't forbidden to go to Prince William Sound, but they had to go on their own time and money. So, many of the people who determine future oil lease sales didn't get out there during the critical days of the nation's worst oil spill. It was only later, during the cleanup phase, that some of our people finally spent time in the field."

The Minerals Management official said that staff members

who had the expertise to clarify many aspects of the *Exxon Valdez* spill were directed not to talk about it publicly. "We had a gag order placed on us," he said. "When people called our office to ask about the spill, we were supposed to refer them to our public affairs office, which would in turn refer them to Washington, D.C. The Department of Interior evidently sent down orders to downplay the damage."

But even more consequential is MMS's current tendency to downplay the potential damage of future lease sales in the preparation of its environmental impact statements, supposedly objective analyses upon which leasing decisions are made. According to a report by the U.S. Congress's Office of Technology Assessment, "The industry has been most eager to probe . . . the Arctic [National Wildlife] Refuge for possible finds. The Interior Department has been too eager for the past eight years to accommodate it. . . . The larger role for MMS in directly managing Alaskan environmental studies may not be the optimum situation. . . . The agency responsible for leasing should not also be in charge of determining what environmental research is necessary, and of supervising subsequent efforts."[16]

Said the Minerals Management official who asked to remain anonymous, "We have a lot of good scientists, but their assessments get axed. They do a thorough job of defining the risks. The package is sent off to Washington, D.C., and what comes back may not be recognizable. It's very demoralizing for good scientists to be told in effect, 'We don't really care how good a job you do. Just put out the environmental impact statements so we can go ahead with the leases.'"

The state of Alaska also acted to perpetuate the myth of safe oil development. No one within state government heeded Dan Lawn's warnings. No one asked Alyeska to prepare a worst-case oil spill scenario. No one insisted that Alyeska prove its equipment capabilities. The Alaska Oil Spill Commission, established by the Alaska legislature two months after the spill to analyze what went wrong, found that the state had failed in its responsibilities to vouchsafe federal regulation, oversee industry operations, inform the public of risk, and ensure proper response capabilities in case of accident.

Two oil-related expenditures in 1988 make the point. The

state legislature denied DEC's request for $252,000 for tanker and terminal inspections, more aggressive enforcement, and reviews of contingency plans. That same year the state gave out $443 million from oil-generated revenues to citizens—just for living in Alaska, each resident received $827. With these kinds of benefits, few Alaskans—from villagers to policy-makers—wish to challenge the myth.

After the spill, many state employees worked their hearts out, often under strenuous and frustrating circumstances. This was particularly true of Dennis Kelso, who was indefatigable in his efforts to ride herd on Exxon. But in addition to just complaining about Exxon, Kelso or the governor could have said what Alaskans needed so badly to hear—something like "We made a terrible mistake in approving Alyeska's inadequate contingency plan. Let's admit that oil development poses some very real trade-offs. All of us in Alaska need to take our environmental responsibilities much more seriously."

Behind the myth of completely safe oil development and transport lies the possibility of another spill. Given the verified actual fact—that there is no way to control a large oil spill—what kind of response should be mounted for the next one?

Six months after the spill, Frank Iarossi said, "If I'm ever faced with a situation like this again, I'll head for Mexico when the phone rings." Although speaking somewhat in jest, Iarossi raised the distinct possibility that another industry executive faced with a large oil spill might not initiate a response at all. Iarossi pursued the underlying problem: "I had the world's biggest checkbook and I could purchase or mobilize anything in the world that would have helped. But once I got things to Valdez, I was powerless to use them. That depended upon the priorities defined by the state—inputs that needed to be developed, permits we needed to use things, plans that needed to be approved."

Unfortunately, in setting its priorities, the state was preoccupied with making certain that none of the liability shifted from Exxon to itself, that nothing endanger the state's lawsuit against Exxon. Governor Steve Cowper acknowledged that this concern "ran through the entire process. . . . No matter what you wanted to do, somebody ran in and said, 'Well, it will have an effect on

the lawsuit.' . . . The liability question was important to everybody but me."[17]

Iarossi explained that "having gone through the hopelessness
of trying to deal without power, I'll never put myself in a place
again of looking at 240,000 barrels of oil on the water. We need
to recognize that there are some absolute limits to what a commercial company can do. We should be ready to fulfill our legal
obligation to pay for the cleanup. But my conclusion is that a spill
like this is clearly beyond what any commercial company can do.
A company should stand ready to support the federal government, but they've got the baton. That's my personal view, not
Exxon's."

The Alaska Oil Spill Commission reached exactly the same
conclusion. "The spiller should not be in charge of a major
spill. A spiller should be obligated to respond with all the resources it can summon, but government should command that
response."[18]

Putting the government in charge does not guarantee an adequate response, but it would prevent the confusion of authority
that paralyzed the initial response to the *Exxon Valdez* spill and
that slowed down activity throughout the cleanup phase. The
next crisis will not be managed any more effectively unless someone has the authority to act very quickly and decisively. "I don't
care if you call him oil spill response dictator or casualty response
dictator," says Iarossi. "But if his title doesn't include the word
dictator, we will miss the whole purpose of having this individual.
This person is going to take some heat and needs skills and a
capability that the average bear doesn't have."

It's true that Coast Guard Admiral Paul Yost, who arrived in
Alaska to "kick some butts and fight this spill like a war," projected the kind of image required. However, to be effective, the
figure in charge would need to have authority that is clearly designated in advance. Further, that spill response "dictator" would
need an intimate familiarity with the local situation, with its geography, resources, and politics. Territorial disputes between
the state and federal government and internecine turf battles
among agencies turn a crisis into chaos, largely because authority that conflicts with local realities paralyzes action. The affected
states and Canadian provinces themselves are likely to have the

greatest knowledge of local circumstances and have their resources readily available during the crucial first hours of a spill.
In short, the necessary authority for spill response should logi-
cally reside with the state. As the Alaska Oil Spill Commission
warned, "Considering the limited capabilities of federal agencies
to respond to a variety of contingencies and the industry's conflict of interest, the state can never rely completely on the U.S.
government or on industry."[19]

The Oil Spill Commission found many shortcomings in the
federal government's National Contingency Plan (NCP), which
Alaska, like other states, has long relied on to provide the personnel and resources to handle large oil spills and other catastro-
phes. "The *Exxon Valdez* response illustrated the emptiness of the
NCP," stated the commission. "It failed to provide the necessary
resources. . . . The government has provided no resources of its
own to handle even moderately sized spills adequately. . . . The
greatest weakness of the NCP was that it failed to establish the
firm, predesignated working relationships that are vital to a successful emergency response."[20]

Even the head of the National Response Center, Coast Guard
Commander Kenneth Rock, was critical of the National Contingency Plan. He said, "It's a good set of rules, but the execution
stinks. There are some very dynamic people who couldn't figure
out how all the rules fit together." An assistant, Coast Guard
Lieutenant Aldo Noto, added that "we should be looking at our
entire crisis response system—at the way the country handles all
environmental incidents. If this were a toxic chemical spill instead of an oil spill, it wouldn't be dead otters washing up on the
beaches, it would be dead people."

In addition to a well-organized response system with clear
lines of authority, what can we do to expand our oil-control capabilities beyond the limitations revealed in the *Exxon Valdez* disaster? Clearly, boom for controlled burning and skimmers for
mechanical recovery need to be available in strategic locations,
but no one should expect them to make a significant dent in a
large spill. Nor can we rely on dispersants. Although, as Dr.
James Butler says, "dispersants would appear to be the only serious control possibility for large oil spills," the dispersant-use
guidelines of most coastal states remain an obstacle to dispersant

use. To avoid the long delays that rendered such use completely ineffective in the *Valdez* tragedy, states may need to streamline their dispersant regulations. However, even where dispersants have been used quickly, either in field tests or actual spills, the chemicals have often been ineffective.

In the end, prevention is the only real defense against large oil spills. As the Oil Spill Commission concluded, "Prevention of oil spills must be the fundamental policy of all parties in the maritime oil transportation system. . . . This disaster could have been prevented—not by tanker captains and crews who are, in the end, only fallible human beings, but by an advanced oil transportation system designed to minimize human error. It could have been prevented if Alaskans, state and federal governments, the oil industry, and the American public had insisted on stringent safeguards."[21]

Admittedly, the tools of prevention—double-hulled tankers, the best electronics, redundancy in critical systems, highly trained crews, and heightened Coast Guard surveillance—are imperfect. Shipping oil in tankers will never be risk-free, but being mindful of this fact will reduce the risk. Realizing that there will be tanker accidents is the first essential step in avoiding them.

Once the pipeline was built, tankers loaded with North Slope crude transited Prince William Sound 8,700 times without accident. This very success fostered complacency, which led to the neglect that added substantially to the danger. Finally, a snowballing of errors and circumstances resulted in a grounding of disastrous proportions. The way to prevent another accident is to fight the complacency, and to do that, we must be mindful of two basic, irrefutable facts—*major spills happen, and when they do, they cannot be controlled.*

Knowing that this oil spill could have been prevented makes the suffering and devastation in its wake all the more painful. Many share the blame. And yet, my own experience with the spill brought me into contact with a wide range of people who rose to the occasion and did whatever they could to help.

Kelly Weaverling fought one obstacle after another to rescue wildlife. Boyd Evison and other Park Service officials put their careers on the line to protect the parks. Valdez Mayor John Devens risked a recall vote when he started criticizing Alyeska; Chuck Hamel and Erlene Blake risked their personal safety by exposing the consortium's misdeeds. Jack Lamb and the Cordova fishing fleet spared no effort to save the hatcheries. Suzanne Marinelli and others volunteered to work under rigorous conditions. Many state and federal employees put in overtime, and some Exxon people pushed themselves to exhaustion trying to contain the oil.

It was, of course, a losing battle, and no one was more aware of this than Dr. Jim Scott. By summer's end, he had treated only a handful of bald eagles, and he knew that hundreds had died. "You still have to save as many as you can," he said. "You do it for the creatures. And you do it for yourself, for who you are inside. We are just another species on this planet, but we've been given the capacity of either protecting other species or destroying other species. I feel we are less human if we don't try to save other creatures regardless of their numbers."

Individual acts of conscience like Dr. Scott's often appear to have little effect on larger environmental problems. But this spill showed that those who cared and decided to act did make a difference, whether in saving a hatchery or saving a single bird. No single individual could overcome the force of the spill: once the oil was loose it was simply overwhelming. But individual commitment resulted in saved lives after the fact. If this energy can be directed at prevention inside as well as outside the industry, we might reduce the impact of major oil spills and begin solving some of the larger environmental problems of which oil spills are symptomatic. For me, one enduring lesson of the *Exxon Valdez* spill is how direct the line is from individual conscience to global problem solving.

This is not to say that initiating environmental reform in a high-tech world is easy. Part of the difficulty is that the conscience-solution link is only one approach to problem solving. Much of the opportunity for change (or the inertia to resist it) resides not with individuals but with large corporations. These entities are not people but conglomerates with no real personalities or feelings of their own. In a given corporation, the "conscience," such as it is, resides mostly with a handful of officers and directors, and in a corporation the size of Exxon this echelon is generally highly guarded and inaccessible to nearly everyone.

Exxon's annual shareholders' meeting seven weeks after the spill demonstrated the distance between corporate management and concerned citizen. Angry protesters, including many of the 6,500 shareholders who had requested admission to the 2,200-seat auditorium, had little apparent effect on the top executives who were developing the company's policies regarding the spill. Virtually all the important decisions had evidently been decided earlier in little-publicized, closed-door sessions. Major shareholders required more direct treatment. By working in private with them, CEO Lawrence Rawl and other Exxon executives diverted the call for more fundamental corporate reforms. Management made a few symbolic gestures toward environmental responsibility, but it deftly turned aside demands for Rawl's resignation and suggestions that Exxon invest in research into and development of alternate forms of energy and energy conservation.

Smooth as it was, Exxon's management made a fundamental mistake in supporting Rawl's refusal to go to Alaska and get out on the beaches, smell the oil, and see firsthand what was really happening. The people Exxon did send to Alaska often created more problems than they solved. Among the citizenry of the state, perhaps the most common take on the situation was that Exxon's people were trying to buy Alaskans off, to create dissension and divide and conquer. Communities desperate for hands-on spill-response experts felt insulted when Exxon sent people from the corporation's public relations department. And Alaskans felt downright manipulated by gag orders on employees of Exxon and its main contractors. The more Exxon tried to save face—with its videos, press releases, and brochures minimizing the spill—the more it convinced the public that it was lying. Lawrence Rawl's presence on the beaches of Alaska could have helped show that Exxon gave a damn—if Exxon *did* give a damn.

As it was, even Exxon's factual reports of what it was doing to combat the spill were derided: people were looking for more than the number of skimmers and beach cleaners dispatched to the spill. They wanted signs of a deeper environmental awareness.

But how to foster a sense of environmental morality within a giant corporation like Exxon? How to instill a commitment to the environment in a corporation's bottom line, in quarterly statements of profit and loss? And who, given the power and extreme self-protectiveness of these huge companies, has the ability to do these things? Claire Atkins, one of the shareholders who wasn't satisfied with Exxon's performance, had an idea. "I am not an environmentalist. I don't go out and pound the pavement," she said. "But I live on a farm, spend a lot of time outdoors, and love animals. And I was very angry that Exxon allowed this to happen. I was going to sell my Exxon stock, but then I found out I could use my position as a shareholder to try to change things."

Exxon's decision-makers are shielded from most lawsuits. Lawsuits filed by the state of Alaska, environmental organizations, and fishermen suffering losses will not take a dime from Rawl's $1,300,000 annual salary. Shareholders, however, can file what is called a derivative suit to hold corporate officers responsible for their actions by having them repay the company for losses their actions incurred. Claire Atkins is only one of some 730,000 Exxon shareholders, but at her own expense she filed suit. She found that a handful of other shareholders were doing the same, and more wanted to join their effort. If successful, they won't suddenly transform Exxon. But they may win a judgment calling for Rawl and other officials (or their indemnity insurance carriers) to pay the company for the losses they caused. And in the process, these efforts may help reinforce the message that corporate officers, like everybody else, must be responsible to the environment.

"It's so horrifying to realize the damage these large corporations can cause," said Atkins. "People have to be accountable. I don't care how rich you are, you shouldn't be allowed to let things like this happen. So many birds and animals died. I want to take my grandchildren to places like Africa and Alaska to see the wild creatures. And I want them to learn that they have to help save these animals. It's critical, very critical. But it doesn't appear that Exxon's officers really care about these things. They have to learn to make environmental safeguards part of our corporation's cost of doing business. They have to hire responsible people. They have to be certain their equipment is safe. If a double-hull tanker is the only thing that's safe, then that's what we've got to use."

Another independent act of conviction came from the Oil, Chemical, and Atomic Workers Union. After the wreck of the *Exxon Valdez*, this union, which represents 40,000 oil workers nationwide, voted to oppose drilling in the Arctic National Wildlife Refuge until a cohesive national energy policy is in place. "I'm for drilling, but there has to be some sanity to the process," said union vice president Robert Wages. "Our stance is certainly not job producing, but we don't believe it's job destructive either. Saying you shouldn't drill in the Arctic National Wildlife Refuge ought not be viewed as heresy by the industry.

"We'd like Congress to take up the nation's energy policy now, before the ghost of the *Valdez* is gone," Wages continued. "As long as that ghost is there, there's not going to be drilling in the Arctic Refuge. When that ghost disappears there will be a subtle, quiet, subterranean move to make sure that they are permitted to drill."[22]

The *Exxon Valdez* experience suggests several convincing reasons for a national energy policy. Alternate energy and conservation measures would reduce dependence on oil, lessening the chance of tanker accidents. More fundamentally, such measures could mitigate the inevitable conflicts between corporate objectives and public values. A national energy policy could be shaped by careful consideration of our need as a species for both a clean environment and long-term supplies of reasonably priced energy.

Perhaps the most compelling motivation to develop a national energy policy is the extent of the industry's deception as laid bare by the wreck of the *Exxon Valdez*. How can an industry with this record of false assurances be trusted to guide the development, transport, refining, and even the use of oil? How can the industry be trusted to avoid disrupting sensitive environments, provide a continuing supply of energy, and help reduce the air pollution and greenhouse warming effects of its products? The broken trust calls for policy and regulation.

There is no arguing the fact that we will need large amounts of oil for some time. Tankers will continue plying the waters off Canadian provinces and every coastal state in the United States. Our need for oil and our reliance on oil companies are not going to disappear overnight. Nevertheless, certain quite achievable objectives in both energy conservation and in alternate-energy development would reduce the risk to such sensitive regions as the Arctic National Wildlife Refuge in Alaska and coastal areas of California and Florida and the fisheries-rich Georges Bank off New England—all targeted by the industry as drilling sites.

But who's going to set the objectives and work toward the goals? Not the industry itself, that much we can be sure of. The responsibility for careful, environmentally sound development ultimately lies with those who use the energy. Diffused as it may be, the ultimate responsibility for problems like the Alaska oil spill lies with industry's silent partners—the consumers. "It wasn't Hazelwood's driving, but the driving of a hundred million Americans that put the tanker on the reef," went one quip that emerged from the spill.

However, it's difficult for most of us to connect the consumption of energy with disasters like that of the *Exxon Valdez*. One who tried is Mark Holdren of Honeoye Falls, New York. In the summer before the spill, he had been sea kayaking among the Shuyak Islands just north of Kodiak. "Who is to blame for the nation's worst oil spill? I am," he wrote to the *Homer News* after the Shuyak Islands were plastered with oil. "You see, I am your typical person living in an affluent suburb. And my lifestyle is choking our planet to death. I rely almost totally on my car to meet my every need. I commute more than 50 miles a day to work. My wife, in her own car, travels hundreds of miles every week. My children, in their own cars, seem to spend more time at a distant shopping mall than they do at home. . . . I am at oil's mercy."[23]

Individually, it's easy to feel that one's effort to use a little less gas or live in a more energy-efficient house has little overall effect. But the math of energy conservation is not only astonishing but also convincing. Improvements in home and business heating efficiency could save as much oil as is delivered by the Trans-Alaska Pipeline—about 2 million barrels a day. Every 1 mile per gallon improvement in automobile fuel efficiency saves about 500,000 barrels of oil a day. A mile and a half per gallon efficiency improvement would save as much oil as is optimistically projected to be under the Arctic National Wildlife Refuge. Energy conservation presents a number of ways to save money, improve national energy security, and help protect the planet. Brooks Yeager, author of *Wasted Energy*, concludes that the most effective way to achieve energy security is to improve energy efficiency: "If the United States could achieve the same energy efficiency per unit of economic output enjoyed by our Western European competitors, our annual energy bill would fall by an astounding $200 billion."[24]

This is $200 billion the oil companies would like to keep on their balance sheets. For the public, the fact that they currently do so represents not only a considerable monetary cost but a tremendous cost to wild places like Prince William Sound as well. We pay the cost in oiled shores, fouled air, polluted seas, and atmospheric changes induced in large measure by our use of hydrocarbons.

In the *Exxon Valdez* spill, Exxon was caught, ironically, by Alyeska's success at dodging regulation—by blocking state regulators and cutting back on safeguards, the consortium eventually victimized one of its own. Within ten months Exxon faced another oil spill cleanup, this one entirely of its own making. On New Year's day 1990, an Exxon pipeline connecting Staten Island and New Jersey broke, spewing 567,000 gallons of No. 2 heating oil into surrounding wetlands, a nesting area for rare wading birds. Exxon workers were warned of the rupture by an alarm, but they treated it as a false alarm—the safety system was known to be defective—and didn't cut off the flow for six hours. Said Albert Appleton, New York City's commissioner of environmental protection, "Exxon has a corporate philosophy that the environment is some kind of nuisance problem and a distraction from the real business of moving oil around."[25]

In lieu of the oil industry accepting its larger responsibilities, public policy backed up with forceful regulators is the only way to institute the safeguards that can prevent the kind of accident that despoiled the coast of Alaska and the wetlands near New York City.

And yet, all too easily, recommendations, safeguards, and even regulations established by law can fall through the many cracks that appear in an undertaking as massive as that of moving oil from its source. Although Congress deemed Alyeska responsible for oil spill response, somewhere within those sister companies are individuals who—here and there, now and then—failed to demand the best safeguards and to challenge the assertion that a large spill could be handled. Most of these persons will remain hidden forever within the corporate ranks. Also, in the state and federal governments, officials throughout the hierarchy—here and there, now and then—allowed the industry to cut corners. They, too, remain hidden, obscured by bureaucratic shadows. In the end we can rely only on ourselves, as consumers and voters, to act on our consciences to save the places on earth we call home.

I remember sitting in the living room of Jack and Paula Lamb in Cordova, discussing their feelings after the Mosquito Fleet's struggle to save the salmon hatcheries. "We ought to be able to trust our government to protect us from this kind of mess," Paula said. "Why do the oil companies just care about the stock market and the bottom line? It breaks my heart the way the whole thing was handled. Look at us—the richest country in the world, and we don't invest enough to clean up our own mess. We have let power and money get out of control. We have to be willing to give up enough to take care of our part of the world."

I hope this tragedy prompts more of us to have some long overdue conversations with ourselves about our personal choices and their consequences for our planet. If we did, more of us might start to see the kind of connection Mark Holdren saw between his lifestyle and an environmental crisis thousands of miles away. Perhaps more Alaskans would share Paula Lamb's conviction that we must never let the benefits of oil or of any other resource development distract us from our primary responsibility to take care of the land and waters.

The Frank Iarossis and Dennis Kelsos—all the highly trained professionals in positions of responsibility—need to get off by themselves, away from their lawyers and the media, and look inward to see if their decisions and actions are morally responsible, in the deepest sense, to the earth. I expect both Iarossi and Kelso have done considerable reflecting as a result of the spill, but the lessons that were thrust upon them are there for others as well.

I'd like the Lawrence Rawls of this world to look in the mirror and see executives who are responsible for far more than a company's annual profit. Should Rawl find this difficult, he might go out to Ohio and chat with Claire Atkins, or come on up to Alaska and visit with Paula Lamb in Cordova or Dolly Reft on Kodiak Island.

And I'd like Alaskans, myself included, to take more time to appreciate how fortunate we are to live in one of the most spectacular and abundant natural environments on earth. This land is good to us—we have to find ways to be more responsible to it.

The process of change starts with one person. And it starts with a personal decision. "It takes great strength to recognize the reflection in the mirror," says Dolly Reft. "Look in the mirror and dig deep within yourself. Don't create an image that isn't there. Act on what you see. The environment is a reflection of who we are. We can't ignore the reflection we see. We have to live with it—today, tomorrow, and forever."[26]

Notes

Introduction

1. Tom Brown, *Oil on Ice* (San Francisco: Sierra Club Books, 1971), 9; comment by Henry Pratt, executive assistant to Alaska Governor Keith H. Miller.

PART I: THE SPILL

1 Passages Through the Sound

1. Unless otherwise noted, quoted comments and dialogue in this and other chapters are from interviews or other personal communication with the author.
2. From "Pilots in Treacherous Waters," Doug O'Hara, *Anchorage Daily News*, April 2, 1989, M11.
3. Commentaries on the accident by Murphy, McCall, Taylor, Blanford, and Woodle are from proceedings of the National Transportation Safety Board (NTSB) hearing in Anchorage, May 16, 1989.
4. Radio transmissions from the *Exxon Valdez* are from U.S. Coast Guard recordings, March 24, 1989.

2 Day One: The First Twenty-Four Hours

1. From testimony at NTSB, May 16, 1989.
2. From Exxon press conference, Valdez, March 28, 1989, recorded by KCHU public radio.
3. Radio transmissions from the *Exxon Valdez* are from U.S. Coast Guard recordings, March 24, 1989.
4. From testimony at NTSB, May 16, 1989.

3 Day Two: "A House on Fire"

1. From testimony at NTSB, May 16, 1989.
2. Comments by Dr. Al Maki at Exxon press conference, Valdez, March 26, 1989, recorded by KCHU.
3. This comment by Governor Steve Cowper was made at a press conference in Valdez, March 24, 1989, recorded by KCHU.

4. From testimony before the U.S. Congress House Committee on Interior and Insular Affairs, field hearing in Valdez, May 8, 1989.
5. Ibid.

4 Day Three: Time Runs Out

1. From Exxon press conference, Valdez, March 26, 1989, recorded by KCHU.
2. Ibid.
3. Ibid.

5 Day Four: The Storm

1. Comment by Frank Iarossi at Exxon press conference, Valdez, March 27, 1989, recorded by KCHU.
2. Ibid.
3. Ibid.
4. From testimony before Committee on Interior and Insular Affairs, Valdez, May 8, 1989.
5. From Alaska Public Radio Network, September 16, 1989.
6. From testimony before Committee on Interior and Insular Affairs, Valdez, May 8, 1989.

6 "It Can't Happen to Me"

1. From "Captain Was Pride of Neighborhood," Kinsey Wilson, *Newsday*, reprinted in *Anchorage Daily News*, April 7, 1989, C1.
2. Unless otherwise noted, quoted comments and dialogue about Hazelwood's student and early marine days are from "Joe's Bad Trip," Richard Behar and Scott Brown, *Time*, July 24, 1989, 42–47.
3. From "Suit Charges Captain Was a Heavy Drinker," *Anchorage Daily News*, April 10, 1989, E1.
4. From Exxon press release, Valdez, April 30, 1989.
5. From testimony at NTSB, May 16, 1989.
6. From "Captain Faces Criminal Probe," *Anchorage Times*, March 29, 1989, A1.
7. From testimony at NTSB, May 16, 1989.
8. From letter to Senate investigation committee. Reported by Richard Behar and Scott Brown, *Time*, July 24, 1989, 45.
9. Robert E. LeResche, "Proposed Probable Cause, Findings and Recommendations of the State of Alaska." Report submitted to the NTSB, July 17, 1989.
10. Ibid.
11. From a letter by Pat Levy to Alaska congressional delegation, February 24, 1984.

PART II: THE RESPONSE
7 The Great Promise

1. Statement by L. R. Beynon for Alyeska Pipeline Service Company, Trans-Alaska Pipeline hearing, Department of Interior, Anchorage, February 25, 1971, exhibit 48, vol. 3.
2. Reported by Charles McCoy, *Wall Street Journal*, July 6, 1989, A4.
3. Ibid.
4. Ibid.
5. Edward B. Deakin, "Oil Industry Profitability in Alaska: 1969 through 1987." Report prepared for the State of Alaska, Department of Revenue, March 15, 1989.
6. Larry Makinson, *Open Secrets* (NP: Rosebud Publishing, 1987).
7. Deakin, "Oil Industry."
8. McCoy, *Wall Street Journal*.
9. Letter by James K. Woodle to Alyeska officials, April 15, 1984.
10. From testimony before Committee on Interior and Insular Affairs, Valdez, May 8, 1989.
11. From "Promises Ring Hollow," Patti Epler, *Anchorage Daily News*, October 29, 1989, A7.
12. From testimony at NTSB, May 19, 1989.
13. Comments made at press conference after NTSB hearing, Anchorage, May 19, 1989.
14. From testimony before Committee on Interior and Insular Affairs, Valdez, May 8, 1989.
15. From testimony before Alaska Oil Spill Commission, Anchorage, August 31, 1989.
16. From "Paper Tiger," Patti Epler, *Anchorage Daily News*, October 22, 1989, A5.
17. Ibid.
18. Ibid.
19. From testimony before Alaska Oil Spill Commission, Anchorage, September 1, 1989.
20. Comments and recommendations by James Card, American Petroleum Institute, Congressional Office of Technology Assessment, and Coast Guard Rear Admiral William Benkert, in "Fight Flares Anew," Stan Jones, *Anchorage Daily News*, October 16, 1989, A1.
21. From "Fight Flares Anew," Stan Jones, *Anchorage Daily News*, October 16, 1989, A1.
22. National Response Team, "A Report on the National Oil and Hazardous Substances Response System." Annual report of the National Response Team, Washington, D.C., March 1989.

8 The Mosquito Fleet

1. Comments at Cordova town meeting, Cordova, March 28, 1989, recorded by KCHU.

2. From Exxon press conference, Valdez, March 27, 1989, recorded by KCHU.

3. Comments made at this meeting were recounted to the author by Gary Hayden, Department of Environmental Conservation, State of Alaska.

9 The Lawyers and the Admiral

1. From testimony before Committee on Interior and Insular Affairs, oversight hearing, Washington, D.C., July 28, 1989.

2. From "Belli Plans to Begin Litigation Today," Beau Brendler, *Anchorage Times*, April 10, 1989, B1.

3. From "Exxon Chief's Statements Don't Square with Facts," David Postman, *Anchorage Daily News*, April 29, 1989, A1.

4. From Exxon press conference, Valdez, March 29, 1989, recorded by KCHU.

5. From testimony before Committee on Interior and Insular Affairs, Washington, D.C., July 28, 1989.

6. From "In Ten Years You'll See Nothing," *Fortune*, May 8, 1989, 51.

7. Interview by Steve Seplocha, KSKA (Anchorage) public radio, March 28, 1989.

8. Letter by Governor Steve Cowper to Lawrence Rawl, April 28, 1989.

9. Facsimile letter by Lawrence Rawl to Governor Cowper, April 28, 1989.

10. "Dispersants and Burning." Report issued by Exxon, March 24–29, 1989, 41.

11. Countersuit filed by Exxon in response to State of Alaska's suit against Exxon.

12. From testimony before Committee on Interior and Insular Affairs, Valdez, May 8, 1989.

13. From "Alaska After Exxon," Jerry Adler, *Newsweek*, September 18, 1989, 50.

14. Admiral Yost's comments in this chapter are from an unpublished interview by Rosanne Smith, KSKA.

15. From an unpublished interview by Harry Hurt III, *Newsweek*.

13 Shorelines

1. From testimony before Committee on Interior and Insular Affairs, Valdez, May 8, 1989.

2. From "Exxon Spurns Offer of Cleanup Equipment," *Anchorage Times*, March 31, 1989, A1.

3. From unpublished interview by Paul Jenkins, Associated Press.

4. Mr. Stevens was repeating a statement made by Exxon CEO Lawrence Rawl at Exxon's annual shareholders' meeting, May 18, 1989.

5. From testimony before Committee on Interior and Insular Affairs, Valdez, May 8, 1989.

6. From a VECO press release, Juneau, April 29, 1989.

7. Comment by Admiral Robbins and the following comment by a DEC official are from an interview by Pamela Abramson, *Newsweek*.

8. From "EPA Chief Likes Bugs that Eat Oil," Craig Medred, *Anchorage Daily News*, August 6, 1989, B3.

9. From Alaska Public Radio Network, September 16, 1989.

10. From testimony before Committee on Interior and Insular Affairs, Washington, DC., July 28, 1989.

11. Cleanup production figures provided by Otto Harrison on Alaska Public Radio Network, September 16, 1989.

12. From testimony before Committee on Interior and Insular Affairs, Washington, D.C., July 28, 1989.

13. From "Now Charges Include Cleaning for TV," Bob Ortega, *Homer News*, May 25, 1989, 40.

14. From speech before Anchorage Chamber of Commerce, Anchorage, October 2, 1989.

14 How Clean Is Clean?

1. Comments by Lee Raymond in this chapter are from an unpublished interview by Harry Hurt III, *Newsweek*.

2. From "In Ten Years You'll See Nothing," 50.

3. From "The Wreck of the *Exxon Valdez*," *Alaska Magazine*, June 1989, 23.

4. Exxon internal memo sent by Otto Harrison to field supervisors, July 19, 1989.

5. From testimony before Committee on Interior and Insular Affairs, Washington, D.C., July 28, 1989.

6. Ibid.

7. Ibid.

8. Ibid.

9. From "Closure Frustrates Fishermen," Joe Hunt, *Anchorage Times*, August 4, 1989, A6.

10. From "Law Provides No Way to Force Exxon to Keep Cleaning," David Postman, *Anchorage Daily News*, July 29, 1989, A10.

11. From testimony before Committee on Interior and Insular Affairs, Washington, D.C., July 28, 1989.

12. From testimony before the National Institute for Environmental Health Sciences conference, Seattle, Washington, July 29, 1989.

PART III: THE WAKE

15 Valdez

1. From "Cities View Spill Ravages Differently," Fred Bayles, *Anchorage Times*, April 11, 1989, A6.

2. From "Valdez Settles Down with Madness," Charles Wohlforth, *Anchorage Daily News*, May 12, 1989, A1.

3. From "Valdez Folks Feel Cheated," Charles Wohlforth, *Anchorage Daily News*, March 30, 1989, A1.

4. From "Normal Responses to an Abnormal Situation," Dr. Richard M. Gist, *Valdez Vanguard*, April 19, 1989, A8.
5. From "Valdez Folks Feel Cheated."
6. Comments by Douglas Baily from an interview by Pamela Abramson, *Newsweek*.
7. Comments by Erlene Blake from an interview by Pamela Abramson, *Newsweek*.

16 Cordova

1. From "Valdez Folks Feel Cheated," Charles Wohlforth, *Anchorage Daily News*, March 30, 1989, A1.

19 Kachemak Bay

1. Don Gilman is mayor of the Kenai Peninsula Borough (similar to a county), which includes the coastal communities of Kenai, Homer, and Seldovia.
2. Comments made at Homer MAC meeting, May 31, 1989.
3. From "Dark Despair Tints Homer's Anger at Spill," Charles Wohlforth, *Anchorage Daily News*, June 17, 1989, C1.
4. Homer MAC meeting, May 31, 1989.

21 Kodiak

1. From "Monigold Pulls Plug on Exxon, VECO," *Kodiak Daily Mirror*, June 15, 1989, 1.

22 The Native Villages

1. Statements by Walter Meganac, Sr., in this chapter were presented to the Alaska Conference of Mayors, Subcommittee of Oiled Mayors, June 27, 1989.
2. From "Sound of Prayer," Debbie McKinney, *Anchorage Daily News*, May 16, 1989, H1.
3. From "Trouble in Tatitlek," *Anchorage Times*, May 21, 1989, B3.
4. From "Sound of Prayer."
5. Ibid.
6. From "Tatitlek Resident: Sad Is Too Mild a Word for Villager's Loss," Francis Lambert-Durdik, *Tundra Times*, April 24, 1989, 1.
7. From "Spill Changes Chenega into Disaster Base," Jennifer Gordon, *Tundra Times*, April 10, 1989, 1.
8. From "Spill Leaves Elder Wondering about the Future," Jennifer Gordon, *Tundra Times*, May 22, 1989, 9.
9. Ukatish and Kvasnikoff comments from "Subsistence Lifestyle Takes a Beating from Spill," Bob Ortega, *Homer News*, August 31, 1989, 1.

Reflections

1. From "Oil Companies Want Spill Evidence Secret," George Frost, *Anchorage Daily News*, December 28, 1989, A1.

2. From U.S. Fish and Wildlife Service, "Total Marine Birds Retrieved Following the *Exxon Valdez* Oil Spill." Anchorage: U.S. Fish and Wildlife Service, December 19, 1989, 1.

3. From "Close Shave Off Morocco," Lisa Beyer, *Time*, January 15, 1990, 38.

4. Three-percent estimate from Alaska Oil Spill Commission, "Spill." Anchorage: Alaska Oil Spill Commission, January 1990, 11; 13-percent estimate from DEC fact sheet, September 12, 1989, compiled by L. J. Evans.

5. From American Petroleum Institute, "Task Force Report on Oil Spills." Washington, D.C.: American Petroleum Institute, June 14, 1989.

6. Ibid.

7. Committee on Effectiveness of Oil Spill Dispersants, National Research Council, *Using Oil Dispersants on the Sea* (Washington, D.C.: National Academy Press, 1989), 247.

8. From an unpublished interview by Joe Hunt, *Anchorage Daily Times*.

9. From "Major Oil Spill: There Is No 'Miracle Cure,'" Dr. I. C. White, *Gard News*, September 1989, 16; and from an interview by the author.

10. Tom Brown, *Oil on Ice* (San Francisco: Sierra Club Books, 1971), 24.

11. From Alaska Oil Spill Commission, "Spill," 17.

12. From "Disaster Shows Emptiness of Oil Companies' Lies," Rep. George Jacko, *Anchorage Daily News*, April 1, 1989, B11.

13. Robert Douglas Mead, *Journeys Down the Line: Building the Trans-Alaska Pipeline* (Garden City, N.Y.: Doubleday, 1978), 317.

14. Edward B. Deakin, "Oil Industry Profitability in Alaska: 1969 through 1987." Report prepared for the State of Alaska, Department of Revenue, March 15, 1989.

15. From "Oil Industry Sets Out to Patch Image," Richard Mauer, *Anchorage Daily News*, November 12, 1989, B1.

16. U.S. Congress, Office of Technology Assessment, *Oil and Gas Technologies for the Arctic and Deep Water* (Washington, D.C.: U.S. Congress, Office of Technology Assessment Pub. No. OTA-O-0270, May 1985), 171.

17. From an unpublished interview by Larry Persily, Alaska Oil Spill Commission, November 28, 1989.

18. From Alaska Oil Spill Commission, "Spill," 40.

19. Ibid., 42.

20. Ibid., 5, 39.

21. Ibid., ii.

22. From "Oil Union Wants Sanity in Drilling," Marjorie Anders, *Anchorage Times*, May 5, 1989, A1.

23. From "We Are to Blame," Mark W. Holdren, *Homer News*, April 20, 1989, 5.

24. Brooks Yeager, *Wasted Energy* (San Francisco, Sierra Club), 3.

25. From "Exxon's Attitude Problem," Barbara Rudolf, *Time*, January 22, 1990, 51.

26. From Alaska Oil Spill Commission, "Spill," 3.

Index